REENGINEERING
HUMAN RESOURCES

REENGINEERING HUMAN RESOURCES

Achieving Radical Increases in Service Quality—with 50% to 90% Cost and Head Count Reductions

LYLE M. SPENCER, JR., PHD

HAY McBER CENTER FOR RESEARCH & TECHNOLOGY

John Wiley & Sons, Inc.

New York • Chichester • Brisbane • Toronto • Singapore

Library of Congress Cataloging-in-Publication Data:

Spencer, Lyle M.
    Reengineering human resources/Lyle M. Spencer.
       p. cm.
    Includes bibliographical references and index.
    ISBN 0-471-01535-0 (cloth)
    1. Human capital.   2. Information technology.
    3. Technological innovations—Management.
    4. Personnel management.   5. Organizational change.
    I. Title.
HD4904.7.S65   1995   95-11736
658.3—dc20

Printed in the United States of America
10 9 8 7 6 5 4 3 2 1

To

my most precious human resources,
my daughters Emily and Julia,
who will inherit a technological wonderland we can scarcely
imagine—and will be prepared.

Acknowledgments

This book draws on studies conducted by many colleagues from McBer and Company, Hay Management Consultants, academic institutions, and most importantly, our clients and colleagues in industry, military, government, education, health care, and religious organizations. I cannot thank by name everyone who contributed to the findings presented here, but I wish to express special appreciation to the following colleagues:

ALLIANT HEALTH SYSTEM: John Morris

CHEVRON: Jay Stright

CAREER SEARCH: David Bachrach

EDS: Paul Pottinger, PhD, Ted Ryan, Mike Cavender

LILCO: William DeMoulis, Jim Flynn, Walter Wilm

MELLON BANK: Dick Ho, PhD

MASSACHUSETTS DEPARTMENT OF REVENUE: Barbara Blakeslee, Michael Bryne

MERCK: Roger Smith, Joyce Gliniewicz, Doug Phillips, David Boch, Andrew Peterson, Len Olsen

NORTEL: Don McCain

TRAINING DEVELOPMENT CORPORATION: Charles Tetro, John Dorrer, Bruce Vermeulen

PPG: Stephen McIntosh

SOFTWARE PRODUCTIVITY CENTER: Capers Jones

SYMMETRIX: Andrea Sodano, PhD

TESSERACT: Christine Dover

WESTINGHOUSE: Wyman Lee

McBer research colleagues Ruth Jacobs, PhD, Sandy Ruby, Bill Treadwell, Katy Hubchen, Kristen Hatch, Teresa Lima

Hay Management Consultants colleagues Chris Dyson, Jacquie McHale, Russ Flint, Jeff Shiraki, Joyce Shields, PhD, Steve Nissenfeld, PhD, Linus Diedling,

George McCormick, Kathy Vestal, PhD, Tom Friedlander, PhD, Lisanne Misrok

McBer's production staff, especially Imat B. R. Badruddin, who produced many figures and tables and cheerfully put up with many revisions.

My editor Michael Hamilton.

Preface

Information technology is transforming human resources (HR) management. Its impacts will include:

Outsourcing

Eighty percent of major organizations are considering outsourcing most HR functions and services.

Automation

Most HR services will be provided by personal computers and interactive voice-response systems.

Integration

HR functions—staffing, performance management, training and development, compensation, and so on—now balkanized among competing fiefdoms of specialists—will be integrated by Integrated Human Resource Information Systems (IHRMIS). These systems will be used directly by employee end-users to get "bundles" of multiple services to solve problems or to achieve personal objectives. Top-line management will have instant access to comprehensive HR "*balance sheets*" and "*profit and loss statements*" for strategic planning.

Radical Decentralization in the Way HR Services are Provided

From HR professionals providing services to line manager and employee self-service directly from workstations.

Dramatic Change in HR Professional Roles and Competencies

HR practitioner roles will change from *doers* to *consultants* for HR services: "Consumer's Guide" compilers, resource brokers, and purchasing agents. Head-quarters training staff will no longer provide training; rather they will advise divisional and field line managers on which training courses to enroll employees and which to purchase from outside vendors. HR practitioners will become *knowledge engineers and programmers:* HR professionals increasingly are being asked to put their expertise "in the box" (i.e., a computer) or on a disk. For example, stand-up trainers are becoming developers of CD-ROM-based interactive video/computer assisted-instruction (IV/CAI) training programs. Compensation, labor law, and benefits administration professionals are programming expert systems that advise manager and employee end users at HR kiosks ("public" personal computers) or on their own PCs.

This book is a survival guide to the HR reengineering revolution. Its objectives are to provide you with:

1. **A practical definition** of HR Reengineering: the radical changes that information technology-integrated HR information systems, worldwide networks, and availability of all HR services on PC screens will cause in HR service delivery and staffing.

2. **Instructions** for reengineering: value analysis, work flow and cost-benefit analysis, with practical tools you can use—software work flow graphics and spreadsheet templates.

3. **People considerations** in reengineering: the competencies HR professionals need to succeed in reengineering, and how employee competencies change with reengineered work.

4. **How to organize and implement** HR reengineering using methods applicable to other staff and business functions: cutting product development concept-to-market cycle time and speeding up order-to-fulfillment customer service.

5. **How to calculate cost savings to make the business case** for investment in equipment, systems development, and employee training needed to reengineer.

The book is organized into the following sections and chapters:

INTRODUCTION

- **Chapter 1. Reengineering Human Resources** provides an executive summary of the book. If you have time only to skim one chapter, this will give you the basic ideas and concepts.

TECHNOLOGY

- **Chapter 2. Information Technology: A Primer for Human Resource Professionals** discusses the extraordinary changes occurring in computing and their implications for HR, and provides definitions of technical jargon you will encounter.

PROCESS

- **Chapter 3. Basics: Activity-Based Costing, Value Analysis, and Work Flow Charting** provides how-to information on the basic tools of reengineering.
- **Chapter 4. Reengineering Concepts** describes the radical new approaches to organizing work made possible by marrying traditional work analysis methods with revolutionary advances in information technology.
- **Chapter 5. Reengineering Human Resources: Functions and Processes** provides ideas and examples of reengineering specific HR functions: HR record keeping, employment (recruitment, selection, placement), succession planning, performance management, training and development, compensation, union and labor relations, and so on.
- **Chapter 6. Integrated Human Resource Management Information Systems (IHRMIS)** describes how worldwide networks will tie together and focus all HR functions to accomplish an organization's strategic objectives.
- **Chapter 7. People** describes the ways employee competencies will need to change in reengineered organizations and jobs of the future.

IMPLEMENTATION

- **Chapter 8. Implementing Reengineering Change: Programs and Projects** describes the steps in reengineering change efforts and projects.
- **Chapter 9. Making the Business Case for Human Resources Reengineering** shows you how to calculate "hard dollar" cost-benefit and return on investment numbers to justify investments in reengineering.

SUMMARY

- **Chapter 10. A National Human Resources System for the Future** discusses organizational and societal implications of reengineering— including the potential displacement of 30% of the U.S. workforce—and how reengineered national "reemployment systems" will arise to redeploy displaced workers.

- **Appendix A. Reengineering Team Readiness Index**, a tool you can use to assess your team's readiness to begin a reengineering effort.

A Note on Computer and Software Tools Computers and software products mentioned by name in this book are not necessarily plugs. Rather, products mentioned illustrate technologies available at the time of writing. Examples generally are from the top three products in market share and/or competitive reviews (in *PC Week, PC Magazine* or *InfoWorld*) in each category: e-mail, document database, automated forms, and work flow management software.

These technologies and product rankings change weekly. In choosing software tools, you will need to keep in touch with your technology gurus or read information systems industry literature religiously. (An example of my own professional evolution: Although a psychologist by training and an HR consultant by vocation, I find I now subscribe to—and spend far more time reading—more computer magazines than HR management, training, and psychology journals).

I strongly believe that reengineering is a wonderful opportunity for HR end-users—managers and employee customers—and for HR professionals. With reengineered HR systems, customers will be able to receive any HR service with perfect quality, instantaneously, on demand, and at the place most convenient to them—their own workstations—anywhere in the world. HR professionals will be freed from low-value-added paper shuffling and be better able to focus their efforts and expertise on higher value-added and more enjoyable service delivery, development, and strategic planning. Everyone will benefit.

LYLE SPENCER

Boston, Massachusetts
September 1995

Contents

PART I   Introduction   1

Chapter 1:   Reengineering Human Resources   3

PART II   Technology   35

Chapter 2:   Information Technology: A Primer
for Human Resource Professionals   37

PART III   Process   51

Chapter 3:   Basics: Activity-Based Costing, Value Analysis,
and Work Flow Charting   53

Chapter 4:   Reengineering Concepts   81

Chapter 5:   Reengineering Human Resources:
Functions and Processes   99

Chapter 6:   Integrated Human Resource Management
Information Systems   122

Chapter 7:   People   144

PART IV   Implementation   161

Chapter 8:   Implementing Reengineering Change:
Programs and Projects   163

Chapter 9:   Making the Business Case for Human
Resources Reengineering   183

PART V   Summary   199

Chapter 10:   A National Human Resources System for the Future   201

Appendix A: Reengineering Team Readiness   210

Bibliography   223

Index   227

PART

I

Introduction

1

Reengineering Human Resources

FUTURE SCENARIOS

Personnel Information and Benefits Administration

Newlywed Diane Surah recently returned to work and needs to update her personnel records.

Sitting down at her personal computer, Diane clicks on the HRIS (Human Resource Information System) icon, enters her password, and pulls up her own personnel file. She enters her new surname and address by overwriting the old ones. She confirms that she wants her paycheck directly deposited in the same bank as before and elects not to change her bank account number and address as yet. Then she adds her new husband's name to her benefits package and designates him the beneficiary of her life insurance policy.

Now Diane simply has to confirm the changes with her password "signature." When she types an incorrect number in her password, the system beeps and displays the error message "Invalid Password—Please try again." This is because error checking and exception control built into the system prevent Diane from entering invalid data. ("Smart" systems also can advise users about choices, for example, an employee's best options from a cafeteria-style flexible benefits plan based on that employee's personal data. Likewise, if childless employees accidentally choose child care as a benefit, they'll be beeped and then tactfully advised.) Diane completes all of her transactions in less than five minutes. When she clicks on the "Confirm" button, all transaction information is instantly entered in her firm's personnel system.

Diane remembers her last contact with her firm's personnel department two years ago (before it reengineered) when she transferred from New Hampshire to Arizona. To change her address she had to complete a minimum of ten steps: (1) go to her boss's secretary, (2) get the secretary to fill out a change-of-address form, which her boss had to sign (3). These steps took a week because her boss was out of town. This form then had to be (4) mailed to the site HR generalist to be checked (5), and then (6) mailed on to corporate headquarters to be (7) entered in the personnel system. This process took an additional two to three weeks.

Diane had moved to Scottsdale, Arizona, to begin work on a critical project. When she arrived at the Hertz counter in the Phoenix airport, she found that her company credit card was invalid. The computer said she had been terminated! Diane used her own credit card. The next two weeks were a nightmare of bureaucracy. Diane met her new boss and explained her problem. He went with her to the Scottsdale-site HR generalist (8), who called the firm's headquarters HR department (9). At headquarters, the personnel representative (10) finally determined that Diane's transfer information had been misentered as a termination.

On Friday of her first week on the job, Diane did not receive a paycheck. Her last paycheck had gone to her old site because her change of address had not been processed—and of course, she did not get a new check because terminated employees don't get paid. This was a major hassle for Diane because she needed to put a deposit on her new apartment. Her boss, chagrined by Diane's reception in Arizona, lent her the deposit money out of his own pocket.

It took Diane, her boss, and the Arizona-site HR generalist three weeks to straighten everything out. Diane (and her boss) lamented the amount of productive time she lost during these weeks: "I should have spent more time working on my mission-critical project—not hassling with Personnel!"

Benefits Information Inquiries

Jack Michaels is in a hospital emergency room at 2:00 A.M., waiting for word about his 15-year-old son Sam, who was found unconscious at a party that was raided by police. A first diagnosis was that Sam had consumed "alcohol and some drugs." Jack is fairly sure that his healthcare benefits cover dependents' emergency room treatment, but what about long-term care should it be needed? What about drug and alcohol counseling? What about legal ramifications, if any? Jack remembers that his cellular computer phone PDA (personal digital assistant) (see Figure 1.1) is in his pocket.

The PDA can connect to Jack's firm's wide area network (WAN) from anywhere in the world. He dials the WAN's access number for Human Resources Services, logs on with his password, and listens to the Interactive

Figure 1.1 A Personal Digital Assistant

Voice Response menu until he hears "Press 3 for employee benefits inquiries." Upon pressing, he is led through submenus:

"Press 1 for health insurance. . . ①"

"Press 2 for hospitalization benefits. . . ②"

"Press 5 for drug and alcohol treatment programs. . . ⑤"

. . . and hears that he and his dependents are covered for 17 days of residential care and 30 sessions of outpatient drug and alcohol counseling.

Jack returns to the HRIS menu by pressing ⑨, then presses ③ to listen to the Benefits menu, until he hears "Press 7 for legal benefits." Listening, Jack finds that his benefits include one free session with a staff lawyer, with referral to lawyers recommended by the company if subsequent legal services are needed.

Somewhat relieved, Jack looks up to find a nurse telling him that Sam has had his stomach pumped and that he will be "one sick kid tomorrow, but okay."

Employment

From a deck chair at the beach hotel in Bali, Derek Driller is job hunting via PDA (see Figure 1.1) and satellite to electronic job posting services. Driller, a free-lance petroleum reservoir engineer, is taking two weeks off after six months in Sumatra working for Pertamina, Indonesia's state oil company. Driller is a professional contract employee, an increasingly common kind of worker. Driller and his counterparts are part of the "virtual" workforce of many oil companies around the world—that is, they are not permanent members of any organization, but they are immediately available (between jobs) to staff projects as needed.

Before leaving Sumatra, Driller signaled his availability by posting his resume, employment contract, salary and benefits requirements, and date of availability to an electronic bulletin board run by his professional association. This bulletin board serves as a job posting system for both employers and employees worldwide.

Fred Auerbach, vice president of Global Oil, needs to assemble a joint U.S.–Russian team of engineers to revitalize secondary recovery of oil from Siberian oil fields. With three clicks of his mouse, Auerbach uses the IHRMIS (Integrated Human Resources Management Information System) job–person matcher to search for engineers with "reservoir," "secondary recovery," "arctic," or "Russian" in the text of their resumes. The IHRMIS sends an active agent—a smart program that searches all on-line employment databases (among them Driller's Petroleum Reservoir Engineer Bulletin Board) to which Auerbach's firm subscribes. The IHRMIS agent retrieves resumes of job-seeking oil engineers who match Auerbach's criteria and downloads them into Auerbach's PC.

Auerbach finds Driller's vita in less than a minute. In fact, he knows Derek from when they worked together at an oil field on Alaska's North Slope. He knows right away that Driller is ideal for the Siberian project. He's got the technical skills, won't go stir-crazy in an isolated arctic environment, and gets along well with the locals. In HR competency jargon, he is "portable" and high in "cross-cultural interpersonal sensitivity."

Via e-mail, Auerbach sends Driller a message: "Strong interest. Contact me ASAP to discuss Siberian project."

Accessing the bulletin board from his lounge chair on the beach, Driller finds that he has three indications of interest from prospective employers. But Auerbach's message stands out. Driller uses his PDA to call his former colleague directly, forgetting that Bali is 12 hours ahead of Chicago. Driller leaves voice mail: "I'll sign up." Auerbach responds that evening and downloads the employee contract to Driller's PDA.

Driller reads the contract on his PDA screen and discusses some changes with Auerbach. By using white-boarding software, both Driller and Auerbach can see and work on the contract as they speak. Driller changes a couple of clauses about home-leave allowances, Auerbach initials them on-screen, and both Driller and

Auerbach sign the completed contract with their styluses. Deal done, Driller heads back to the beach for a moonlight swim.

Team Placement

Bette Fernia, systems development manager for SysLink Inc., needs to assemble a multidisciplinary team to integrate the information-processing departments of two banks, one in Florida and one in Latin America. This project requires an unusual mix of skills:

- Bilingual fluency in English and Spanish (Information Systems technical).
- Technical expertise in integrating two incompatible hardware and software systems: IBM mainframe running DB2 and two UNISYS minis running UNIX.
- Vertical market expertise in automating reengineered bank back office transaction processing.
- Cross-cultural team leadership and conflict resolution skills to get two competing departments' IS professionals to work together effectively under challenging conditions: heavy deadline pressure and the prospect that half the team will be laid off when the banks merge.

At her PC, Bette clicks on the HRIS icon, followed by "Team Builder" and then Job/Role Requirements to specify competencies needed by team members: language skills, technical skills, industry knowledge, and interpersonal competencies.

When she has defined the job role requirements, she then clicks on the "Find Team Members" button. The computer immediately searches the personnel information records of the 30,000 regular and contract employees available to the firm, and identifies those system professionals who meet Bette's language, technical, business, and personal competency requirements.

The "Team Builder" then optimizes, sorting different combinations of employees, to find a dream team comprising the smallest number of people who bring all the necessary skills to the team and are most likely to work well together. Candidates must have language and the teamwork and cooperation competencies but need not have every technical competency. The team must include at least two workers with all of the required skills. "Renaissance" employees who bring the most competencies to the team reduce the total number of people needed and are worth more in "pay for competence" compensation.

The IHRMIS recommends several dream teams, with alternates for each "best pick" employee in case some are unavailable. The system's recommendations include performance management objective statements, development plans, and compensation ranges for each prospective team member based on his or her competencies. With a few more clicks, Bette e-mails each candidate a request for his or her time availability to work on the integration project.

On-line Coaching and Training

Win Lee Su—an M.B.A. from a top business school with a reputation as a bril-
liant corporate staff analyst—is in his first line job: South Georgia Territory
Sales Manager. Win knows he was given this job to get line experience—and to
see if he had the right stuff to stay on the fast track to an executive position.

This morning, Win faces a confrontation with one of his top salespeople, Joe
Bloggs. A customer has complained that Joe "was drunk again when he called on
us and embarrassed me in front of my boss. If you want to keep our account, you
had better get Bloggs to shape up."

Win has met Bloggs, who has been with the company for many years, has lots
of friends, and has a good sales record despite his well-known fondness for bourbon.

New to the territory and 20 years his junior, Win doesn't feel he knows how to
handle a confrontation with Bloggs. He clicks the IHRMIS icon on his PC, and then
on Management Advisor/Drug and Alcohol Abuse/Confronting an Employee.

A window (see Figure 1.2) opens in the upper-right corner of the screen and
plays a video that describes

1. The company's policy on providing assistance to an employee with a
   substance abuse problem.

2. The steps of a confrontation interview with a specific point to be made at
   each step: acceptance of a contract that includes participation in a treatment plan, standards of behavior on the job, and so on.

The program then asks if the viewer would like to see an example of a confrontation interview. When Win clicks on yes, he sees a ten-minute tape of a
confrontation interview illustrating the steps and points the manager should
make, typical employee responses (denial, etc.), and how a manager can deal
with each of these.

At the conclusion of the video, the program suggests that the manager watch
the example interview several times to get the maximum benefit from this on-
line modeling training. Thus prepared, Win calls Bloggs and asks him to meet
him in his office.

Bloggs, after a bad week and a worse weekend, suspects he may be about to get
fired. He walks to the HR Benefits kiosk (conveniently located between the Men's
and Women's rest rooms), clicks on the human resource management icon, and then
on Employee Assistance/Drug & Alcohol/Telling your boss you have a problem.

A window (see Figure 1.3) opens in the upper-right corner of his screen and
plays a video that

1. Describes the rights and benefits company policy offers an employee
   with a substance abuse problem.

2. Then asks the viewer if he or she would like to see an example of how to
   inform the boss that he or she is seeking assistance.

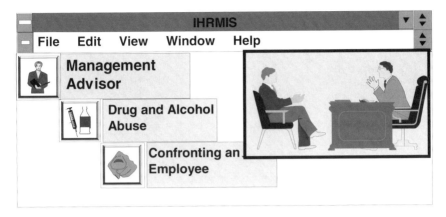

Figure 1.2 An On-line Management Advisor Screen

When Bloggs clicks on yes, he sees a ten-minute tape of an employee telling a boss about a decision to seek assistance for a personal problem, and how the employee can get help instead of getting fired. Thus prepared, he heads off to his meeting with Win.

Human Resource Assets: Training Needs Assessment

When Fiona Prokovief, CEO of Global Transport (GT), boots her computer in the morning, her "wallpaper" (opening screen) shows a message:

> **BUSINESS ALERT:** Sales are down 26.4% in Eastern Europe.
> **Probable causes**
> Customer Satisfaction: down 16.8%
> **Human Resources Indicators**
> Front line Employee satisfaction: down 19%
> Compensation: 6.2% below market
> Competence fit scores: 64% (std: 85%)
> Training plan: 0-23% completed

During the night, various active agents—small expert system software programs triggered by a timer—have been calling GT's business and human resources databases around the world. These agent programs are part of an Executive Information System (EIS) that automatically uploads and analyzes data, looks for patterns and problems that may explain business results, and reports its findings to top management.

Prokovief knows that front line employee satisfaction is a leading indicator for customer satisfaction: approximately six months after employees become dissatisfied,

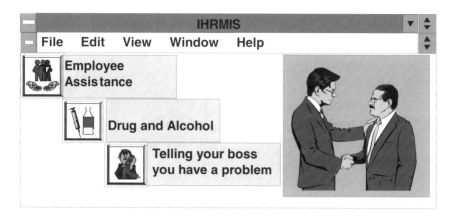

Figure 1.3 An On-line Employee Assistance Screen

customers become dissatisfied and sales decline. GT's EIS has flagged compensation, competence, and training as possible explanations for poor employee morale, which may be causing customer unhappiness and lost sales.

GT subscribes to several compensation firms' salary surveys. These firms' active agents continually poll a sample of clients' compensation databases to monitor salary trends for several hundred key jobs. GT's compensation agent has polled Hay Management Consultants' compensation database for operations and IS professionals in Eastern Europe, compared these data with GT's current salary practices, and found that GT's pay for key jobs has drifted 6.2% below market—a likely cause of employee dissatisfaction.

Prokovief picks up the phone and asks her compensation analyst to get back to her with recommendations for changes in GT's compensation policy for Eastern Europe. (And she makes a mental note: if the compensation staffer had been on his toes, he would have seen the trend on his computer screen and proposed a remedy *before* it became a problem. *Superior* HR staff are always *ahead* of the curve, not behind it. Woe be to those who find out about a problem when a senior executive calls.)

Prokovief next drills down (asks the computer for more detailed information) on high, average, and low customer service competency levels of employees in Eastern Europe as a whole, and then by country: Poland, Hungary, and the Ukraine (see computer screens in Chapter 6).

She finds Hungary is above the Western European average level in customer service orientation. Poland is below average, and the Ukraine is a full three levels below the customer service orientation standard GT expects of all of its employees.

By double-clicking on each country, Prokovief can drill down even more to view data by office location: Gdansk, Budapest, or Kiev. She can immediately see how many employees have completed GT's customer service orientation training (available on CD-ROM) at all GT offices worldwide. Twelve hours of customer service orientation training is mandatory in the first month of employment for all employees. She sees a 95%+ completion rate in Poland and Hungary and 0% completion rate in Ukraine. She immediately e-mails the Ukraine general manager and training director with a request for an explanation and a plan to bring customer service orientation levels up to GT standards.

Prokovief can access the current competency level and training status of any one of GT's 44,000 employees instantaneously by any aggregate: country, office, salary grade, function (e.g., sales, finance, manufacturing), demographic category (e.g., gender, race). Countries, offices, and individual employees are color-coded: green, if competencies are at or above GT standards; yellow, if data are one to two just-noticeable differences below standards; and red, if three or more just-noticeable differences below standards, meaning "**critical for improvement!**"

Prokovief's EIS provides her with up-to-the-minute assessment of GT's most valuable assets, its human resources.

The vignettes above—all true stories, and all possible with technology available today—illustrate ways HR can be reengineered:

1. Employees can enter routine administrative changes and get information on benefits *directly, by themselves*—from almost anywhere in the world—using their own PCs, PDAs, or HR kiosk workstations linked to their firm's HRIS.

2. Line managers themselves can recruit and select needed workers on-line, using job–person matching expert systems linked to the firm's HRIS and external bulletin boards, and do it much faster than most HR departments can provide this vital service. Candidates can include not just current employees, but anyone in a worldwide virtual workforce network of potential contract workers.

3. Training can be delivered "just-in-time" by computer interactive video performance support systems available on employees' PCs or PDAs.

4. Comprehensive information about a firm's human resource assets—the competencies of its employees—can be immediately available to top management for remediation, succession planning, or strategic analysis. Executives can get on-line answers to such questions as:

   ■ Do we have the right skills to compete effectively with our domestic and international competitors?

   ■ Do we have people with the right skills to launch a new product, service, or strategic market initiative? If we do not, why?

   Is recruiting not finding candidates with these competencies?

   Is our selection system ineffective in hiring for these competencies?

   Are we training to these competencies?

   ■ How many employees have completed required training and been assessed to have competencies at the standards we require?

- Are we giving people feedback on their competence and performance appraisals?
- Are we rewarding employees (e.g., via skill or pay demonstration, or development of critical competencies)?

VISION

This is the vision for reengineered HR in the future:

All human resources services available instantaneously, on demand, at the place most convenient to an employee: his or her own workstation, anywhere in the world.

WHAT IS REENGINEERING?

The term reengineering usually is credited to former MIT information systems professor Michael Hammer who defines it formally as:

> "The fundamental rethinking and radical redesign of business processes to achieve dramatic improvements in critical, contemporary measures of performance, such as cost, quality, service and speed (p. 32) . . . (using) state-of-the-art information technology, an essential enabler, since it permits companies to reengineer business processes." (p. 83)
>
> "Business reengineering means starting over from scratch. . . At the heart of business reengineering lies the notion of *discontinuous thinking*—identifying and abandoning the outdated rules and fundamental assumptions that underlie current business operations." (pp. 2–3)[1]

"Macro" reengineering means rethinking whether work should be done at all (vs. eliminated), or if essential, whether work, products, and services should be provided by the firm, or "outsourced"—purchased from outside vendors. Triage rules for work elimination, outsourcing versus DIY ("do it yourself"), and reengineering are shown in Figure 1.4. *Only if work is essential and strategic is it worth reengineering*: a firm should not reengineer a business it is not familiar with.

"Micro" reengineering can be defined as:

> **Radical** redesign of workflow processes, using **Information** systems technology: networked personal digital assistants (PDAs), which I will define as all types of personal computers and smart phones; with People competent and empowered to do the whole job for their customers (or themselves) at their first point of contact with a customer (or the information system), to achieve dramatic (50% to 90%) improvements in quality and productivity.

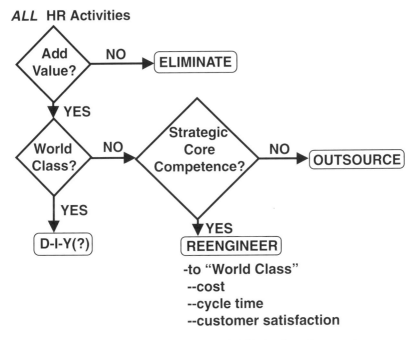

Figure 1.4 Flow Diagram for Work Elimination, Outsourcing Versus DIY, and Reengineering

What's New About Reegineering?
(And why it won't be just another passing fad)

Skeptics legitimately ask, "What's new about reengineering? Is it simply the latest in a long list of management fads? The same old stuff in new jargon?"

I personally believe that reengineering includes two new elements: use of networked PDAs *communications* and *expert systems* support tools as well as traditional data and word processing devices, and the assumption that work can be radically (as opposed to incrementally) changed to produce radically *(50% to 90%)* greater time, cost, productivity, and quality improvements.

Networked PDAs

Reengineering is made possible by the fact that PDAs are now:

- cheap enough for virtually all employees to have one.
- user friendly enough for all employees to be able to use one.
- *networked—so every computer and employee can be connected to and communicate with each other.*

What is new is that networked PCs have finally reached a critical mass of power, affordability, accessibility, and user friendliness and are beginning to deliver their long-promised productivity gains.

In the last 50 years, information technology has increased human ability to improve productivity an incomprehensible 30 orders of magnitude, 10^{30}, the ratio of the diameter of an atom to that of the Milky Way Galaxy (see Chapter 2). Until very recently, despite the hundreds of billions of dollars invested in computers, there has been virtually *no* increase in service sector productivity. Reengineering is nothing less than humankind's fulfillment of the long-heralded information revolution, which will be as massive and sweeping as the Industrial Revolution was 200 years ago. The word reengineering may be dismissed a year from now and some other jargonistic term (current candidates include work transformation and reinvention) given to the changes brought about by the information revolution. But the fundamental process of using information technology to rework everything human beings do will continue irrespective of what the process is called.

Radical Productivity Gains

Figure 1.5 compares the incremental 2% to 3% improvement assumptions of TQM (total quality management), the last fad, with the radical discontinuous 50% to 90% improvements in productivity and service possible with reengineering, on a continuum from "little i" to "BIG I" improvement.

Reengineering is the necessary successor to TQM because TQM incremental improvement increasingly is perceived as simply "too little, too slow." Firms

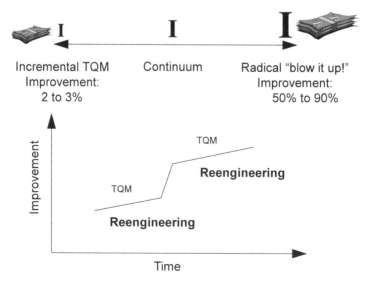

Figure 1.5 Radical "BIG I" Productivity Improvement with Reengineering

need radical process improvements to survive, remain competitive, and gain competitive advantage.

In fact, TQM and reengineering are by no means mutually exclusive. As will be discussed in Chapters 3 and 8, both share many concepts (e.g., Supplier => Input => Process => Output => CUSTOMER work flows, with emphasis on CUSTOMER).

Reengineering produces dramatic quantum increases in productivity improvement approximately every three to five years, when technology advances make radical changes in work possible. (For example, as will be discussed in Chapter 2, the next quantum jump will be *voice recognition*. By the year 2000, keyboards and mice will be as obsolete as typewriters. Everyone will talk to their computers. The ability to perform almost all work by voice commands will offer yet another opportunity to totally rethink and reengineer work processes.) TQM methods provide the fine tuning, debugging, slightly inclined incremental improvements between reengineering quantum leaps.

Key Ingredients

The key ingredients in reengineering are *information systems technology, process, and people*, as suggested in Figure 1.6.

Information Systems Technology

Reengineering is enabled by extensive use of networked, integrated personal computers, which make it possible to process virtually all HR paperwork electronically and automate the delivery of most human resources services. As important as PCs themselves are the communication links among them, which permit information on any machine anywhere to be communicated to any other at (potentially) the speed of light. (Chapter 2 discusses PC network and software tools available for reengineering HR services delivery.)

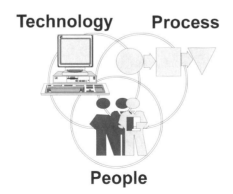

Figure 1.6 Reengineering Essentials: IS Technology, Process, and People

Process

Reengineering makes use of classic industrial engineering work-analysis methods: cost benefit/value analysis, work flow charting, and systems and operations analysis. Nothing new here: all of these methods have been around for 100 years. Knowing how to use these methods is, however, a basic prerequisite for actually doing reengineering. (Chapter 3 provides instructions for activity-based costing, value analysis, and work flow process improvement methods).

People: Empowered—and Competent—Employees and Teams

People are frequently neglected in reengineering projects, perhaps because most reengineers are former IS professionals, accountants, or MBAs. Yet anyone with any experience with reengineering knows that people are the most important ingredient: reengineered work flows do not work without empowered and competent employees able to use them.

Empowerment in reengineered work means that employees closest to customers are given the authority to do the whole job as case managers for their customers. For example, with an expert systems computer that qualifies loan applicants, a 17-year-old bank teller can ask a customer eight questions (e.g., Do you own your home? If "yes," how long have you owned your home? etc.) and *on the* s*pot* approve a $1,000 personal loan. Before reengineering, this loan could only be approved by a bank officer after many steps, many pieces of paper, and somewhere between two and six weeks.

The obvious people question is "How many 17-year-old tellers are competent to do the enlarged job of teller plus loan officer?" Competencies required are not just technical (the ability to operate the expert system). More important are motivation, maturity, and interpersonal competencies: the willingness to take responsibility for making significant financial decisions as well as interpersonal skills to calm angry customers denied loans, and the like. (The very significant changes in people competencies required to do reengineered work are discussed in Chapter 7.)

HUMAN RESOURCE COSTS AND VALUE-ADDED

Figure 1.7 shows the approximate percentage costs and value-added of present human resources systems in most organizations.

Sixty percent of human resource costs, activities, and people is devoted to administration: record keeping, compliance, and bureaucratic paper shuffling.

Thirty percent of costs and efforts is devoted to HR services delivery: recruiting, training, counseling, succession planning, performance management, selection assessment, equal opportunity, and the like.

Ten percent of costs and effort is devoted to strategic planning: compensation, executive development and succession planning, and ensuring that the firm has the human resources it needs to compete effectively in future years.

Figure 1.7 HR Costs and Value Added

The value-added by each layer of the pyramid is *inverse* of its cost. Administration costs 60% of total human resources efforts but adds only 10% value. At best it keeps the firm out of court. Services delivery costs 30% and provides 30% in value-added. Human resources strategic planning probably accounts for 60% of the value-added by the HR function and costs only 10%.

The implication is obvious. Reengineering logically starts at the bottom of the pyramid, where the deadly combination (opportunity!) of *high costs* and *low value-added activities* offer tempting targets. Administrative functions should be eliminated, outsourced, or automated wherever possible (and cost-effective) to free resources for higher value-added HR activities: services delivery and strategic planning.

Figure 1.8 shows the impact of reengineering human resources: 50% cost and head-count reduction. Reengineering scissors are applied almost exclusively to administrative tasks (see Chapter 9). Reengineering has just begun to nibble at the costs of human resources delivery (e.g., automation of training, using computer-assisted instruction, interactive video and distance learning via teleconferencing) and has barely touched HR strategic planning.

Figure 1.9 shows the reengineering order of battle.

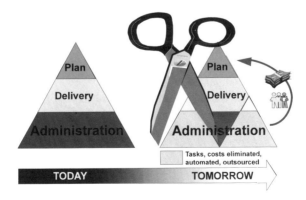

Figure 1.8 The Impact of Reengineering Human Resources

REENGINEERING HR

1. Clean up Administration: "No paper!"

 Everything by phone or on screen

2. Deliver "Virtual" Services

 Just-in-time (on demand) to clients at place most convenient to client: his/her workstation

3. Develop EIS for Strategic Planning

 Executive Information Systems help recruit people who can do reengineered jobs and provide competitive advantage

Figure 1.9   Reengineering Order of Battle

Reengineering Phase I Clean Up Administration

Phase I focuses on eliminating, outsourcing, or automating all routine administrative paperwork. Powerful reengineering concepts here are Customer Do-It-Yourself (DIY) and No Paper! (i.e., employees and managers process all their own HR transactions on PC screens or via voice-response telephones). Examples include everything from employee personal data changes to expert-system-facilitated on-screen performance appraisals. Figures 1.10 and 1.11 show a *before* versus *after* reengineering work flow for a standard personnel transaction (e.g., a promotion in a Fortune 500 company).

Before reengineering, a typical transaction included the six major and 49 minor steps shown in Figure 1.10.

> **1.** A manager initiated a change (1.1) by asking his/her secretary to retrieve an employee's paper files (1.2), then generated a paper form (1.3), which was retrieved by the manager's secretary who typed it, copied it, filed a duplicate copy, and then mailed it on to the manager's manager (1.4).

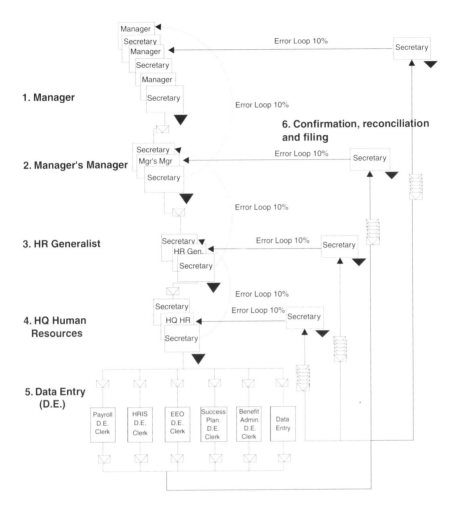

Figure 1.10   An HR Transaction Before Reengineering

2. After his/her secretary opened and delivered the mailed form to his/her in-box (2.1), the manager's manager (MM) then checked "approved" or "disapproved" on the form (2.2), which was retrieved by the MM's secretary, who copied it, filed a duplicate copy, and then mailed it on to the site HR generalist (2.3).

3. After his/her secretary opened the mail and carried the form to his/her in-box (3.1), the HR generalist further checked and approved or disapproved the form (3.2), which was retrieved by the MM's secretary, who copied it, filed a duplicate copy, and then mailed it on to (a minimum of one)

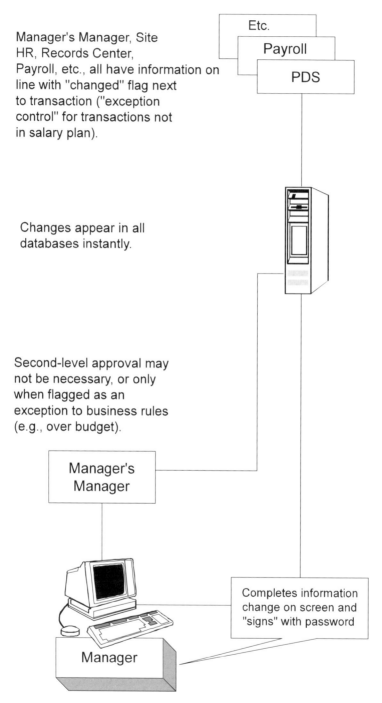

Manager's Manager, Site
HR, Records Center,
Payroll, etc., all have information on
line with "changed" flag next
to transaction ("exception
control" for transactions not
in salary plan).

Etc.

Payroll

PDS

Changes appear in all
databases instantly.

Second-level approval may
not be necessary, or only
when flagged as an
exception to business rules
(e.g., over budget).

Manager's
Manager

Completes information
change on screen and
"signs" with password

Manager

Figure 1.11   An HR Transaction After Reengineering

corporate headquarters' HR specialist (3.3).4. After his/her secretary opened the mail and carried the form to his/her in-box (4.1), the HQ HR specialist(s) further checked and approved or disapproved the form (4.2), which was retrieved by his/her secretary, who made seven copies of the form, filed one, and then mailed the others to (in this real case) six different HR and payroll database data entry clerks (4.3).

4. Each personnel system (HR records center, payroll, EEO/AA, Labor Relations, Benefits Administration, etc.) data entry clerk opened his/her mail (5.1), checked the form and entered transaction data in his/her database (5.2), filed a paper copy of the form (5.3), and mailed (5.4) a confirmation of the data change back to the HQ HR specialist(s), HR generalist, the manager's manager, and the manager, at four steps each, a total of 24 steps for the six clerks.

5. Each manager's secretary opened (6.1) the confirmation form, reconciled it against his/her filed copy of the original change request, stapled the original and the confirmation together (6.2) and refiled (6.3) them—at three steps each, a total of 12 steps for the four secretaries.

Note that duplicate data records, each a piece of paper occupying a file folder in the file cabinet, are maintained in ten different places, and these are in addition to identical electronic data files on six separate computer databases.

The work flow represents the best case for a transaction processed in this firm. Often, more than one corporate HQ HR specialist, representing Compensation, EEO/AA, and so forth, would get involved, multiplying Step 4 time and costs.

Further, this scenario assumes *no errors*, when in fact, the firm's error rate averaged 10%. Errors follow a "1-10-100" rule: if it takes one minute and costs $1 to do it right the first time, it takes 10 minutes and costs $10 to fix it *during* the process, and 100 minutes and $100 to fix it if it comes back (i.e., causes problems for an end-user customer. Recall Diane Surah's "termination" at the Phoenix Airport Hertz counter due to data entry error.)

Figure 1.11 shows the reengineered process *after* implementation of the firm's integrated human resources management information system. There is one, or at most, two steps.

1. The manager simply completes the information change on his or her PC screen, signs it with his or her password, and clicks on "Confirm/Send."

The IHRMIS has expert system error checking, or exception control, built into it. When a manager tries to enter a promotion that violates a business rule, for example, includes a salary increase that exceeds the department's budget, promotes an employee who lacks the competencies to perform a higher-level job, or does not meet the firm's affirmative action guidelines, the computer beeps and displays a message: "Salary out of range"; "Person doesn't meet competency criteria for promotion"; or "Promotion of this candidate will cause you to miss your affirmative action goal."

The expert system gives the manager an opportunity to reconsider and perhaps revise his or her decision to promote a candidate.

If the change is not beeped, it is instantly forwarded to everyone else in the organization who needs to check or approve it. If no approvals are needed, the change automatically updates a single IHRMIS database that serves all HR functions, payroll, strategic planning, and every manager and employee in the firm.

2. OPTIONAL: Second-level approval by the manager's manager. Higher-level management review may be conducted on an exception-only basis, and usually it is not needed at all. Even without expert system exception control, only 15% of decisions need to be approved by a higher level of management and only 3% of changes by two or more higher levels. With the IHRMIS, only 5% of transactions need a second approval step. When needed, the manager's manager simply clicks on "Confirm/Send," and the change automatically updates the IHRMIS database.

Note who goes away between the *before* and *after* reengineering work flows: secretaries, data entry clerks, and middle people—managers and HR generalists. Going away may or may not mean layoffs. Often reengineering efficiencies increase managerial and support-staff spans of control or service: a manager can supervise 15 subordinates instead of 10, or a secretary serve five managers instead of three.

The spreadsheet in Tables 1.1 and 1.2 show the activity-based costs of the HR transaction before and after reengineering. Assuming one level of approval needed for 5% of transactions, the *after* work flow cost savings are 76.4%, a total of $23.74 per transaction in labor costs and out-of-pocket expenses for mail, and $2,089,340 for the 100,000 transactions a year that occur in this firm. In this case, reengineering's promise of 50% to 90% cost reductions is clearly realized.

Reengineering Phase II
Development of Virtual Services Delivery Systems

Many HR services (e.g., benefit selection advice and training) can be performed via expert systems at the HR kiosk and training programs on CD-ROM. Phase II is development of hardware and software systems that can deliver all HR services just-in-time (instantaneously, on demand) at the place most convenient to end-users—their own workstations. Examples include Driller's job hunting, Win's on-line coaching and training, Joe Bloggs' employee assistance information and referral, and Auerbach and Fernia's computer-assisted recruitment and selection transactions.

Table 1.1 Activity-Based Costs for the HR Transaction Shown in Figure 1.10 Before Reengineering

Analyst: Lyle Spencer
Work Flow: HR transaction: promotion
Costs × Baseline=___ Alternative:

STEP	Labor Costs: Who does it?	Cost per Time	Time Unit	Labor Cost	Cash Outlay	# of Trans.	Cost per Unit	Total Cash Outlay	Total Cost
		Salary/Year × Overhead × Time Unit (260 days, 2,080 hrs, 124,800 min./yr)							
1.1 Mgr has secty pull folder	Mgr	$0.64	2	$1.28				$0.00	$1.28
1.2 Mgr's secty	Secty	$0.27	2	$0.53				$0.00	$0.53
1.3 Mgr reviews salesplan, increase	Mgr	$0.64	10	$6.42				$0.00	$6.42
1.4 Secty retrieves, types files, duplicate	Secty	$0.27	2	$0.53				$0.00	$0.53
1.5 Mgr signs	Mgr	$0.64	2	$1.28				$0.00	$1.28
1.6 Secty sends to Mgr's Mgr for approval	Secty	$0.27	2	$0.53				$0.00	$0.53
2.1 Mgr's Mgr signs	Mgr's Mgr	$0.64	2	$1.28				$0.00	$1.28
2.2 Mgr's Mgr's Secty sends to Mgr's Secty	Secty	$0.27	2	$0.53				$0.00	$0.53
2.3 Secty files, mails to HR	Secty	$0.27	3	$0.80	Postage	1	$0.29	$0.29	$1.09
3.1 HR secty opens, sorts	Secty	$0.27	1	$0.27				$0.00	$0.27
3.2 Secty gives to HR Generalist	Secty	$0.27	1	$0.27				$0.00	$0.27
3.3 HR Generalist approves, gives back to secty	HR Gen	$0.64	1	$0.64				$0.00	$0.64
3.4 Secty mails copies to HQ HR	Secty	$0.27	1	$0.27	Postage	1	$0.29	$0.29	$0.56
4.1 HQ HR secty gives to HQ HR manager	Secty	$0.27	2	$0.53				$0.00	$0.53
4.2 HQ HR manager signs and gives back to secty	HQ HR Mgr	$0.64	1	$0.64				$0.00	$0.64
4.3 Secty files and sends copies to data entry	Secty	$0.27	1	$0.27	Postage	6	$0.29	$1.74	$2.01
5a Payroll data entry–mails completed forms	Clerk	$0.27	4	$1.07	Postage	1	$0.29	$0.29	$1.36
5b HRIS data entry–mails completed forms	Clerk	$0.27	3	$0.80	Postage	1	$0.29	$0.29	$1.09
5c EEO data entry–mails completed forms	Clerk	$0.27	3	$0.80	Postage	1	$0.29	$0.29	$1.09
5d Succes. plan data entry–mails completed forms	Clerk	$0.27	3	$0.80	Postage	1	$0.29	$0.29	$1.09
5e Ben. admin data entry–mails completed forms	Clerk	$0.27	3	$0.80	Postage	1	$0.29	$0.29	$1.09
5f Data entry	Clerk	$0.27	2	$0.53				$0.00	$0.53
6a HR Secty receives, reconciles files	Secty	$0.27	2	$0.53				$0.00	$0.53
6b Mgrs Secty receives, reconciles files	Secty	$0.27	2	$0.53				$0.00	$0.53
6c HQ secty receives, reconciles files	Secty	$0.27	2	$0.53				$0.00	$0.53
6d Mgr's mgr secty receives, reconciles files	Secty	$0.27	2	$0.53				$0.00	$0.53
TOTALS	Per trans.		62	$23.28				$4.06	$27.34
	# trans.			100,000				100,000	100,000
	Total			$2,328,333				$406,000	$2,734,333

23

Table 1.2 Activity-Based Costs for the HR Transaction Shown in Figure 1.11 After Reengineering — and Before After-Cost Saving Benefits from Reengineering the Work Flow

ANALYST: Lyle Spencer

Full Labor Cost Calculation Formula

WORK FLOW: HR transaction: promotion

Salary/Year × Ohd Mult____Time Unit____ (260 days, 2,080 hrs, 124,800 min. /yr)

COSTS × BASELINE ALTERNATIVE: STEP	LABOR COSTS Who does it?	#	$Cost/ Time	Time Unit	Total Labor $Cost	Cash Outlay Costs	#	$Cost/ Unit	Total Cash Outlay Costs	Total $Cost
1. Manager enters changes in computer	Mgr	1	$0.64	10	$6.42				$0.00	$6.42
2. Manager's mgr approval (optional)	Mgr's Mgr	1	$0.64	0.1	$0.06				$0.00	$0.06
									$0.00	$0.00
TOTALS	Per transaction			10.1	$6.48				$0.00	$6.48
	# transactions				100,000				100,000	100,000
	Total				$648,083				$0.00	$648,083
	Savings				$1,680,250				$406,000	$2,086,250

Reengineering, Phase III
Executive Information Systems (EIS) for Strategic Planning

Phase III is development of expert system executive information systems (EIS) to improve HR strategic planning: recruiting, selecting, training, motivating, and maintaining the performance of the people who can do the reengineered jobs and provide competitive advantage in the "Year 2000" firm. Fiona Prokovief's on-line ability to monitor Eastern European workforces' customer-service orientation competencies and employee completion of training are examples of an HR EIS in action.

IMPLICATIONS OF REENGINEERING
FOR THE HUMAN RESOURCES FUNCTION

Reengineering has major implications for human resources professionals: automation, outsourcing, integration, decentralization, destaffing, and changes in professional roles and competencies needed to perform effectively in the future.

Automation: Most (70%+) HR services will be provided by personal computers and interactive voice-response systems connected to a central HR database. Data generated by thousands of daily HR transactions will be monitored by smart agent software programs, and findings regarding the moment-to-moment state of the firm's human resources assets will be reported via EIS to top management.

Outsourcing: The most profound of HR reengineeering will be outsourcing. A Conference Board survey indicates that 80+% of large U.S. organizations are considering outsourcing most or all of human resources. Major service firms preparing to provide HR services on an outsourced basis include:

- Systems integrators: EDS, Andersen, IBM
- Payroll firms: ADP, Ceridian, many large banks
- Financial services firms: American Express, Fidelity, Merrill Lynch
- Big Six Accounting firms: Andersen, Coopers & Lybrand
- HRIS Software vendors: Ceridian/Tesseract, ADP/PeopleSoft, Dun&Bradstreet
- Temporary Agencies: Kelly, Manpower, Temporaries Inc.

and various strategic alliances among these providers.

The temporary firms will offer other organizations the most radical proposition: "you don't want to 'own' employees—just lease them from us, and we will take care of all human resources."

Outsourcing options are created and made practical by information systems that permit "virtual" performance of any HR service anywhere by anyone. Employees could not care less whether "payroll" is in Bombay or Bulgaria as long as their checks are deposited on time.

Integration: HR functions—staffing, performance management, training and development, compensation, and so on—now balkanized among competing fiefdoms of specialists, will be integrated by IHRMIS (see Chapter 6) and used directly by employee end-users to get bundles of multiple services to solve problems or achieve personal objectives, as shown in Figure 1.12. Top-line management will have instant access to comprehensive HR balance sheets and profit-and-loss statements for strategic planning.

> *To make sure that staff is helping rather than hindering the line, staff departments must justify their budgets to the operational units on the theory that operations pay for them. Cuts in middle management staffs are ranging from 20% to 40% . . . to improve efficiency from 30% to 50%.*
>
> *Business Week* cover story, April 25, 1983

Radical decentralization in the way HR services are provided: from HR professionals providing services to line manager and employee *self-service* directly from their workstations. Increasingly, often-heard policies such as "Human Resources Management is the *line manager's* responsibility" and "Career development is the *employee's* responsibility"—now mostly rhetoric—will actually be implemented using expert system "HR Advisors" available on-line to all employees.

Integrated INFORMATION for Top Management Strategic Planning

HR SERVICES

ORG & JOB DESIGN   STAFFING DESTAFFING   PERF. MGMT.   DEVELOPMENT   COMPENSATION   ORGANIZATION DEVELOPMENT

Integrated SERVICES to Line Management and Employee Customers

Figure 1.12   Data "Bundled" by Human Resource Information Systems to Integrate Services for Managers and Employees and to Provide Information to Top Management for Strategic Planning

Decentralization of HR staff from headquarters to line and field business units has been under way for the last 15 years. The early 1980s recession chilled whatever bloom remained on the M.B.A. rose. The hordes of corporate staff that had accumulated during the 1960s and 1970s conglomerate era increasingly came to be seen as despised overhead people who *cost* money, as opposed to value-adding line manufacturing and sales employees who *made* money. Firms responded by cutting staff and dispersing corporate HQ HR specialist staff to the provinces—to line field offices and sites—to be generalists.

Currently under way is a second and much more profound decentralization: that of HR services provided by HR professionals to their line manager and employee customers. In the future, line managers and employees essentially will serve themselves (empowerment!), aided by a user-friendly silicon HR advisor expert system in the PC on their desk or at the HR kiosk.

Destaffing: 50% across the board, HR head count and cost reductions. As shown in Figures 1.10 and 1.11, the middle people (secretaries, clerks, middle managers, and HR generalists) go away when line managers and employees perform their own HR functions. Current data suggest reengineering HR results in 50% across-the-board HR head count and cost reductions. Chapters 6 and 8 show where these savings are.

HR reengineering is not, however, simply cutting heads in the HR function. Strategically, there aren't enough of them to make any difference. As shown in Figure 1.13, HR rarely represents more than .9% to 1.0% of a firm's total costs. The entire HR function could be eliminated without significantly improving most firms' cost structure.

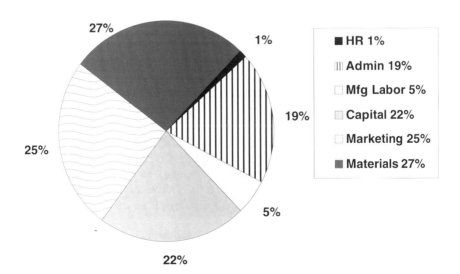

Figure 1.13 Human Resources Department Costs as a Percentage of Total Company Costs

A more strategic way to think about reengineering HR costs—and *potential benefits*—is shown in Figure 1.14.

Benefits from reduced customer costs. Firm manager and employee customer time spent interacting with the HR function costs *three times* what the HR function itself costs. Changes in HR work flows that save *customer* time can increase customer satisfaction and result in significant cost savings.

Benefits from reduction in HR vendor costs. Vendor costs (health insurance and pension benefits, HRIS, etc.) average 15% to 16% of a firm's costs, 15 times the cost of the HR function. Clearly savings from alternative sourcing or vendor agreements can result in significant cost savings benefits.

Improving the return on the firm's "human organization" assets. By far the most valuable HR reengineering will be strategic interventions that increase a

Figure 1.14 "Human Organization" Costs as a Percentage of Total Company Costs

firm's return on its human organization—typically 50% to 70% of its total costs. For example, as will be shown in Chapter 7, competency-based HR practices can improve a firm's human assets productivity as much as 30%. A 3% productivity increase in 50% of a firm's productive assets is worth 1.5%—a 50% return on an HR function costing 1% of a firm's resources.

Dramatic change in HR professional roles and competencies. The remaining HR professionals will be very different from the administrative paper shufflers of the past. HR practitioner roles will change from "doers" to the consultants for the doers: HR services "consumer's guide" compilers, advisors, resource brokers, and purchasing agents who help line managers and employees decide which HR services to purchase from outside vendors. Headquarters training staff will no longer provide training, but will advise divisional and field line managers on which training courses to send employees and which to buy from contractors. Top-level HR specialists will continue to provide advanced advice and knowledge not yet built into the HR expert systems. (Effective expert systems will know their own limitations, referring users to human experts when appropriate, e.g., "There is a 33% chance that this action violates the Family Leave Act of 1993. Click here to contact Marta Shark, Esq. Corporate Labor Relations Counsel").

Knowledge engineers and programmers. HR professionals increasingly are being asked to put their expertise "in the box" (i.e., a computer) or on a disk. For example, stand-up trainers are becoming developers of CD-ROM-based interactive video/computer assisted-instruction (IV/CAI) training programs available on disk or via teleconferencing or modem to provide distance learning for employees worldwide. Compensation, labor law, and benefits administration professionals are programming expert systems that advise manager and employee end-users at HR kiosks (public personal computers) or on their own PCs.

WHAT'S IN IT FOR THE CUSTOMER?

A powerful lesson from the TQM movement is that everything begins and ends with the customer. What is quality HR service value-added from the line manager's and employee–customer's perspective? Studies of customer perception of service quality include:

1. **Response Time.** From the moment I am aware I want the service, how long does it take to get it? Ideal: Service is delivered just-in-time—instantaneously, on demand—when I want it.

2. **Convenient Location.** How far do I have to go to get it? Ideal: I can get it where I am, when I want it, without any (or an absolute minimum of) movement, travel, or inconvenience on my part.

3. **Reliability.** If it's a product, does it work and continue to work? If it's information, is it accurate? Up-to-date? *Ideal:* The service gives me what I want.

It delivers what I expect. It *always* works. It is *always* 100% accurate and current (current usually means accurate; old data is usually inaccurate).

4. **Tangibles.** Is it clean? Private? A nice smoke-free training room, not cramped, with good lighting? *Ideal:* The physical environment not only does not distract from delivery of the service, it enhances it (e.g., a very nice training environment but not so stunningly beautiful as to be distracting). Privacy and security—knowing one's personal information, medical records, and personal problems are kept confidential—are important tangibles in HR service environments. HR kiosks should be enclosed private spaces like phone booths with doors.

5. **Empathy.** Does the service provider understand and genuinely care about me? *Ideal:* I feel understood immediately and feel that the service provider truly wants and will make every effort to help me in any way he/she/it can.

6. **Assurance.** Is the service provider credible and trustworthy? Can I count on its being there when I need help? *Ideal:* I know that this service provider is the best (heart surgeon, labor lawyer, etc.) in the world or is at least state-of-art and backed up by the best, if needed.

Other service quality criteria found in some studies include:

Empowerment. The service gives the customer a sense of control or mastery, leaving the customer feeling *more* confident and competent that he or she can solve the problem alone next time.

Stimulation. The service provides variety, novelty, or challenge; it excites or engages something *new*.

Aesthetics. The service is attractive (e.g., stunning graphics in beautiful colors on a computer screen).

Fun. Getting the service is an enjoyable experience, not boring and frustrating, and you don't have to fight with a computer to get it to do what you want it to do. "Fun" is probably a product of other service quality dimensions: empowerment, stimulation, and aesthetics.

The challenge in HR services delivery is how to *improve* customer service—provide all service quality criteria as well as or better than they are being provided now—while still achieving 50% to 90% productivity increases and cost reduction. Response time, convenient location, and reliability are easy with technology. Computers, when properly programmed and debugged, almost always provide routine data faster and more accurately than people do, and are often considered equally or even more credible (notwithstanding garbage in, garbage out).

Resistance to automation of HR services usually centers on *empathy*. One would think that the hardest service criterion for a computer to deliver is the sense that it *cares* about the service recipient. Can a nonhuman service robot provide the human touch, a caring manner? Three encouraging tales:

Eliza, the Computer Expert System Psychotherapist

Eliza is a computer program developed by MIT computer science professor Joseph Weizenbaum in the 1960s to test artificial intelligence ideas about human–computer interactions. This program essentially acts as a nondirective Rogerian psychotherapist. Rogerian therapists reflect: they repeat whatever their clients say in a caring, questioning "tell me more" tone.

When you load Eliza, the screen displays a welcoming message: "Hi! I'm pleased you want to talk with me. What would you like to talk about?" If you type "I'm angry at my girlfriend/boyfriend," the computer, using psycholinguistic analysis, identifies the feeling word "angry" and object (girl*/boy*) in your sentence and asks you: "*Why* are you angry with her/him? Tell me more." The program continues a slightly stilted but plausible conversation, politely prompting you to explore your thoughts and feelings for as long as you want to play with it.

To Weizenbaum's astonishment, the finding regarding computer empathy was that MIT students and other adults who used Eliza actually *preferred* the computer shrink to human psychotherapists. Clients found the computer *more* caring, *more* accurately empathic, and *more* responsive. And, of course, Eliza was always available, 24 hours a day, with complete privacy, on students' own terminals, *free*, or at least immensely cheaper than a $100-an-hour, hard-to-get-an-appointment-with human therapist.

Weizenbaum's experiment has created its own professional literature with many reasons being advanced for people's preference for Eliza, including the suggestion that most professional human therapists are not very good. Assessment scores from taped therapy sessions have shown that the empathy level of shrinks is no better than that generated by the computer.

Little Old Ladies and ATMs

When ATMs were first introduced in the early 1970s, the sizest, ageist, sexist assumption was that "little old ladies" would not use the machines. The presumed reason: female senior citizens' main source of human interaction during the week was gossiping with friends while standing in the teller line to cash their social security checks. This assumption proved to be nonsense. Early ATMs were rejected by people of all sizes, ages, and sexes because they were not user friendly; in fact, they shortchanged customers and ate their bank cards. As soon as ATMs were debugged and delivered reliable service, little old ladies used them as willingly as anyone else. LOLs don't like to waste time standing in line any more than people of other sizes, ages, or sexes.

I recently encountered this objection again in reengineering Canada's Income Security and Pension (social security) system. Senior citizens were assumed to be unwilling to use interactive voice response (IVR) telephones to get and check their benefits. Once the phones were reengineered for greater user friendliness (louder volume; bigger, more readable keys to compensate for seniors' less acute hearing and sight), older customers accepted IVR without resistance.

Computer Software Firm Voice-Response Help Desks

A personal experience: I had great difficulty installing an early version of the software program I am using to write this book. The computer screen told me to insert installation Disk 5, and when I did, it gave me an error message: "Can't find Disk 5." After two hours of trying, I gave up and called the help desk. I got a voice-response robot that said, "If you are having problems with installation, press 1." When I pressed ⓵, the robot said "If you get the message 'Can't find Disk 5, when you know you have put Disk 5 in your disk drive,' press 1." When I pressed ⓵, the robot said, "Use EDLIN or NotePad to edit the BUFFERS = line your CONFIG.SYS file to BUFFERS = 50. Then try installing the program again."

This worked—the voice-response help had solved my problem in less than a minute. Obviously, the "Can't find Disk 5" bug was the manufacturer's problem. A quality installation program *automatically* edits users' CONFIG.SYS and AUTOEXEC.BAT files to specifications required by the program being installed. The voice-response help also requires a fair degree of computer literacy—knowledge of what EDLIN, NotePad, and CONFIG.SYS files are and how to use them. But because the voice-response system understood and solved my problem quickly and efficiently, I *felt* understood and helped. Indeed, I felt the help system was almost magic: it read my mind, anticipating exactly what my question was and what advice I needed. (Obviously, when the manufacturer found the bug in its installation program, it knew it would be inundated with calls. So it had a smart help desk expert system developer program the voice-response system to give customers the solution to this often-asked question *fast*.)

My hypothesis is that if a computer or voice-response system provides the service you want quickly and responsibly, it will be perceived to have "understood" you (i.e., to have been empathic). The issue with automation is not automation itself but *user friendliness*: good human–machine interface or usability engineering. Automation is readily accepted if it works, especially when the robot is more responsive, helpful, and fun to interact with than the average harried HR clerk. Playing with modern graphical point-and-click user interfaces is much more fun than filling out personnel department paper forms. Reengineering human resources may offer the paradox of better HR service without humans.

HR professionals who want to see the future of interaction with their clients should spend some time at Chuck E. Cheese playing video games with kids. They will see stunning color, sound, animation, and moment-to-moment challenges as aliens appear to be dealt with at the rate of several a second. And they will see mesmerized children and adults accomplishing very complex cognitive tasks (interactivity at the speed of thought) while having an outrageous amount of fun.

Compare state-of-the-art video games to the typical corporate training program, even your firm's best interactive video computer-assisted instruction training. Business is many years behind entertainment in the development of compelling use of computers. (Aside: A hopeful trend for humankind is that, for most of human history, technological innovation has been driven by war: metallurgy for swords, naval architecture and navigation for warships, aeronautical engineering for fighter planes and bombers, nuclear engineering for the atomic and hydrogen bombs, radar for detecting German bombers approaching Britain, rocketry and telemetry for missiles, computers themselves for cryptography and missile guidance—the examples are countless. For perhaps the first time in human history, technology is now being led by *entertainment*. Consider the special effects in "Star Wars" (the movie, not the anti-ballistic missile system of the Cold War), or the animated dinosaurs of "Jurassic Park."

Today's young workers, members of the MTV generation, are highly conditioned to very sophisticated multimedia, verging on virtual reality. It is likely that they will *prefer* interaction with sophisticated computers to traditional HR bureaucrats who aren't as colorful, animated, smart, or *fast.*

REENGINEERING AND THE CORPORATE (AND HUMAN) LIFE CYCLE: CREATIVE DESTRUCTION, REBIRTH, RENEWAL, GROWTH AND (RE)EMPLOYMENT

Labor economists' estimates (see Chapter 10) suggest reengineering may eliminate 30% of jobs in the U.S. economy, a change "as massive and wrenching as the Industrial Revolution." Reengineering is nothing less than the transition from an industrial to an information economy. While it will cause temporary upset and require most people to learn new technologies and change the way they work, reengineering is the first step in a cycle that will lead to greater affluence and a high level of civilization for all.

Reengineering is what the great Austrian economist Joseph Shumpeter called creative destruction—the breaking down of old ways to free resources for new and higher uses. As shown in Figure 1.15, reengineers are to bloated, inefficient organizations what flies are to garbage: they break the mess down into clean elements, freeing underutilized resources (primarily people and capital) to be recombined to create higher value-added products and services. At the end of an economic era, reengineering accomplishes the creative destruction needed to free resources for the birth of the next economy. Some of today's businesses—those that restructure and adapt fast enough to achieve rebirth by renewal—and many new businesses, born to seize the opportunities of the new economy, will drive the next life cycle of (re)birth and growth to maturity. This natural life cycle will create much more wealth in society and provide many more employment opportunities for those with the requisite skills.

HR professionals' role in this natural process is not to resist but to humanely assist and even *accelerate* it.

First, every HR professional must become a reengineer—leading, training, and facilitating the transition to new ways of working, including relentless

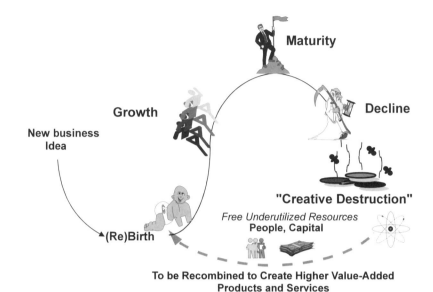

Figure 1.15   Reengineers' Role in "Creative Destruction" in the
Corporate Life Cycle

elimination of low value-added admininstrative paperwork; "virtual" delivery just-in-time of value-adding services to employee–customers; and much greater focus on strategic HR planning and intervention to create and sustain competitive advantage.

Second, HR professionals must lead and faciliate the retraining and reemployment processes needed to prepare the entire U.S. work force—most importantly, the 25 million workers who may be displaced by the information economy/reengineering revolution and the underclass who are unprepared to participate in even the current economy—for the economy of the future.

This is a sufficiently exciting and daunting challenge to employ and motivate every HR professional, including public and private school educators at all levels, for the next generation. The 50% to 90% head count reductions promised by reengineering are much more an opportunity than a threat. These reductions will occur in low value-added administrative paper shuffling, freeing us to focus on much higher value-added efforts to prepare ourselves, our colleagues, and our organizations for the economy of the future.

ENDNOTE

1. (1983, April 25). The Shrinking of Middle Management. *Businessweek*.

PART

II

Technology

2

Information Technology: A Primer for Human Resource Professionals

This chapter provides a brief history of information technology, emphasizing the concepts, terms, and tools HR professionals need to understand. Reengineering's radical improvements in productivity are made possible by enormous increases in computer *power, connectivity, user friendliness*, and *artificial intelligence*. The bottom line: soon *anyone* will be able to *use* a computer *anywhere*, from his or her desk, pocket, or wrist. These PCs will connect to any data the corporation, other information providers, or society wants to make available.

POWER

In the 45 years of the computer age, computer processing power has increased an incomprehensible 30 orders of magnitude, 10^{30}, the ratio of the diameter of an atom to that of the Milky Way. From the 1970s to the present, computer power has doubled each year, a trend known as Moore's Law, after Gordon Moore (founder of chip maker Intel), who first observed it. This means computer power increases at 2^{year}, about one million times (five orders of magnitude, 10^5, 2^{20}) every 20 years. And there is no end in sight to this trend: research on nano-computers (transistors made of individual atoms or organic molecules) predicts that Moore's Law will apply well into the next century.

To put this awesome power increase in perspective, consider the following: if automobile technology had increased at the rate of computer technology, a Rolls Royce Corniche costing $150,000 in 1970 (15 miles to the gallon, 120 miles per hour) would cost $.15 in 1990, go around the world 667 times on a gallon of gas, at 42,000 miles per *second*, 20 percent of the speed of light.

The combination of the Watt steam engine and the sun-and-planet gearing system that launched the Industrial Revolution increased manufacturing productivity 15 times, a little better than one order of magnitude. Between 1770 and 1851, worker productivity from all sources increased about 300-fold, just over two orders of magnitude (10^2). The Industrial Revolution forever changed the dynamics of everything: family life, government, cities and farms, language, art, religion, and our sense of time and place in the cosmos.

In 45 years computer power has increased 28 orders of magnitude (10^{28}, 10 followed by *28* zeros) *more* than the technological changes that launched the Industrial Revolution.

Paradoxically, this phenomenal increase in power has had *no* impact on knowledge worker productivity until recently. A famous cover story in *Fortune* magazine in 1986 headlined "The Puny Payoff from Office Computers" noted that "hundreds of billions of dollars have been spent on computers with no noticeable increase in productivity." Many studies have shown that while the use of computers has spread throughout American industry, productivity of white-collar employees has essentially remained flat. Nobel Prize-winning Stanford economist Robert Solow has joked, "Computers have shown up everywhere except in the productivity statistics."

Reengineering is just beginning to harness the 10^{30} increase in humankind's ability to process information. What this increase in power will mean in future years can scarcely be imagined.

A Brief History of the Computer

The evolution of the computer is shown in Figure 2.1. In the beginning was the mainframe, a room-sized behemoth that cost $2 million to $30 million, required a special air-conditioned environment called "the glass house," and had to be attended 24 hours a day by IS "priests and acolytes" to keep it running.

Next came the minicomputer, a $100,000 to $1 million downsized version of the mainframe. The minicomputer launched such companies as Digital Equipment, Data General, and Prime Computer (all now in trouble because they missed the *next* major downsizing, the personal computer).

Third came the PC in two versions: a high-end engineering workstation costing $10,000 to $80,000, and a low-end truly personal computer used primarily for word processing and spreadsheet analysis. High-end workstations were used primarily by engineers for graphics and mathematically intensive computer-assisted design and data analysis. Early PCs, for example, Wang word processors, were dedicated to single tasks. However, Wang paid a heavy price for failing to realize that its $10,000 word processing PC could be replaced by a $1,000 PC that featured not only word processing, but also offered spreadsheets, desktop publishing, graphics, communications, and many other useful business functions.

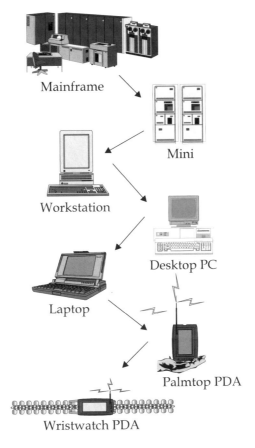

Mainframe

Mini

Workstation

Desktop PC

Laptop

Palmtop PDA

Wristwatch PDA

Figure 2.1 Evolution of the Computer: Ever Smaller, Ever More Powerful

PCs have gotten steadily smaller: from bulky desktops to 10- to 30-pound "lunchboxes" and laptops, to five-pound notebooks and, recently, two- to three-pound subnotebooks. Pen-based personal notebook computers about the size of a clipboard have downsized to personal digital assistants (PDAs) called palmtops, many equipped with wireless cellular phone connections that permit sending and receiving voice and data anywhere. A wristwatch computer with wireless communication abilities, the Timex Data-Link, is already being sold by a joint venture of Timex and Microsoft.

Beyond wristwatch computers are computer chips implanted directly into human bodies. Computer chip-driven heart pacemakers have been used for 25 years. Experiments using computer chips with direct connections to human nerves help amputees move robot hands and legs, help the blind see, and the deaf hear.

The trend in computer power is obvious: making the PC more powerful, cheaper, smaller, lighter, and more portable, so everyone can have and use one anywhere.

CONNECTIVITY: COMPUTER-TO-COMPUTER COMMUNICATIONS

Network connections are as important as computers themselves. Computers are evolving from stand-alone word, data, and graphics *processing* tools to *communications* devices. Most reengineering solutions depend on the ability to send data from one computer to another and to access information available on computers elsewhere in the organization or the world.

A Brief History of Computer Communications

At first, there were no computer-to-computer connections. All data input and output were handled by people dealing directly with a single computer, usually a mainframe. (Ironically, PCs initially were as isolated as early mainframes: accessible to the single person who used them but unable to communicate with others.)

Dumb terminals came next: up to several hundred teletype machines, or later, keyboards with screens (but with no computing ability themselves) connected to a mainframe or minicomputer. Dumb terminals used the principle of time sharing: each terminal submitted its task or request for information to the mainframe. If the central computer, the spider in the center of the web, was fast enough, a dumb terminal's user had "virtual" access (i.e., the user felt he or she was using the mainframe directly). In fact, mainframes rarely were fast enough to handle all of their dumb terminals virtually: dumb terminal users would type something on their screens and nothing would happen. The cursor would blink for seconds or even minutes before the central computer got around to responding. Mainframe-dumb terminal architectures were called master–slave systems— perhaps because this is how they (or the "glass house" priests—technicians who run mainframes in special air conditioned rooms called glass houses) made end-users feel.

The touch-tone phone, increasingly important in HR reengineering, is a dumb terminal. It can send voice and keyboard data to a computer server and receive voice data back, but it cannot *process* data. Pagers with beepers ("call your office") or LCD displays are also dumb terminals—able to receive but not process information.

Smart terminals are personal computers (i.e., personal workstations with computing power). PCs can upload and download information to and from a central computer server and also process information using resident word processing, spreadsheet, presentation graphics, and database software programs. This architecture is called client-server, where the client is the PC—and the PC user—and the central computer is the server (contrast this term with master-slave!).

Client–server architectures are extremely important in reengineering and downsizing information systems. Key concepts and terms useful for you to know include:

File–server architectures **(smart client, dumb server***)*.   The client, the PC on your desk, is smart. The file server—whether a mainframe, a mini, or a large, fast PC—is dumb—and can be thought of as simply a huge hard drive.

All processing is done on the client PC. For example, if you wanted to search for all employees in California making more than $25,000 a year, your PC would request the employee file from the server HRIS database. The server would not process anything: it would simply download the file for all employees in your organization into your PC. The database program in your PC would then sort this database to find the employees who match your criteria.

Client–server architectures **(smart client and smart server***)*.   In true client–server architectures, both client and server are smart—and together are optimized to do what each does best: the processing operations that each can perform most efficiently. Powerful servers are best at processing large amounts of data, so for the task of finding California employees earning more than $25,000 a year, the server would sort its database on these criteria and download to your client PC only those employees meeting the criteria.

PCs are good at processing data to end-users' unique specifications, so you can use your own word processing and spreadsheet programs to analyze and present data your way.

Client–server architectures are evolving very rapidly to become enterprise computing networks strung together by LANs (local area networks, usually serving two to 100 people in the same department or physical office) and WANs (wide area networks, high-speed telephone and fiber optic connections between many LAN sites).

Figure 2.2 shows a typical client–server LAN/WAN enterprise computing network. A mainframe in the United States sits in the center of the web. It has two minicomputer satellites—one in London, serving Europe, Africa, and the Middle East, and one in Singapore, serving Asia Pacific. Each company office has a powerful PC server that serves individual employees' desktop and notebook PCs. Any employee has access to any data anywhere in the system. A consultant working in a Thai oil refinery first queries the local server in Bangkok for the data she needs. If the office server doesn't have it, the query is sent automatically to the larger Asia Pacific server in Singapore. If this server doesn't have the information, it queries the U.S. and London mainframes. A smart database program called an active agent flies around the system asking every connected computer, "Do you have the data my client needs? If not, forward me to the next server." When the active agent finds the data, it returns and displays the data on the requesting client's screen. Whether the agent finds the requested data in the Bangkok, Boston, or Budapest database is transparent (not noticeable) to the client (if the system is fast enough).

Global, regional, and office servers keep each other up-to-date by replicating or synchronizing their databases, usually at least once every 24 hours. Essentially, every server reports to every other server any data that has changed during the day so that all store the same data.

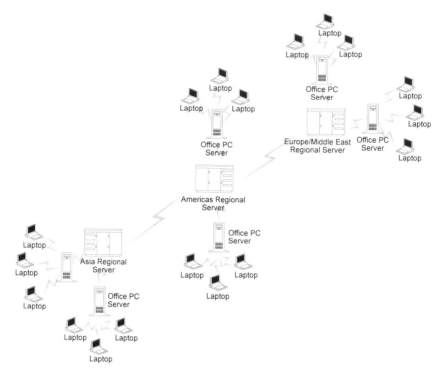

Figure 2.2 A LAN/WAN Worldwide Client Server Computer Network

USER FRIENDLINESS: EVOLUTION OF THE HUMAN–COMPUTER INTERFACE

Interface "user friendliness" is the benefit of immensely more powerful computing.

Physical Interfaces

Technicians initially communicated with computers by throwing physical switches on and off. Later, switches gave way to punched cards and paper tape, laboriously created using a keyboard attached to a keypunch machine.

Keyboards

The human interface was the keyboard (each key a physical switch in a more user-friendly package); the actual interface with the computer was paper with holes cut in it representing data the computer could read. (I vividly remember key-punching thousands of computer cards, all holding fewer data than a modern 3.5-inch floppy drive, when doing my doctoral dissertation in the late 1960s.)

Next came keyboarding on clunky teletype machines (electric typewriters) that input data directly into a computer.

Then came keyboards with computer screens, first attached to the dumb terminals mentioned above, and later to PCs. For the first time, one could see what one was typing.

Twenty-five years later, the ubiquitous touch-tone phone is the latest keyboard used increasingly to input data to computers.

Screen Interfaces

Screen-oriented computing has itself evolved from *character-based* to *graphical* user interfaces. Character-based screens initially offered just text and numbers, no icons, no graphics. (Character-based computer programs increasingly are emulating graphical user interfaces.)

Graphical user interfaces (GUIs, pronounced "gooeys"), introduced by the Apple Macintosh and later by Microsoft's enormously popular Windows program, let users communicate with computers with pointing devices like fingers (*touch screen* technologies) and *mice* by touching or clicking on picture icons (in addition to typing numbers or characters using a keyboard).

Pen Notepad Interfaces

Pen or notepad computing lets users write directly on a computer screen with a stylus or even their fingers. Handwriting recognition is still in its early stages, but already any worker who fills out forms or prescriptions, or sketches designs, can write directly on an electronic clipboard and touch a "Send" button to transfer any data to an electronic database.

Voice

The next obvious advance in human interface with computers is simply telling them what to do verbally with a microphone. Practical voice recognition programs (20,000- to 80,000-word-vocabularies) currently cost $500 to $1,000 (Dragon Dictate™, IBMs's Digital Voice) but are dropping in cost and increasing in accuracy at the rate of Moore's Law. It also is very probable that within a few years computer users will not have keyboards. (In a wonderful "Star Trek" episode, a Trekkie travels back in time to the 1990s, finds a PC, mistakes the mouse for a microphone, and gives the PC several verbal instructions. Nothing happens. Baffled, the Trekkie shakes the mouse, speaks louder, then tries to make sense of the keyboard—keyboards and mice being technologies so primitive as to have been lost in the mists of history.)

At present, most phone interfaces with computers use the phone as a keyboard rather than for true voice data input. Genuine voice data input and output applications, however, are beginning to appear. For example, employees can query their

401(k) retirement fund balance by carefully pronouncing each number in their personal identification number (PIN): "one . . . seven . . . three." A *voice recognition* program in the benefit database computer can translate these numbers into data and verify the requester's access rights. The computer's *voice synthesis* program can then read the balance to the employee by translating data into spoken words.

Future Physical Interfaces

New interfaces such as *heads-up displays* and *neuro-implants* are already used in entertainment (virtual reality games) and medical research. Heads-up displays allow fighter pilots to guide a missile merely by glancing at a target. A low-power laser bounced off the pilot's eyeball tells the computer where the missile needs to go. Neuro-implants at present are limited to detecting, processing, and transmitting nerve and muscle twitches to control artificial limbs. But the science fiction dream of a neuro-implant, a computer wired directly to the human nervous system, is already a fact.

Language Interfaces

Language concerns both what data—text, sound, voice, video images, or senses—the computer is processing, sending, or receiving from a user and how much work the user has to do to put the data in a form the computer can understand.

Code Computer programming languages have evolved in generations. In the beginning was very hard code in First Generation machine language (0101111110111111100100100010) and in Second Generation assembly language (LX, M X8, OLDMAS)

Then came *relatively* easier code in Third Generation compiled languages such as C, COBOL, and BASIC, for example

IF GROSS => $5000 THEN TAX RATE = .4 ELSE TAX RATE = 3

TAX = GROSS-TAX RATE

NET = GROSS-TAX

Next was near-English code in Fourth Generation languages (Compute Net Pay from Gross Pay and Tax Rate).

Finally, NO code was needed in Fifth Generation languages, which let users develop their own applications (e.g., database queries), by pointing and clicking on graphic icons, as shown in Figure 2.3.

Beyond code and physical indication of what you want the computer to do are *natural language systems,* either written or spoken. With a natural language parser one can type or say into a microphone, "Find all employees in California making more than $25,000 a year, with women in green and men in red." The computer will understand this command and execute it without the user having to write any queries or point and click on a series of defining words.

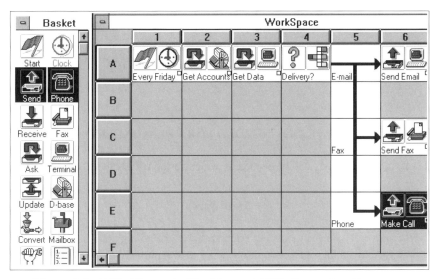

Figure 2.3   Edify Electronic Workforce: A Fifth Generation Computer Language—No Code, Just Drag an Icon to Tell the Computer What You Want It to Do

ARTIFICIAL INTELLIGENCE

Computer smarts—the extent to which the computer can mimic human thinking processes—have advanced from computation and data storage, to expert systems, to learning and even creativity. Computers frequently are derided as simply big, dumb calculators, and in fact until very recently, that was all they were. Computer smarts have evolved from calculators to file cabinets (i.e., databases) to decision-supporting expert systems with "artificial intelligence" that can ask users questions, interpret data, and provide specific management advice such as:

IF your Organizational Climate "Clarity" score is below the 40th percentile, *THEN*

1. Give a vision speech linking your workgroup's goals to the mission, vision, and strategy of the firm.

2. Install a Performance Management System that monitors and gives every subordinate weekly feedback on his or her progress in accomplishing professional goals—and how these accomplishments impact the workgroup's and the firm's own goals.

3. Take a course to increase your managerial coaching style.

Beyond rule-based expert systems are heuristic *neural network programs* that can learn, find *new* patterns, and discover rules and algorithms human users did not program into them. Neural network programs can be fed personality and managerial style data on successful and unsuccessful managers on Friday, left to try millions of algorithms over the weekend, and report to the Succession Planning Committee the algorithm that offers the best predictive validity on Monday morning.

TECHNOLOGY NEEDED FOR REENGINEERING

Tools, in the order they will be needed in reengineering HR, include the following.

Hardware

1. Phones: By far the most cost-effective interface with a computer is a *phone.* Studies of personnel transaction costs (labor plus amortization of equipment and programming) found:

Phone	PC (employee desk)	Kiosk	Paper
$1.75	$2.75	$2.75	$6–$150+

Phones have many advantages. Everyone has one or has access to one. Everyone knows how to use one (a simple touch-tone phone, at least). At less than $10, phones are cheap. Phones can provide voice prompts, or on-line help, which tell you how to use them (e.g., "Press '1' if . . .") Interactive voice-response systems using touch-tone phones can automate an estimated 50% to 70% of all routine HR transactions.

2. Personal computer or PDA: Employees should have access to a PC or a PDA to enable them to enter or retrieve data that is too complex to be entered or accessed by phone (e.g., forms or spreadsheets). Ideally, all employees will have their own PDA on their desk, lap, pocket, or wrist. A way to start is to give employees access to a kiosk: a public personal computer on a pedestal or in a booth. Kiosks can be placed strategically just outside the main door to the cafeteria, next to the ATM, between restrooms, and other places employees are likely to pass several times a day. For firms starting reengineering efforts, kiosks offer many advantages:

- A quick, cheap way to get started: the firm does *not* have to buy everyone a $2,000 PC.
- An opportunity for "usability testing." Can, will, employees use the kiosk? If not, why not? What problems are they having? Observing employee behavior while using the kiosk PC can provide powerful feedback to systems developers on how to improve the system's user friendliness.
- Employee training: users become familiar with the computer and the HRIS *before* it lands on their desks.

■ Marketing: ideally, employees will begin to wonder: "Why do I have to walk to the kiosk when I could have the same data and HR services on my own PC?"—and instead of resisting, start to agitate for implementation of the new system.

3. Networks: A LAN (local area network), linking your PC to your department's server and colleagues' PCs, and perhaps a WAN (wide area network), linking your PC and LAN to other LANs around the world, require servers, connectors, and cables—and software (often included or bundled with the network hardware).

Small peer-to-peer networks suitable for 2 to 50 users require only PCs, cables, and plug-adaptor boards or connectors. Peer-to-peer LANs let users share files, printers, and e-mail messages among them. Any PC on the LAN can act as either the server sending files or the client receiving files. Artisoft's LANtastic™, Microsoft's Windows for Workgroups™, and Novell's Netware Lite™ are the leading peer-to-peer LAN vendors, supplying both hardware and software.

For larger LANs and WANs, one or more powerful servers with cables and connection devices called bridges, routers, and gateways, are needed to connect servers and client PCs. The current leading network software is Novell Netware. (Other names you will hear include Banyon, DECNet, IBM LAN Server.) In the future (perhaps by the time you read this), networking software will almost certainly be built into PC operating systems (e.g., IBM's OS2.1 and Microsoft's Windows 95 and NT).

Network technology is rapidly advancing to include voice, white boarding (systems that let two users see and work on the same screen simultaneously), images (still pictures), and real time (30 frames-per-second) video. Video conferencing hardware (a small video camera that sits on top of a PC monitor and video compression card in the PC) now cost $1,000 to $5,000 but are dropping rapidly in price. It is likely that all PCs will soon be multimedia capable, providing picture phone voice and video communication with any other similarly equipped PC on the network.

PCs on a client–server network can mimic many more advanced software systems used in reengineering (e.g., document databases and e-mail). For example, all personnel policy, procedure, and legal manuals, benefit plans, training course catalogs, and so on, can be put on a public directory on the server hard drive. Any employee can access, browse through, and download any of these documents, in whole or part, to his or her PC. Each employee can have his or her own directory on the server, with a subdirectory named mail. Any colleague can save a note, memo, document, or spreadsheet to any employee's mail directory. This in effect is what e-mail programs do via more user-friendly screens.

Network systems development and administration are highly technical specialties—perhaps the fastest growing new profession in the United States at this time. As an HR professional you do not need technical knowledge to network computers, but you do need to know how networked PCs can automate HR services. Advice: brainstorm your ideal system, following the reengineering HR vision and concepts discussed in Chapter 4, and see your network administrator or vendor for how to implement it. Better still: include the LAN developer, administrator, and vendor in your brainstorming session, a method of systems development called JAD/RAD (joint application development/rapid application development). JAD/RAD sessions that involve HR subject matter experts, customers, and techies together can cut the cycle time to implement a new system by 90%.[1]

Software

1. E-mail: Once you have a network, it helps to have software to send messages around on it. As noted above, e-mail software is not absolutely necessary—you can achieve many of the same benefits simply by saving to server directories named "public, or for workgroups or individual employees." E-mail software, however, makes sending, receiving, routing, and administering the communication system much easier and user friendly—users can simply click on mailbox icons. Leading e-mail vendors are Lotus with CC Mail™, Microsoft with MS Mail™, and WordPerfect Office™. Each enables you to send virtually any file—text, spreadsheet, graphic (and soon, video)—you can produce on a computer to anyone anywhere on the network or through access to external networks like MCI Mail.

E-mail messaging will replace fax communication. Almost all faxes are produced on a PC, printed out, walked to a paper-fax machine, faxed (turned back into an electronic file), printed out on the receiving machine on paper—and often reentered on another PC. Current e-mail-cum-fax programs let users e-mail their faxes to a common fax connected to a server, which saves one round of printing and walking paper. A better system is for electronic files to stay electronic: e-mailed from screen to screen and saved to an electronic file so users need *never* create, touch, move, or file a piece of paper.

E-mail systems can confirm whether your message has been received. Some e-mail systems even let you retrieve a message (if it hasn't been accessed) should you change your mind and think better of it. Advanced e-mail features include artificial intelligence screening (rule-based message handling) you can program to recognize and delete junk e-mail, or automatically route to colleagues incoming inquiries, orders, or "to do's." E-mail software already includes voice annotation and will inevitably include multimedia.

2. Forms flow/work flow software: *Forms flow* software combines e-mail with forms design templates that let you draw on a screen any form you use in business (e.g., job description, performance appraisal, job application form, time sheet, travel and expense forms, and the like). Forms flow programs either include or connect to e-mail systems so that you can fill out a form, sign it with your employee number or password, and send it on to the next person who needs to take action on it and send it to a central database.

Work flow software enables users to program complex routing of forms among many users or approvers, with decision rules and exception controls built in ("If recommended salary increase is within budget, forward to payroll; IF NOT, forward to requestor's manager for approval"). The combination of e-mail and forms flow software have great potential to clean up the paperwork administration of human resources. The leading vendors of forms/work flow software at present are Delrina Form Flow™, Microsoft Electric Forms Designer™, and WordPerfect InForms™, Action Software™, Edify Electronic Workforce™, and Scitor Process Charter for Windows™ (which provides the ability to track, graph and simulate work flow, time and cost).

3. White-boarding software: This software permits two or more users to see and work on the same document at the same time, entering or changing data or drawing on the document on their screens from anywhere their computers can connect. Some white-boarding software includes teleconferencing: a window in a corner of the screen with a talking head view of the colleague one is working with. White-boarding software eliminates the need for physically shipping bulky manuscripts, the need for engineering drawing or advertising layouts, and the need for individuals to travel in order to work on a shared project.

4. Document database: This is a large database with e-mail and forms flow capabilities. At present, only one document database, Lotus Notes, is widely available. (A similar product, Microsoft "Exchange," is expected to be included with Windows 95 to be released in late 1995.) Notes enables an organization to make virtually all personnel manuals, policy statements, labor law announcements, training programs, health and benefits advice, job postings—*anything* now on paper—on-line and accessible via e-mail to all employees from their PCs wherever they are. Notes can also distribute sound and video files of multimedia presentations and training programs.

Notes includes key word and some natural language search capabilities so that one can search, for example, "American Disabilities Act" and "self-control" to see if a requirement of emotional self-control discriminates against employees with epilepsy.

Notes also has a forum or bulletin board discussion database feature that lets you converse by typing messages, responses, and comments to the bulletin board. A U.S. employee can post a message "See memo x for some neat ideas that our London office has come up with for reengineering job application submissions—could we use this approach in other countries?" An employee in Jakarta could add, "Here's how we would need to do it in an Asian Islamic country."

5. Teleconferencing software: It enables two or many co-workers in remote locations to see and converse with one another on their PC screens. Interviews, meetings, and work sessions (aided with white-boarding software) can be conducted without moving people or pieces of paper. Teleconferencing software usually is sold as a hardware–software package, which includes a small video camera with a microphone that fits on top of a PC monitor; a video card that handles video compression and transmission, which must be installed in the PC itself; and communications software. The leading vendors of telecommunications packages are Intel ($2,000) and AT&T ($5,000); prices of real-time video conferencing over "POT" (plain old telephone) lines are expected to drop below $1000, and perhaps to $500, per PC in 1995.

Teleconferencing is likely to have its greatest impact in eliminating travel, enabling face-to-face meetings, and for its use as a training tool. Any human resources meeting, hiring interview, counseling session or training program can be "telecommunicated" from/to any number of people anywhere. Interviewing a potential candidate in Hong Kong, or conducting simultaneous "distance learning" training for employees at many sites around the world, can be done without anyone having to physically move from his or her PC or PDA.

6. Integrated Human Resource Management Information Systems (IHRMIS): These are shared databases that serve all human resource functions: selection, performance management, succession planning, training and development, and compensation. Chapter 6 describes an IHRMIS in detail.

SUMMARY

Advances in information systems technology (IST) have made computers small, cheap, user friendly, and smart enough so that everyone can *have* one, *anywhere,* connected to *any* information, anywhere—and can *use* one to do bigger jobs than they are doing at present. Chapters 5 and 6 discuss ways IST is being used to transform work.

ENDNOTE

1. Martin, J. (1990). *Rapid Application Development.* New York: MacMillan.

PART

III

Process

3

Basics: Activity-Based Costing, Value Analysis, and Work Flow Charting

Reengineering has its intellectual roots in industrial engineering cost and value analysis and operations research—systems and work flow analysis. A working knowledge of three of these methods—activity-based costing, value analysis, and work flow charting—are prerequisites for reengineering.

ACTIVITY-BASED COSTING

Activity-based costing (ABC) is a new method of cost accounting that measures the cost of specific activities or steps in work flows that produce product or service outputs. ABC differs from traditional cost accounting in that it delineates overhead costs far more precisely. Overhead costs are all costs not easily assigned to a specific productive activity, for example, occupancy (office rent and utilities), general management and staff (secretaries), equipment depreciation (PCs, copiers), and other administrative services (human resources, accounting, legal, and the like).

Traditional cost accounting buries overhead costs by attaching them to the hourly wage costs of direct or "touch" labor—people who actually make things. This system worked fairly well when the ratio of overhead people and costs to direct labor was small. For example, as recently as 1960 there were two touch labor workers for every one overhead worker. Today direct labor is rarely more than 10% of total costs even in manufacturing firms. (General Motors' direct labor is about 12%, and on any given day, one-third of United Auto Workers are in classes or serving on labor management committees, not making cars.) In high-tech firms such as Apple Computer, direct labor is less than 1%, a proportion too small to show on a pie chart.

In traditional cost accounting, overhead costs are added as a percentage to direct labor hourly wage and fringe costs to provide what is called a full or fully loaded cost per unit of worker time. For example, if direct wage and fringe cost is $18/hour, and overhead (all other company costs) 100% of direct costs, total cost of labor per hour is $18 plus overhead costs (100% × $18 = $18) = $36/hour.

In today's firms, overhead costs are anywhere from nine to several hundred times direct labor costs (i.e., almost *all* costs are what has traditionally been called overhead). This leads to absurd fully loaded labor costs calculated as $18/hour wage direct labor and fringe plus $4,879 overhead cost/hour = $4,897 full labor cost/hour.

The problem with traditional cost accounting is that if overhead is not broken out and measured precisely, it is invisible. Managers can't get a handle on it, discover where it occurs, or take action to reduce it. ABC breaks overhead costs out for all to see and eliminate, outsource, or reengineer.

Types of Costs

Activity-based accounting uses basically four types of costs: direct cash outlay, labor, overhead, and capital.

Direct Cash Outlay Costs

These are nonlabor costs of products and services the firm pays for directly with out-of-pocket cash. Examples are shown in Table 3.1.

Table 3.1 A Cash Outlay Activity-Based Costing Worksheet

Cash Outlay Costs	# Units	Cost per Unit	Total Cash Outlay
Travel:			
Airfare Boston <=> San Francisco	1	$ 1,200.00	$ 1,200.00
Bus into San Francisco	2	$ 16.00	$ 32.00
Per diem hotel and meals	3	$ 185.00	$ 555.00
Materials:			
Course workbooks	25	$ 125.00	$ 3,125.00
Consultant days	3	$ 2,000.00	$ 6,000.00

Calculating cash outlay costs is very easy: Simply multiply the *number* of the cost (i.e., two round-trip tickets from Boston to San Francisco) by the *cost per unit* (in this case $1,000 per ticket) to give the total cash outlay cost: $2,000.

Labor Costs

This is the cost of workers' time—salary plus fringe benefits per unit of time worked or paid (e.g., 260 days, 2,080 hours, 124,800 minutes in a standard year).

In U.S. industry, fringe benefit costs currently are running about 35% to 37% of salary per year. Fringe benefits costs have two components: *time paid but not worked,* roughly 30 days of vacation, holiday, sick, and personal leave time (on average, about 30 days off/260 days paid = 13.5%); and *fringe cash outlay costs,* social security and unemployment taxes, health insurance, pensions, and other benefits paid for by the firm (on average about 22% to 23% salary paid per year).

Figure 3.1 shows the noncash time paid but not worked and cash components of fringe benefits. Fringe benefits cost calculations can be slightly tricky because it is easy to double account for the 13.5% of time paid noncash benefits, roughly one-third of total fringe benefits. Most firms use time paid per year (including time paid but not worked) as base salary. The formula for labor costs plus fringe benefits is therefore salary per 260 days, 2,080 hours, 124,800 minutes multiplied by 1.225, where this number, called a fringe benefits multiplier, adds cash outlay fringe costs to salary costs.

Overhead Costs

These are all other costs added to workers' salaries plus fringe cost per unit of time. Overhead costs, as defined earlier, are costs of items that provide general

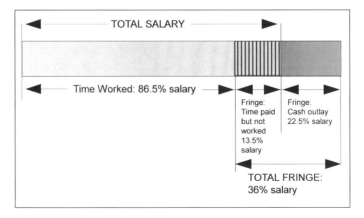

Figure 3.1 Components of Full Labor Costs

benefit to the firm and are not easily attached to specific people, products, or services, such as the following:

- Office occupancy: rent (or amortization on the building owned by the firm), lights, heat
- Managers, support staff (secretaries)
- Other services: legal, accounting, human resources
- Miscellaneous: the CEO's salary, the company jet, the corporate penthouse in Manhattan, etc.

Fully loaded costs are overhead costs added to salary plus fringe costs per unit of time worked as a percentage to calculate a typical overhead percentage. In American firms, this is about 140%, so:

> Full cost per worker unit of time (labor plus fringe benefits plus overhead) = 1.225 salary per year × 140% (1.225 salary per unit of time) = 3 × salary per time paid in a standard year (260 days, 2,080 hours, 124,800 minutes).

The amount you multiply salary per year by 3 to fully load labor costs for fringe benefit and overhead, is called an overhead multiplier.

By far the easiest way to get labor cost data is to get a cost schedule for employees in various pay grades from your controller or financial analyst. This approach has two major benefits. First, it saves you doing a lot of arithmetic. Second, it covers you politically. If anybody asks, "Where did you get those crazy numbers?," you can reply with confidence, "*Finance* gave them to me!"

Capital Costs

These are cash outlay costs that have a useful life of more than one year and are treated differently for tax purposes. Capital costs are amortized or expensed using a formula (usually a straight line method), which divides the total costs of the capital item by its useful life in years. For example, a $2,000 computer that has a useful life of three years would be expensed or charged off at $2,000 ÷ 3 years = $667/year.

ABC tries to attach capital costs expenses more precisely to specific activities. HR professionals rarely have to worry about capital costs because costs of computers, training rooms, overhead projectors, CD-ROM players, and other capital items used in the delivery of HR services usually are buried in overhead. This simplifies accounting, but it is dangerous.

For example, if a firm invests $300,000 in a CD-ROM-based customer service training program offered to 1,000 customer service representatives over a number of years, the costs per trainee would be charged off at $300,000 ÷ $1,000 trainees = $300 per customer service rep trainee.

This approach is better than burying the capital cost of the training in HR overhead, where it will be attached to all employees' labor costs per time unit. The customer service training course proves to be of little value, yet it costs a lot. It drives up all HR professionals' apparent labor costs; it makes the HR department look "fat"; and it may invite an across-the-board head count reduction. The better approach offered by ABC is to break out, target, and write off the ineffective customer training course investment, lowering the HR department's overhead and, hence, labor costs.

ABC is essential in reengineering efforts to calculate the cost side of a cost–benefit equation and to identify benefits from *before* minus *after* cost savings, as shown in Table 1.2 in Chapter 1. Almost all benefits from reengineering HR result from reduced costs (see Chapter 9). The secret of showing benefits and the return on investment in reengineering is knowing how to calculate costs.

ABC is easy, like doing a budget. To do an ABC analysis of a work flow, you fill in a spreadsheet. Figure 3.2 shows a spreadsheet with the questions you want to ask. What are the steps involved in the work flow? What's the first (second, third, etc.) thing that happens? And then for each step, the following questions are asked about labor costs and cash outlay costs: Who (what employee labor cost) is involved in the step? How many people of the same title or pay level are involved? How much does each labor person cost per minute, hour, or other time unit? Or if you are calculating their cost-per-time unit, how much do they make in salary per year?

You may need to calculate this cost using the following equation:

$$\frac{\text{Salary per Year} \times \text{Fringe or Overhead Multiplier}}{\text{Unit of time}\,(260\ \text{days},\ 2{,}080\ \text{hours},\ 124{,}800\ \text{minutes in the year})}$$

Quick exercise: Using the equation above, calculate your own full labor costs, salary plus fringe plus overhead. (Easier: Get a labor cost schedule from your financial analyst or comptroller!)

How much time does each labor person spend on the step? Usually your time unit will be minutes, but it also can be hours, days, weeks, months, or years. There are two basic ways to get labor time data: Use units of time spent on a step or task directly—the micro approach; or calculate labor costs from percentage of time spent on a step or task—the macro approach.

Micro unit of time method: Simply ask workers, "How long does it take you to do step X?" Enter this number (usually minutes) in the spreadsheet.

Macro percentage of time method: Ask, "What percentage of time in a given day, week, month, or year do you spend on the step?" Then multiply this percentage by the worker's full costs per time unit. For example, if an employee

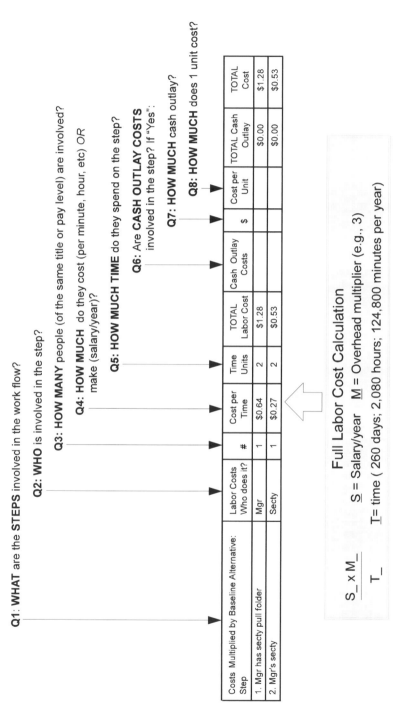

Q1: WHAT are the **STEPS** involved in the work flow?

Q2: WHO is involved in the step?

Q3: HOW MANY people (of the same title or pay level) are involved?

Q4: HOW MUCH do they cost (per minute, hour, etc) *OR* make (salary/year)?

Q5: HOW MUCH TIME do they spend on the step?

Q6: Are **CASH OUTLAY COSTS** involved in the step? If "Yes":

Q7: HOW MUCH cash outlay?

Q8: HOW MUCH does 1 unit cost?

Costs Multiplied by Baseline Alternative: Step	Labor Costs Who does it?	#	Cost per Time	Time Units	TOTAL Labor Cost	Cash Outlay Costs	$	Cost per Unit	TOTAL Cash Outlay	TOTAL Cost
1. Mgr has secty pull folder	Mgr	1	$0.64	2	$1.28				$0.00	$1.28
2. Mgr's secty	Secty	1	$0.27	2	$0.53				$0.00	$0.53

Full Labor Cost Calculation

$$\frac{S \times M}{T}$$

$\underline{S}$ = Salary/year $\underline{M}$ = Overhead multiplier (e.g., 3)

$\underline{T}$ = time (260 days; 2,080 hours; 124,800 minutes per year)

Figure 3.2 ABC Analysis of a Work Flow

says, "Yeah, I probably spend 10% of my time every day just filling out copies of that form and walking them to accounting," the ABC of this activity is found by the equation:

$$\frac{10\% \,(\text{time on task}) \times \text{Salary} \times \text{Overhead Multiplier}}{260 \text{ days per year}}$$

The micro method has the advantage of being more specific. Steps in the process are decomposed into smaller units, making it easier to identify specific steps that can be eliminated or reengineered. The disadvantage is that people may estimate their time incorrectly so that when all the minutes of all the work flows in which they are involved are added up, the total is *more* than 100% of their total time and costs.

The macro method has the advantage that worker time allocated cannot exceed 100%—everything will add up credibly—and it can be used for large sample value analyses. The disadvantage is that it is less specific: It may not break out value-added from nonvalue-added steps.

Total labor costs for each row are calculated by multiplying the *number* of labor people involved by their *cost per unit of time* by the *number of units of time* that are involved in the step. Total labor costs for a step—or all steps in a work flow—are calculated by summing the "Total Labor" column in the spreadsheet, as shown in Table 3.2. Are any cash outlay costs (travel, materials, consultants, mail, etc.) involved in this step? If yes: How many units are used? And how much does one unit cost? Total costs per step are found by adding total labor cost

Table 3.2 A Labor Activity-Based Costing Worksheet

			LABOR COSTS		
Step	Who does it?	Units	Cost per Minute	Units per Step	Labor Cost
1.1 Mgr has secty pull folder	Mgr	1	$0.64	2	$ 1.28
1.2 Mgr's secty	Secty	1	$0.27	2	$ 0.53
1.3 Mgr reviews salary plan increase	Mgr	1	$0.64	10	$ 6.42
1.4 Secty retrieves, types, files, duplicates	Secty	1	$0.27	2	$ 0.53
1.5 Mgr signs	Mgr	1	$0.64	2	$ 1.28
1.6 Secty sends to Mgr's Mgr for approval	Secty	1	$0.27	2	$ 0.53
Totals per Transaction				20	$10.57

and total cash outlay cost by row and by summing the total cost column at the far right of the spreadsheet.

Expected Values

Expected value analysis is the calculation of the cost or value of an event, which happens only a certain percentage or probability of the time. The equation for an expected value (usually abbreviated as "E(v)") is E(v) = p × A, where p = the percentage or probability of the event from 0 to 1.00 (100%), and A = the cost in dollars of the event if it does occur.

Recall the reengineered HR transaction discussed in Chapter 1: "Sometimes the boss's boss gets involved." This event is a branch event, as shown in Figure 3.3.

One branch represents those times when the boss's boss gets involved. This happens 1 time in 20—5% of the time—or with a probability of .05 for any random HR transaction. The cost of this event is the probability, .05, multiplied by the Amount—event: 2 minutes × $.64/minute = $1.28 = $.06.

The other branch represents those times when the boss's boss *doesn't* get involved. This happens 95% of the time and costs nothing (A = 0), so the expected value of this (non)event = .95 × $0 = $0.

The total expected value of branching events is the total of the costs of each branch, in this case, $.06 + 0 = $.06. This amount is added to the cost of every reengineered HR transaction to capture the $1.28 cost of the one transaction in 20 that goes to the boss's boss.

Note that the probabilities or percentages associated with branches have to add up to 1.00, although, practically, you can ignore branches that have zero cost amounts because their cost will always be zero. You can use the Number of Units (#) column in an ABC worksheet to enter probabilities or percentages; these are essentially fractional units of a cost.

Figure 3.4 shows an expected value analysis of the 1-10-100 cost-of-quality rule: If it costs $1 to do it right the first time (80% of transactions), it costs $10 to

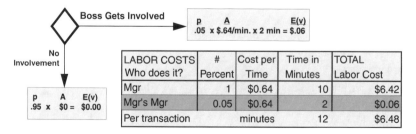

Figure 3.3 An Expected Value Calculation for an Event Having Two Branches, One with an Amount Greater than Zero, and the Other with a Zero Amount

$$\underline{p} \quad \text{x} \quad \underline{\$A} \quad = \quad \underline{E(v)}$$

– **Do it right the first time:**	80%	x	$1	= $ .80
– **Catch error and fix *before* it goes out:**	15%	x	$10	= $1.50
– **Have to fix *after* error comes back:**	5%	x	$100	= $5.00
Total Expected Value (cost) for a transaction:				$7.30

Expected Value					
COSTS	# (%,p)	Cost/Unit	TOTAL COSTS	Percent Total Cost	Cost: 100,000 Transactions
1. Do right the first time	0.80	$ 1.00	$0.80	11%	$ 80,000
2. Catch error and fix *before* it goes out	0.15	$ 10.00	$1.50	21%	$ 150,000
3. Fix error *after* it comes back	0.05	$ 100.00	$5.00	68%	$ 500,000
TOTALS	1.00		$7.30	100%	$ 730,000

Figure 3.4 An Expected Value Analysis of the 1-10-100 Cost of Quality Rule, an Event with Three Branches

fix it if you catch a mistake before it leaves your office (15% of transactions), and it costs $100 to fix it when it has been returned by the irritated customer because it was defective (5% of transactions). Note that 89% of the cost of this transaction is for fixing errors. This cost of quality is typical for HR and other service operations. I have seen operations in which error rates to customers were as high as 30%. World-class service operations (e.g., L.L. Bean's mail-order business) have error rates below .15%.

Validation of Costs Data

The way you turn a "guesstimate" into an honorable statistic is to get ten guesstimates and find their mean and standard deviation. When in doubt repeat your analysis or have two or three other people do the analysis independently. Compare your numbers, see where you differ (differences usually are a result of assuming more or fewer steps, people involved, and times to do step tasks), and reach consensus. You also can calculate basic statistics—averages and standard deviations for several analyses of the same task. With these statistics you can state with confidence: Even if we use the lowest (or highest) value, at the 5% or 95% confidence interval, we can safely assume the work flow costs *at least (at most) $xxx.xx.*

Activity Value Analysis

Activity value analysis (AVA) is a method of rating the products and services produced by work flows and the steps or tasks in these work flows on such criteria as "customer value-added, business value-added, no value-added," to identify products, services, and steps that can be eliminated, outsourced, or re-engineered. As will be discussed in Chapter 8, most reengineering efforts start (or should) with a value analysis of all of the firm's human resources activities.

AVAs include the following steps.

1. Employees, managers, and consultants create a "dictionary" of:

   - All products or services (e.g., promotion transaction) produced by their department; each is given a product/service code number.

   - All task activities needed to produce product or service outputs (e.g., type promotion request form); each is given a task activity code number.

   - All employees in the department, identified by number. (The computer database has the master salary and cost per unit of time schedule.)

2. Employees fill in an AVA form similar to that shown in Table 3.3. On this form employees record their:

   - End products (e.g., a piece of paper or a completed service; the specific task activities they engage in to produce the end product; the value of each activity in producing the quality end product).

   - Amount of time (either as a percentage of time or actual time units) they spend on each activity.

   The computer then calculates task activity labor costs from the employee's name, title, or pay grade.

3. AVA data are entered into a spreadsheet or database and analyzed. For small departments, any spreadsheet with a sort capability can be used. Large departments or organization-wide AVA require a database program designed to produce AVA reports. AVA data can provide many valuable reports, for example:

   - No or low-value-added products or services—and their costs and the employees who perform them—are obvious candidates for elimination and redeployment.

   - Activity costs from no value or low value to high value and high to low cost are clearly displayed, as shown in Table 3.4.

These reports help analysts see immediately how much no-value and low-value activities are costing and which steps cost the most. No-value and low-value activities are candidates for elimination (e.g., all of the secretary's typing and filing steps in the analysis above), especially the "manager signs form" step, which has no value and high cost (why sign a form you have just made out?). High-value but high-cost activities should be outsourced or reengineered.

Various telling ratios and graphs can be created from AVA data, for example, the ratio of low- or nonvalue-added work to essential work by steps (8:1 or

Table 3.3 An Activity Value Analysis for an HR Transaction Showing Customer, Business, and No-Value-Added Activities— and Who Does Each

| | VALUE ADDED | | | | | VALUE ADDED | | | |
	End Product/ Service	Product/ Service Code	To C = Customer B = Business N = None	Value 1 = High 2 = ? 3 = Low	Task Activity	T.A. Code	To C = Customer B = Business N = None	Value 1 = High 2 = ? 3 = Low	Person	Person Code
	1. Promotion Transaction	101	B	1	1. Mgr has secty pull folder	201	N	3	Mgr	200
					2. Secretary retrieves	101	N	3	Secty	100
					3. Mgr reviews salary plan, increase	202	B	1	Mgr	200
					4. Secty retrieves, types, gives to Mgr to sign	101	N	3	Secty	100
					5. Mgr signs	203	N	3	Mgr	200
					6. Secty copies, files duplicate, sends to Mgr's Mgr for approval	101	N	3	Secty	100
					7. Mgr's Mgr's Secty opens mail, gives to Mgr's Mgr to sign	101	N	3	Mm / Secty	101
					8. Mgr's Mgr signs	303	?B	2	Mm	300
					9. Mgr's Mgr's Secty retrieves, copies, files duplicate copy, sends to Mgr's Secty and HR Generalist	101	N	3	Mm / Secty	101

Table 3.4 A Value Analysis Report Showing Activities Sorted in Ascending Order of Value and Descending Order of Cost—the Most Expensive No-Value Activities Appear First for Easy Identification

Task Activity	T.A. Code	To C = Customer B = Business N = None	Value 1 = High 2 = ? 3 = Low	VALUE ADDED			
				Person	Person Code	% Time (Time Unit)	$ Cost
4. Secty retrieves, types, gives to Mgr to sign	101	N	3	Secty	100		$1.33
5. Mgr signs	203	N	3	Mgr	200		$1.33
6. Secty copies, files duplicate, sends to Mgr's Mgr for approval	101	N	3	Secty	100		$1.33
7. Mgr's Mgr's Secty opens mail, gives to Mgr's Mgr to sign	101	N	3	Mm Secty	101		$1.33
9. Mgr's Mgr's Secty retrieves, copies, files duplicate copy, sends to Mgr's Secty and HR Generalist	101	N	3	Mm Secty			$1.33
1. Mgr has secty pull folder	201	N	3	Mgr	200		$1.28
2. Secty retrieves	101	N	3	Secty	100		$0.53
8. Mgr's Mgr signs	303	?B	2	Mm	300		$1.33
3. Mgr reviews salary plan increase	202	B	1	Mgr	200		$6.42

82.5% in the above analysis) or cost ($9.79 to $6.42, roughly 67% in the above analysis), or a cumulative cost of activities by value chart as shown in Figure 3.5.

- *Work fragmentation* charts show the full-time equivalent (FTE) time spent producing a given product or service, or the time spent on a specific activity divided by the number of people performing the activity. For example, if one FTE of work is performed by one person, the work fragmentation percentage is $1 \div 1 = 1.00$, 100%. If five people are doing the one FTE of work, the fragmentation percentage is $1 \div 5 = .20$, 20%. A low percentage indicates that work is widely fragmented and probably could be combined and performed more efficiently by one person or team.

- *Work distribution reports* show each employee's percentage of time and costs spent on customer VA, business VA, and NVA work. People spending any percentage of their time on NVA work are obvious candidates for redeployment.

WORK FLOW ANALYSIS

Modern work flow analysis methods are derived from the general systems model shown in Figure 3.6. A *processing system* receives inputs and transforms them into outputs, which the processing system sends to a receiving system. In business, the firm is the processing system and its market or customers the receiving system. Outputs can be metered (i.e., their cost, quality, and sales measured) and this information fed back to the processing system to improve its performance.

The Total Quality Management movement highlighted the importance of paying attention to feedback from receiving systems (i.e., customers). Japanese industrial engineer Ishikawa Karou's famous NOAC principle is *the next organization as customer* (i.e., the internal recipients of your work should be looked at as valued customers rather than as annoyances). This perspective is shown in Figure 3.7.

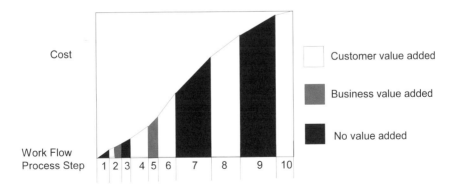

Figure 3.5   A Cumulative Cost Chart Showing Customer, Business, and No-Value-Added Steps

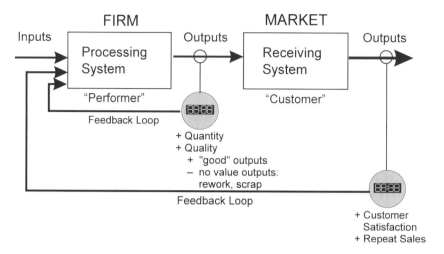

Figure 3.6 The General Systems Model Showing "metered" Outputs, Which Provide Feedback to the Processing System

Anyone inside or outside the organization who supplies inputs, information, or requests for service to you are "upstream" suppliers. Anyone who receives the output of your work "downstream" is a customer.

Figure 3.8 shows what is being called the process revolution in American industry: the shift from emphasis on hierarchical functions to process flows. U.S. firms traditionally have been organized in terms of functional bureaucracies R&D, manufacturing, and marketing—and are now often disparagingly called silos or stovepipes—to suggest that information flows only up and down, not across.

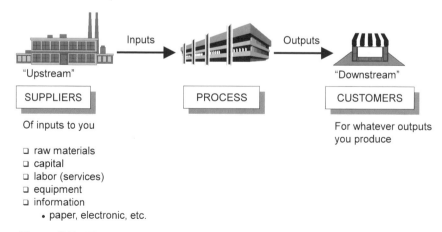

Figure 3.7 "Upstream" Suppliers and "Downstream" Customers in Any Work Flow Process

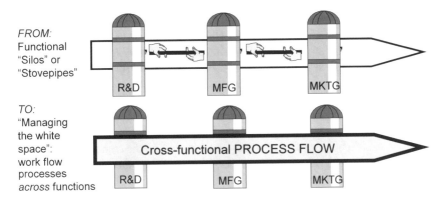

Figure 3.8 The Process Revolution in American Industry

A law of production systems is that inefficiencies occur at *points of interface*—whenever a task or product is handed off from one functional organization to another. This realization has led to an emphasis on "managing the white space on the organizational chart," or focusing more on how products, services, or orders from customers flow from one functional box on the organizational chart to the next.

Improving Work Flows

The basic ideas for improving work flows can be organized in terms of inputs, processes, and outputs.

Inputs

Get inputs just-in-time. Arrange with your suppliers to get whatever inputs or data you need from them at the exact time you are ready to process them. This will minimize the following problems:

- Excess inventory: stacks of paper you will have to search through at some future time to do your work. Fifty percent of white-collar work has been found to be set-up time (searching for needed information), and scrap (doing faulty work over)

- Rush-order overtime: getting too much work too late, causing unproductive work-until-midnight frenzy—and burnout

- Waiting downtime: sitting around with nothing to do because a supplier has not provided you with the information you need

Get inputs in better condition to reduce processing work needed to convert inputs into desired outputs. For example, in the bad old days, I would show up at my tax accountant's office the first week in April with a dirty laundry bag full of crumpled receipts. The accountant would charge me for the two days it took him to sort these receipts into income and deduction categories.

One year he gave me a set of organizer envelopes, each keyed to an income tax form category: medical expenses or educational expenses. I thought this was neat, a freebie that helped me get myself better organized. Of course, what the accountant had done was to get me to do some of his work: He had transferred the data organization task back upstream to his supplier, me.

A couple of years later, he gave me a tax data organizer form to fill in, with each data entry field keyed to the computer tax program he used. This form increased my organization and further decreased his work. Now all his secretary had to do was reenter the data I had put on the form into the computer.

Currently, instead of a paper form, he gives me a computer disk. I do the data entry for him as well as the data organization. I mail the disk back to him, he puts it in his floppy disk drive, computes my taxes, prints out my tax return, sends it back to me to sign and send on to the government and then he sends me a bill.

The next step, obviously, is for me to modem the data to him directly, eliminating physical mailing of the floppy disk, and for him to modem my tax return to the IRS, eliminating the paper tax return.

What my accountant has done each time is move processing upstream to me, the supplier, in a way that I perceive as a *higher* rather than a lower level of service, and that gets him the data he needs just-in-time and in progressively better condition.

Eventually, my accountant friend will be reengineered out of at least the grunt work of his tax preparation business. There is no reason that the state and federal Internal Revenue Service cannot provide tax preparation software on electronic bulletin boards that any citizen can download into their own PCs. Taxpayers can enter their tax data directly on the screen. All calculations will be performed for them automatically and the IRS will know that at least the arithmetic is right. The completed income tax return can then be uploaded to the IRS with a credit card number to pay the tax due. This process would save the taxpayer and the IRS an enormous amount of paperwork.

Another example of reduced processing work is professionals' direct entry of word processing data. Ten years ago most professionals in my firm wrote proposals and reports in blurry pencil on yellow legal pads and handed these pieces of paper to their secretaries, who walked them to desktop publishing (DTP). In DTP, typists attempted to decipher the scrawls and reentered the data on a word processor. An ABC accounting exercise suggested that this process cost about $2.50 a page. As an incentive to get professionals to learn to type and do their own text data entry, I went to a direct billing system: Drafts turned in on paper would be charged $2.50 a page, while drafts turned in on disks and also walked by the secretary to desktop publishing ("sneaker LAN") would be charged $1 a page. Professionals' bonuses depended on the profitability of their projects. Want a bigger bonus? Learn to type, and reduce costs on your projects. Today, of course, professionals do most of their own desktop publishing proposals, reports, and marketing presentations. Headcount in desktop publishing has been cut in half. The data that does go to desktop publishing now goes by e-mail over the LAN.

The implications of these examples should be obvious: HR should enable end-user suppliers to provide HR with the input data it needs, just-in-time, in perfect condition, by PC via LAN or modem. The on-screen forms provided by the HRIS will lead/force users to organize data in exactly the way most easily processed by HR. Spell checking, error checking, and exemption controls built into the system will ensure highest quality inputs.

Processing

Process steps that cannot be moved upstream to suppliers or downstream to customers should be reengineered to eliminate low- or non-value-added steps and waiting time between operations, and enable the process step to be done by the least expensive worker available or by a computer. Specific methods and ideas for doing this are presented in the rest of this chapter and in Chapter 6.

Outputs

Output efficiencies can be identified by asking your downstream customers, "How can I save you work? How can my outputs to you be changed to give them to you just-in-time and in better condition?"

Very often customer suggestions include:

- *Stop sending low-value-added outputs* (i.e., printouts, approvals, and memo forms routinely ignored or tossed). For example, every week for ten years, I received a six-inch-thick printout reporting all the financial transactions in my organization. Not once in ten years did I ever look at it. I routinely put it into my briefcase and took it home for my children to draw on. Finally, I wised up and told my controller, "Mike, I don't ever want to see this paper again. If there is anything I need to know about the financial state of the company, I want you to tell me. If there are any numbers I need to see, I want you to put them on one sheet of paper." I subsequently received one or two phone calls a month, and rarely more than one sheet of paper.

- *Improve outputs by providing fewer or lower levels of service.* Less is often more. Patients facing abdominal surgery used to spend one day in the hospital before their operation, fasting and drinking lots of water to purge their systems. After the operation, they had to spend two more days in a recovery room. It turned out these patients could just as easily prepare and recover in their own beds at home rather than in an $850-a-day hospital bed *and much preferred to do so.* Home versus hospital preparation and recovery made no difference in quality (percentage of good surgical outcomes or recovery rates). In fact, postsurgical infections were fewer with home recovery (hospitals are full of germs).

- *Facilitate customer DIY self-service* (i.e., move process and output creation downstream to the customers themselves). The health care example above illustrates movement of work both upstream (fasting and drinking water) and downstream (recovering at home).

Implications for HR: Most paperwork HR managers and employees receive is considered not a help but a burden, as in "More (expletive deleted) bureaucracy from HR!" Many managers consider the words, "I'm from HR and I'm here to help you!" as among the most frightening words they can hear.

How to Do a Work Flow Analysis

A typical work flow analysis includes the steps described on the next several pages.

1. **Identify a work flow to reengineer.**
   Criteria include:

   - High customer impact and customer complaints (e.g., a key process is not meeting your customers' needs).

   - High business impact: when the work flow is performed, often in high volume, takes a lot of people's time and, above all, costs a lot.

   - Blatant inefficiency: The work flow includes many nonvalue-added steps, for example, data reentry, duplicate files, redundant copies (kept forms exchanged).

   - (Too) many people are involved almost always a sign of poorly designed, duplicated, and fragmented work.

   - "Just-in-case" inventory buffers: stacks of paper sitting around in case they are needed.

   - Many approval layers, and checking and control steps.

   - Unacceptable (uncompetitive) cycle times.

     The three main processes and cycle times in any business, are:

     a. Product development: concept-to-market time

     b. Sales: prospect identification-to-order time

     c. Order fulfillment: order-to-delivery (customer receipt of the product or service) or order-to-collection (payment) time

     In HR processes, order fulfillment is a customer service inquiry-, request-, or complaint-to-resolution time. Unacceptable cycle times are indicated by "Why does it take HR four months to process a new hire and six weeks to get a change of address right?"

   - The process annoys you or your team. It makes everybody angry so lots of people have the energy to work on it.

2. **Enlist the cooperation of the people doing the work.** The participative approach to reengineering is to teach workers reengineering methods and

ask them to analyze their own work flows versus "doing it to them" (using outside experts or consultants to analyze work flows and recommend changes). Participative approaches assume that employees doing the work:

■ Know their jobs and where improvements can be made in work flows.

■ Naturally resent inspection and implied criticism by outside efficiency experts.

■ Are much more likely to implement changes they had a part in proposing.

Employees asked to participate in reengineering efforts may need to be reassured about job security. To many people, reengineering means downsizing and layoffs. Not surprisingly, employees are not likely to suggest improvements that will get them fired. Hence, whenever possible, emphasize that:

■ Any work force reductions will be made by attrition or transfer to other jobs with retraining. Employees will be rewarded for good ideas. (If layoffs are inevitable, you can subtly suggest that workers who enthusiastically support the reengineering effort are the ones most likely to stay, and that the converse is equally true: Those who resist, actively or passively, will be the first to go.)

3. **Chart all the steps in the work flow, even the most trivial.**
   You can use:

■ Paper work flow analysis worksheets (see Figure 3.9).

■ Black or white boards.

■ Yellow stickies on a wall.

■ Software: any presentation graphics or program (Shapeware's Visio™, Scitor's Process Charter™, Microsoft PowerPoint™, Lotus Freelance™, or Micrographics Draw™).

Which tool should you use? The easiest! Free-form paper sketches, even the back of an envelope, can work as well as more elaborate work flow charting tools. Software programs have the advantage of speeding the creation of very nice charts for presentations, especially when charts must be changed a number of times.

Figure 3.9 shows a typical work flow chart with space for charting both current and proposed steps in a work flow, noting the type of step performed by circling the appropriate symbol:

■ ACTION: Fill out a form on paper or screen.

■ MOVE: Walk, mail, modem a piece of paper or data.

■ DELAY: Form sits in in-box or e-mail directory, waits for approval.

PRESENT — WORK FLOW STEPS	Act	Move	Delay	File	Decision/Control	VALUE C,B,NR,N	TIME Cycle Elapsd Time	COST Labor (Who?) Expnse (What?)	# Units (Work Time)	$Cost/ (Time) Unit	$Cost/Step	NOTES
Employee walks to HR Office	□	(circle)	D	▼	◇	N	10	Empl.	10	$ 0.46	$ 4.60	Eliminate
Empl explains request to HR Clerk	(circle)	⇨	D	▼	◇	C	3	Empl.	3	$ 0.46	$ 1.38	Empl. enter data at workstation, send electronically to database
HR Clerk fills out form	(circle)	⇨	D	▼	◇	N	3	Clerk	3	$ 0.29	$ 0.87	Eliminate
Form sits in out box (save: 1 day=16hrs)	□	⇨	(circled D)	▼	◇	N			960	Act		Eliminate
TOTAL							976		16		$ 6.85	
Proposed							-3		-3		$ (1.38)	
=Saving							973		13		$ 5.47	

Notes header: >ELIMINATE:Low,?, no value/control/ file stps? >Send electronically?>Automate: computerize?>Combine steps in one person, team?

PROPOSED — WORK FLOW STEPS	Act	Move	Delay	File	Decision/Control	VALUE C,B,NR,N	TIME Cycle Elapsd Time	COST Labor (Who?) Expnse (What?)	# Units (Work Time)	$Cost/ (Time) Unit	$Cost/Step
[none]	□	⇨	D	▼	◇						
Empl enters transaction directly on kiosk screen	(circle)	⇨	D	▼	◇	C	3	Empl.	3	0.46	1.38
[none]	□	⇨	D	▼	◇						
[none]	□	⇨	D	▼	◇						
TOTAL											
Proposed							3		3		$ (1.38)
=Saving											

Figure 3.9 Work Flow Analysis Worksheets

- FILE: Save paper in file folder, data to computer disk or database.
- DECISION: Route form on the basis of condition.
  or
- CONTROL: Check form for quality, accuracy, completeness, and then if
- OK, send; if not, return to be fixed.

Figure 3.10 provides a key to work flow analysis symbols with examples and possible alternatives to how work is done for each in an existing step.

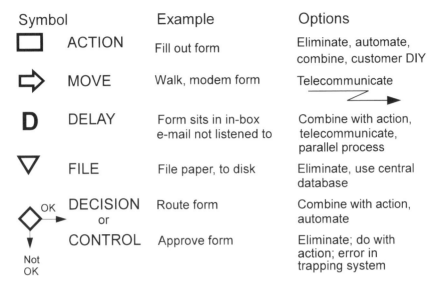

Symbol		Example	Options
□	ACTION	Fill out form	Eliminate, automate, combine, customer DIY
⇨	MOVE	Walk, modem form	Telecommunicate
D	DELAY	Form sits in in-box e-mail not listened to	Combine with action, telecommunicate, parallel process
▽	FILE	File paper, to disk	Eliminate, use central database
◇ OK	DECISION or	Route form	Combine with action, automate
Not OK	CONTROL	Approve form	Eliminate; do with action; error in trapping system

Figure 3.10 Common Work Flow Charting Symbols with Examples and Alternative Suggestions

The cycle (elapsed) time the step takes

- ABC data: labor and cash outlay costs, time worked or cash outlay units, and cost per (time) unit, used to calculate the total cost of the step. (Note that elapsed time and time worked should be equal for steps involving labor. Delay steps involved elapsed time, but not time worked.

- Notes: comments on the value of a step, or reengineering alternatives to it.

A note on work flow analysis grammar: While there is an international standard for work flow charting symbols (American National Standards Institute ANSI/AIIM MS4, built into Visio's Flowchart stencil), almost no one follows it. In practice, work flow analysts tend to develop their own preferred symbols and grammar. A WFA grammar should include the data shown in Figure 3.11.

In traditional work flow charting, symbols were labeled with the action "what's done" (verb) inside the symbol, Secretary, and the "who does it" (noun) outside the symbol.

The grammar used in the examples in this book puts the "who does it" noun inside the symbol, and the verb outside or on a verb symbol, for example, a straight arrow for physical movement or a zigzagged arrow for electronic movement. The people involved in a step are given prominence because in HR work flows, labor is by far the greatest cost. Steps in the work flow are cascaded from upper left to lower right in time-sequential order, as shown in Figure 3.12.

Grammar	Subject Labor "Who"	Verb Action	Object Used in Action	Object Acted Upon	Destination Preposition	Destination Object
Example	Secretary	walks	feet	form	to	Manager
Example	Manager	modems	modem	screen data (form)	to	IHRMIS database
Example	HR specialist	telecon- ferences	picture phone	image of self	to	colleague in Jakarta

Figure 3.11   Elements of Work Flow Charting "Grammar"

Symbols (footsteps for walking), "zap" lines for electronic communication, or downward-pointing black triangles for filing, are not just cute, they enable analysts to see at a glance the potential steps for reengineering.

IDEF is a WFA grammar mandated by the U.S. Department of Defense and widely used by other government agencies and firms that deal frequently with the government such as defense contractors and

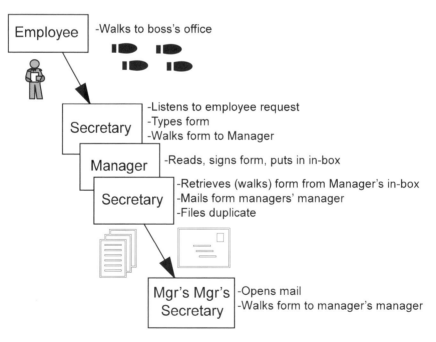

Figure 3.12   An Upper Left to Lower Right Work Flow Chart
with Explanatory Symbols

aerospace firms. IDEF WFA charts must include these five elements (shown in Figure 3.13):

- *Inputs*: people, things, data transformed by the Activity process
- *Controls:* output quality standards; rules, policies, procedures the Activity process must follow
- *Mechanisms:* input resources not transformed by the Activity process (e.g., the people "doers" of the activity, software, computer, equipment, and facilities)
- *Activity* process: in IDEF always labeled with a verb-noun phrase (e.g., Conduct workshop)
- *Outputs:* of the Activity process

IDEF diagrams cascade steps in a work flow down and to the right, and permit any step to be "decomposed" into smaller component steps, as shown in Figure 3.14. IDEF's advantages include:

- Explicit listing of "Controls" identifies the whys of work flow steps. Silly NVA policies, rules, and procedures are exposed for questioning, modification, or elimination.
- Industrial strength (albeit expensive) software is available to automate IDEF WFA charting of very complex (e.g., > 1,000-step) enterprise

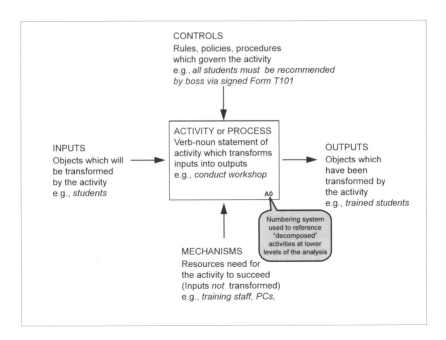

Figure 3.13 Elements of an IDEF Work Flow Analysis Chart

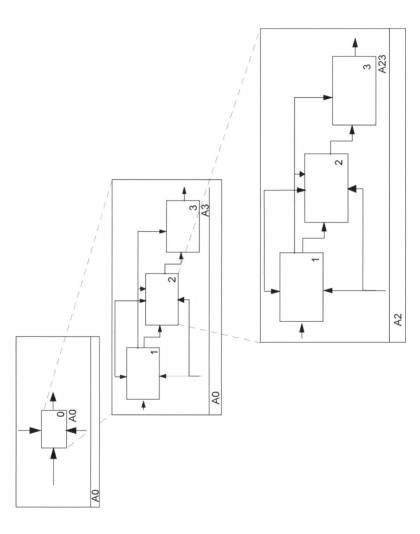

Figure 3.14 An IDEF Work Flow Diagram Showing Steps "Decomposed" into Smaller Component Steps

processes. IDEF software aids entry, tracking, and summary of activity costs, work times, cycle delay times, and values of steps, simulation of "what if" changes in work flow, and compilation of comprehensive dictionaries or glossaries of inputs, controls, mechanisms, activities, and outputs referenced in the analysis.

■ *Decomposition.* IDEF methods and software keep track of "drilldown" decomposition of work flow steps into smaller component steps.

Any step in a process can be infinitely decomposed into smaller steps. A question beginning work flow analysts always ask is how far they should decompose work flow steps. For example, one typology has the following levels:

a. *Motion.* This is the least part of the task (e.g., "reach for phone")

b. *Element.* This is part of a task (e.g., "schedule one meeting")

c. *Task* (e.g., one boss-subordinate meeting)

d. *Intermediate product* (e.g., a development plan signed by appraisal form signed by boss and subordinate)

e. *End product* (e.g., a complete Performance Appraisal, with all forms signed by boss and subordinate)

The appropriate level of decomposition depends on the scale of your analysis. A very high level analysis, like the general systems model shown above, may lump all firm functions in one box process. Most of the HR work flows shown in this book concern a task (manager signs form) or cluster of tasks performed by the same person at the same time (secretary retrieves signed form, copies original, mails original to HR generalist, and files duplicate copy) level.

The traditional rule has been decompose one level more detailed than you think you need to (e.g., "files form" into elements like "opens file drawer, pulls file folder, looks through file folder to find form"). A step taking two minutes may seem too small to be worth recording or calculating the cost, but such steps, if performed dozens or hundreds of times in a week, add up in time and cost. Documenting them can lead a reengineer to see that, "it would be smarter to save all records to a server database hard drive, saving many minutes and pieces of paper which add up to saving file cabinets and secretaries."

4. **Value the problems.** Calculate the baseline costs of the present work flow. Follow the ABC steps described above to calculate labor times and costs, cash outlay costs of material, equipment, services, travel, per diem, and so forth.

Note that the work flow analysis worksheet combines the templates for labor (who) and cash outlay (what) costs to save space. Also record any baseline quality or quantity metrics (e.g., error rates).

5. **Question the value-added of each step and brainstorm alternatives to how it is done now.**

Value Analysis: Start with the most expensive steps, your "low-hanging" fruit are your best bets for reducing costs, and ask about each step:

- Is there any customer value-added (CVA)?
- Is there any business value-added (BVA)?
- Is it required by policy, standard operating procedures manual, legal, or regulatory mandates, but otherwise adds no value (no value-added but required: NR)? NR steps indicate a need to change outdated policy and procedures or to lobby furiously to get unnecessary laws and regulations changed.
- Is it a no-value-added (NVA) step that should be eliminated?

You can also rate steps on a value scale (e.g., 1 = essential; 2 = some value; 3 = no value). This is sometimes needed to sort data using software that requires numerical values.

Brainstorm alternatives. Alternatives are shown in the last column of Figure 3.9.

- *Eliminate* steps that produce no customer or business value-added.
- *Combine* steps performed by others earlier or later in the work flow. (As discussed in the next chapter, a fundamental principle of reengineering is to have as few people involved in a process as possible. One person or one team should perform as many steps simultaneously as possible.)
- *Computerize* (e.g., process forms on a PC screen rather than on paper; move data by e-mail, LAN, WAN, or modem; file on a server hard drive rather than in a folder).
- *Delegate* checking and approval steps to one front-line employee who often costs less.

6. **Document the proposed new work flow.** Document the changes you want to make (and why) in the center notes column using the right-hand side of the work flow analysis worksheet (see Figure 3.9), in exactly the same way as for the current work flow.

7. **Value the solution.** Calculate the costs of the proposed work flow.

Again follow the ABC steps described above to calculate labor times and costs, cash outlay costs of material, equipment, services, travel, per diem, and so on. Also note the cycle (elapsed) time the new work flow takes to produce a product or service, and any product or service quality and quantity improvements.

8. **Estimate time and cost savings and other benefits by comparing proposed and present work flow data.** At the bottom of the work flow analysis worksheet there is a template for subtracting proposed work flow times and costs from present times and costs to estimate savings. Cycle time and cost savings data are critical for marketing reengineering proposals, that is, convincing others to invest the time, training, and capital to make the new process work.

9. **Try out the new work flow.** Get typical employees—those who will be using the new work flow—to try it out (usability engineering). (Do not use a typical reengineer or subject matter expert who designed the new work flow to test it.) Watch workers carefully to see where they have problems with the system. Errors are users' intuitive attempts to use the system and provide key feedback to systems designers about how to make the system more user-friendly.

   - Debug and fine tune systems interfaces (computer screens) using employee feedback. Plan for at least two prototype revision cycles.

   - Validate the value of the proposal: Determine whether the new work flow yields the expected savings in time and cost. Where does the new work flow yield the expected time and cost savings, and where does it fall short?

   Remember: In testing new work flows, there is always a learning curve. The new work flow may initially be *less* efficient, take *longer*, and cost *more* than the old system because people haven't learned it. Measure the actual time and costs to perform the new work flow when people have stopped improving (i.e., when their learning curve plateaus). A few hours or a few days of trial usually is sufficient.

   Usability testing is very powerful. It virtually guarantees that there will be no "puny payoff from office computers," because the time and cost savings from the reengineered process are known. Usability testing also helps plan for implementation, where employees have problems with the new system and need extra training or learning times are known. Implementation goes much more smoothly when obstacles to the new process have been encountered and overcome.

10. **Implement the new work flow.** Implementation steps include:

    - Communicate how the new work flow will work (e.g., by posting and talking through the new work flow, with explanation or the reasons for changes).

    - Orient employees by walking them through the new process.

    - Train people in the new work flow (i.e., how to use new PCs or software).

- Post productivity statistics publicly (i.e., on a large chart on a wall where every employee can see them). Seeing that time and cost savings are being achieved is a powerful reinforcer.

- Give individuals feedback on their performance, and provide coaching advice and support in ways to improve.

- Reward employees who adapt quickly to the new work flow and increase productivity.

- Replace employees who do not or will not adapt to and use the new work flow process. This sounds harsh, but it is a reality of every reengineering effort. The ultimate choice for employees is adapt or leave. The choice for management is train or replace.

11. **Follow up, evaluate, and document the benefits of the new work flow.** Check to ensure that the new work flow is being used and that people aren't relapsing. In reengineered work flows, changes are often so dramatic (e.g., everything on computer screens rather than on paper) that relapse is difficult, if not impossible. However, some skeptics and dinosaurs may maintain shadow paper files or procedures for some period of time after the transition to the new work flow has been made.

12. **Value the result.** Document the time and dollar cost benefits of the new work flow versus baseline data collected on the old work flow in step 4: labor time and outlay costs saved, reduced cycle time, and improved product and service quality.

13. **Publicize results, and reward the people who helped.**

- Always let the client process owners take the credit.

- Publicize successful employees and ideas, employees whose suggestions were used, and employees who participated. Tangible rewards can include new computer equipment or software, travel to conferences, or opportunities to participate in more challenging reengineering projects.

- Provide gain-sharing monetary rewards where possible.

SUMMARY

Activity-based costing, value analysis, and work flow analysis provide the basic skills needed to reengineer. The next chapter shows how these methods have been advanced to achieve radical improvements in productivity.

4

Reengineering Concepts

Reengineering concepts build on activity-based costing (ABC), value analysis, and work flow charting methods discussed in the previous chapter. Some concepts are extrapolations of industrial engineering principles, and some are genuinely new concepts enabled by advances in computer and communication technology as discussed in Chapter 2. Examples in this chapter are purposely taken from a variety of industries and functions other than HR to stimulate "out of the box" thinking. The challenge: How might each concept be applied to reengineering HR?

RETHINKING WORK

The most fundamental reengineering concept is to rethink work from scratch. All businesses, products, services, and the work flow activities needed to produce them should be rethought from a blank piece of paper (or screen!). Reengineering's assault on existing work occurs first at a macro and then a micro level.

We'll concentrate first on macro reengineering. The fundamental concept of value analysis is "eliminate the nonessential, simplify the essential." Macro reengineering means automatic consideration of three basic alternatives, in the following order: eliminate, outsource, automate (reengineer). For example, the CEO says to the vice president of Human Resources, "I'm taking a third out of your budget starting January 1—either eliminate your low-value activities or figure out how to deliver them more efficiently." The CEO is suggesting a zero-based budgeting approach to force reconsideration of everything the Human Resources department does. The three basic alternatives are:

- *Eliminate* low-value services and activities.

- *Outsource* services and activities that can be provided more cheaply, or at a higher quality, or both, by outside vendors.

- *Reengineer* activities that are too strategically important to outsource, in order to cut costs and improve quality.

Eliminating means not wasting time or money reengineering a business, product, or service you shouldn't be in—just get rid of it. General Electric CEO Jack Welch is famous for telling his managers that they must be number one or two in their markets or they will be sold: "If you are not one or two, get there, or get out!"

Outsourcing means not doing anything that you can buy more cheaply and/or at a higher quality from a vendor. James Bryant Quinn asserts the toughest version of this rule: If your firm is not the best in the world (or at least the best in town) in providing a service (highest quality at lowest cost), you should outsource it. You don't do payroll as well as Ceridian, ADP, or your bank's direct-deposit system? Hire Ceridian or ADP's Service Bureau or your bank to do your payroll. Can't manage your pension fund as well as Fidelity Investments can? Hire them to do it. Can't recruit as quickly or find as high-quality candidates as your headhunter? Let him or her do it.

Outsourcing relies heavily on a free market concept, hardly new with reengineering. External vendors of HR services are every HR department's natural competitors—and a readily available source of competitive cost, cycle time, and quality data against which internal HR services can be measured. When internal services slip beneath the competition on any of these metrics, they should be outsourced. The mere threat of outsourcing keeps internal service professionals on their toes. Hence, all firms should continually perform *make* versus *buy* versus *ally* analysis—and buy or ally for services that can be provided cheaper in-house.

The only caveat is that a firm should not outsource or ally for a strategic strength or core competence (e.g., unique technologies, information systems, supplier or customer relationships). Firms must retain and strengthen those competencies where they can create unique value and competitive advantage. It will be argued in Chapter 7 that a firm's only sustainable competitive advantage is its people. A key challenge for HR is to identify those HR services (e.g., recruiting, selection, or training) that genuinely add value and world-class competitive advantage. These functions should not be outsourced—they are key proprietary intellectual assets of the firm.

Reengineer only when a business, product, or service is too valuable to eliminate and too strategically important to outsource should it be restructured to get it to world-class cost, cycle time, and quality performance.

Reengineering continues the "eliminate, outsource, automate" process the next level down into an organization's critical workflows—radically eliminating nonvalue-added activities, outsourcing what vendors can do better, and automating or delegating to end-users essential activities to save time and money.

NETWORK PCs SHARE CENTRAL DATABASES

The second core reengineering concept is making all information available on-line to all employees (suppliers and customers), using client–server database architectures discussed in Chapter 2. Reengineering principles that follow from this concept include:

Capture data once, at its point of origin, and *never* reenter data. Many personnel work flows involve employees or applicants filling out forms on paper, which are then reentered by personnel clerks onto a computer. In Maine's fragmented social services systems, the same client information may be requested as many as 72 times by different social service agencies (see Chapter 10 for a discussion of National HR Systems for the Future).

The obvious reengineering solution is for an employee or client to enter data once, at a PC or kiosk, into a central database available to all HR functions and managers. This central database must be reliable and secure, yet permit easy access to data by authorized persons. Otherwise, people will begin to maintain shadow files and duplicate databases, keeping pieces of paper "just in case" or cluttering their PC hard drives by downloading information that only needs to be on the server.

Process Information Close to Those Who Use It (i.e., on End-Users' PCs)

The server maintains the masses of data, which are word processed and spreadsheet analyzed by the employees who need it.

Chapter 6 describes how a shared HR database will integrate all HR functions in the future. In an Integrated Human Resource Management Information Systems (IHRMIS), every personnel transaction is entered when and where it occurs. Every employee worldwide has instant access to most data on a need-to-know basis. (The only exceptions are the performance appraisal ratings and salaries of peers and superiors and confidential medical records.) Data is reliable because it is constantly updated just-in-time. Employees can generate any reports or get any information they need at their own workstations.

Common access to HR data greatly simplifies many HR tasks. For example, if an employee needs to enter a child care application or medical benefit reimbursement data for a child, the form comes up on the screen with 95% of the necessary information already filled in. The computer already knows the employee's name, social security number, date of employment, and children's names, ages, and medical conditions. All the employee has to do is enter any new or changed information to get the desired service.

Make Customers and Suppliers Part of Your Information System

The core concept here is to extend your information system "upstream" to suppliers and "downstream" to customers to get data you need from them or to them just-in-time, in better or perfect condition. Innovative retailers Wal-Mart, Levi-Strauss, and Benetton use customers' cash registers as just-in-time inventory-reordering systems. The computer behind the cash register knows how many jeans are in stock, so when size 40/39 is low, it automatically reorders from the manufacturer. Manufacturer and customer inventory is "warehoused" in delivery trucks enroute from the factory to retail stores. Suppliers receive instant feedback on customer buying preferences (e.g., "green and purple striped sweaters are flying off the shelves in our southern New Hampshire stores this weekend; have the factory produce more of these colors—Benetton)." Powerful on-line market research keeps these firms ahead of competitors.

Automatic reordering systems make selling automatic: Customer orders flow in without any intervention by customer or seller. The computer simply says, "reorder, ship, debit my firm's account." These systems reduce selling and collection costs by eliminating the need for many salespeople and bill collectors.

HR suppliers to firms include unemployed individuals in the general population; headhunters; college placement offices; and numerous vendors of health insurance, benefits and pension administration, software, and the like. Potential employees in the "virtual work force" should be on-line to the HR department via the Internet or electronic job-posting bulletin boards that hold resumes of candidates worldwide. An HR staff person or line manager can search for candidates by demographic characteristics, technical skills, competencies, and other job–person matching criteria (e.g., using key word queries for *black chemical engineers* with an *M.B.A.,* preferably from a *European business school*, fluent in *French*, knowledgeable in *tetracycline* production, willing to *relocate* to Francophone *Africa* to *manage* a *pharmaceutical plant*—and find potential candidates instantly). Benefit vendor data and employee information requests about medical, dental, legal, child care, and other benefits as well as the current status or value of their 401(k) plan, and so forth, can be supplied immediately by telephone or computer modem access to the HR database.

No Work:
Enable Do-It-Yourself Customer Self-Service

Now we're ready to discuss micro reengineering. At the micro level, concepts for reengineering those products, services, and work flows that the firm decides to keep include no work, enabling DIY (Do It Yourself) customer self-service. The vision for HR service in the future discussed in Chapter 1 is essentially the DIY concept: Every employee, potential employee, or other stakeholder has immediate access to any HR product or service anywhere in the world, without having to move from his or her workstation (PDA, telephone). DIY HR systems enable end-user customers themselves to get HR products or services they need.

Examples of the DIY concept (with cases from other functions and industries to stimulate your thinking) include:

- *Salad bars.* Clients have to move to the bar, but (if the bar has an ample selection) can choose only and exactly what they want to eat, just-in-time, when they want it. Self-service is almost always faster than waiting for the waitperson.

HR example: "cafeteria" benefits and career development plans (some with expert system help) that help employees select benefit and training options with the most value to them.

- *Automatic Teller Machines (ATMs), employee benefit kiosks.* Customers have to go to the ATM but get faster service than having to walk to the bank and wait in line to see a teller.

HR example: Employee Benefits kiosks. Employees have to go to the kiosk but get faster service than having to walk to the personnel department and wait. Kiosks deliver services at a third to a quarter of the cost of human service providers.

- *GE answer line.* A voice-response computer (or backup human consultant) helps you fix your refrigerator or garbage disposal by talking you through the repair. "Is it plugged in? Try pressing the little red reset button on the bottom." The customer doesn't have to move, and if the voice response or human consultant is competent, he or she gets high quality service just-in-time.

HR example: HR help desks, such as Meridian Bancorp's "TESS"[1] (The Employee Self-Service System) and Mellon Bank's "HR4YOU,"[2] which handles 550 calls a day, 125,000 a year, with six FTE HR help desk service representatives.

- *Diagnostics, repair instructions, and spare parts in the machine.* Modern copier machines have interactive video screens that talk copier operators through common repairs. A pleasant speaking head says, "Open breaker panel B, pull out the charred piece of paper" or "The toner cartridge is empty. You will find a replacement cartridge in the parts drawer down at the bottom right. Replace it using the following steps . . ."

  The best repair instructions include advice on how the operator can avoid the problem in the future. Frequently the operator finishes the process feeling empowered: "Hey, this is easy. I can fix this the next time myself or prevent it from occurring." No movement of the customer is required; perfect-quality help is given just-in-time.

HR example: Employees don't yet come with operating and repair instructions or spare parts for improving work performance, but bracelets and "smart" identification cards already store personal medical data (allergies, needed medications) and other information on microfilm, magnetic strips, and memory chips. There is no reason why "personnel folder" data, including occupational preference, preferred managerial style, and other "what motivates me" information could not be carried by any employee (or available from the HR server).

- *Computer program help screens.* Press F1 or click on Help. A Wizard (Microsoft), Coach (WordPerfect) or Advisor (Lotus) will tell you how to perform the function you want. As described in the future scenarios in Chapter 1, "living" help screens can provide multimedia on-line training, coaching, legal, and management advice.

No Workers (or the Fewest Possible)

A basic reengineering principle is to involve as few workers as possible (other than the customer) in any process. This principle is implemented by automation, combining tasks so that one worker (or team) can do the whole job for the customer at the first point of contact, using the cheapest, most competent multi-skilled workers.

Automation

The ultimate application of this rule is having no workers, achieved by enabling customer self-service use of a "service robot"—computer, interactive voice-response (IVR) phone, or vending machines like ATMs and benefit kiosks. Recent research by Edify Corporation, a leading vendor of IVR software, indicates that 70% of all HR transactions[3] can be handled by IVR systems connected to HRIS databases. A major objective is to combine tasks so one person or team can do the whole job at the first point of contact with the customer.

A traditional rule of worker and managerial authority and responsibility has been that 85% of service transactions or decisions should be made by the first worker the customer encounters. Only 15% of transactions or decisions should need to be "bucked" to a second level of management, and only 3% to 5% bucked to a third or higher level.

- Reengineering benchmarks are much more aggressive. For example, employees in the Massachusetts Department of Revenue (DOR) handle 55% of taxpayer transactions at the first point of contact. DOR's reengineering goal is to first-point-of-contact transaction completion to 95%. Canada's Income Security and Pension (social security) system's reegineering objective is to handle 99% of citizen inquiries at the first point of contact. MasterCard customer service representatives hold the world's record for first-point-of-contact service: 99.9%—that is, only one transaction in 1,000 gets bucked any further into the bureaucracy.

  Empowered (and competent) front-line workers, acting as account or case managers for their customers, increasingly approve loans, process insurance claims, fill orders, and resolve customer complaints on the spot for their clients without handing off these tasks to other workers or managers. One result is flatter organizations with fewer middle managers: When front-line people do the whole job, managers and staff are not needed.

Least Expensive, Most Competent Workers

A basic rule of industrial engineering has always been to design work so that it can be done by the cheapest (least-skilled) worker. This principle is erroneously decried as causing jobs to be "dumbed down," turning people into mindless robots, cogs in a machine.

In fact, reengineered work usually requires *higher*, not lower, skills. Employees capable of doing the whole job for their customers, at the first point of contact, need to work at their highest level of competence. More skilled and more highly paid workers actually become less expensive when cost effectiveness or productivity is considered: Productivity = outputs (units of product or service produced) ÷ inputs (labor hours × cost-per-labor hour). More competent workers cost more, so the input denominator in the productivity equation is larger but produce much larger output numerators, so the productivity dividend increases. Charles Handy[4] describes a "1/2 × 2 × 3" workplace in the future in which *half* the number of people, paid *twice* as much, do *three* times as much work. Here are some examples.

Multiskilled Water Meter Installers.   Before reengineering, a crew of four workers was needed to install a water meter: (1) The laborer dug a hole; (2) the mason bricked in the hole; (3) the plumber connected the pipes to the water meter; (4) the electrician connected the wires to the meter; (5) the mason finished bricking in the hole; and finally, (6) the laborer refilled the hole with dirt. This took four workers three hours: 12 person hours at an average wage of $13.75 an hour, a total cost of a $165 per meter installed.

After reengineering and multiskilling (the laborer learned enough masonry, plumbing, and electricity to install the water meter), *one* worker went out, dug the hole, bricked it in, connected the pipes, connected the wires, finished the masonry, and refilled the hole with dirt. This took the one multiskilled worker four hours, a 200% productivity increase—and even at $20 an hour premium for multiskilled labor, it cost but $80 per meter installed, a 52% cost reduction.

Why the reduction from 12 hours to 4 hours? Before reengineering, one person worked in the hole while three others stood around watching and waiting to do their part of the work. The multiskilled laborer/mason/plumber/electrician works continuously, without any slack time, and does three times as much work for 45% more pay.

Health Care Delivery.   A fundamental rule in health care reengineering is to take people to the highest level of their licensure. This means, for example, that nurses in most states are trained and legally licensed to perform minor surgery and pre-scribe drugs—in fact, they can provide *80%* of the health care services physicians generally provide. Licensed practical nurses (LPNs) or registered health care tech-nicians (RHCTs) can do 80% of what nurses do. (Nurses spend 50% of their time doing paperwork, which can be done by clerks, or automated out of existence.)

Taking health care professionals to the highest level of their licensure results in a dramatically restructured health care system, for example, a staffing ratio of one phy-sician to five nurses to 25 RHCTs. Even if better paid, nurses' and RHCTs' services cost far less than physicians' services. Reengineering saves health care costs by mak-ing the highest use of lower-paid but equally competent employees.

As will be discussed in Chapter 7, this restructuring in health care requires dramatic changes in the roles of service providers and in inpatient customer expectations. Physicians, traditionally the "doers" of health care, increasingly will become trainers, coaches, consultants, and managers of front-line-care delivery; ultimately they will perform only the most advanced diagnostic and intervention procedures (e.g., bipass surgery). Customers will have to change the expectation that they will automatically see a "real doctor" and learn to accept, even prefer, receiving most care from a competent but much less expensive nurse or RHCT. (A patient will expect to see an M.D. only if at death's door.)

More radically, health care is becoming increasingly DIY. Self-administered insulin injections for diabetes have been standard for 50 years; home self-administered kidney dialysis for 20; DIY pregnancy and cholesterol tests are available at any drugstore. "Tele-medicine," remote diagnosis by teleconferenc-ing, and even tele-surgery, in which a surgeon controls a robot scalpel to operate on a patient 3,000 miles away, are already common in major medical centers. When most home computers include teleconferencing and DIY tests are avail-able for most common health problems, diagnosis and prescription can be done wherever a patient customer is.

Mellon Bank's HR4YOU Help Desk.   Mellon's "help desk" HR generalists, with expert system support, combine the benefits of "multiskilling" and "func-tioning at highest level of licensure" to provide twice as much service at half Mellon's previous costs. Before the HR4YOU help desk, HR specialists costing $28.00 an hour, received 20,000 calls from Mellon employees. Calls averaged two minutes and cost $2.00. Nine thousand (45%) of these calls were callbacks because the specialist didn't have the information the employee needed and had to look it up or refer the employee to someone else.

HR4YOU help desk generalists, costing $13.50 an hour, reduced calls to 11,000 by achieving 85% customer satisfaction at first point of contact. Calls averaged 90 seconds and cost $1.00. Mellon saved 73% by reducing calls by 45%, using skilled generalists who cost half what specialists cost—and achieved a higher level of customer service. Key to Mellon's success is its skilled help desk representatives and an expert system database that (1) pops up a profile of the employee requesting help, including a log of all previous contacts with the help desk recording the employee's problem, information sought, and the help desk's response; and (2) a help screen listing answers to the ten most frequently asked questions, then the next ten, and so on, with "drill down" ability to get more detailed information if needed. The help desk continually monitors customer requests to establish their Pareto distribution, the ten questions that account for 80% of employee calls, to "tune" its expert system.[5]

Cross-Disciplinary Development Teams. Many professional work flows—for example, development of training programs and computer software—involve specialist teams handing off from silo to silo across functional walls, as shown in Figure 4.1.

A training or systems analyst starts by knowing absolutely nothing about user requirements, calibrating patriot missile radar, or what an end-user wants to see on his or her PC screen. Over time, the analysts figure this out (i.e., their productivity rises from 0% to 100%) but at the cost of the learning curve time lost (shown as shaded areas in Figure 4.1).

At the end of the analysis process, the analyst/experts develop lengthy memoranda or specifications that they then "throw over the wall" to the training or systems design professionals, who start by knowing absolutely nothing about the task. After much time spent explaining findings and arguing about data, the designers prepare extensive design instructions that they throw over the wall to developers or programmers.

Again, the new team spends much time trying to understand the designers' instructions. Curriculum developers produce lengthy and detailed training manuals, which they throw over the wall to the trainers. Few trainers are willing to

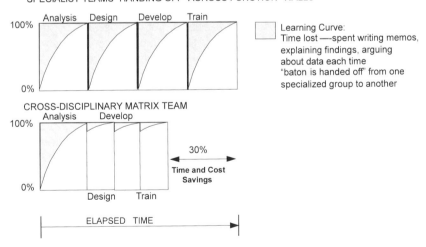

Figure 4.1 Time and Cost Savings with Cross-Disciplinary, Cross-Organizational Teams in Which Tasks Are Combined and Performed by the Fewest Possible Number of Team Members

teach by rote what somebody else has written, so the trainers often redesign and rewrite the course to reflect their own styles.[6]

The solution to the specialists' handoff problem is a cross-disciplinary matrix team that stays with the project from beginning to end. For example, a training analyst, designer, developer, and trainer all go to a military base and immerse themselves 16 hours a day in the details of calibrating a missile radar. Systems analysts, designers, and developers work together with end-users in JAD/RAD (joint application development/rapid application development). End-users are included on the team so that they can provide continual usability testing feedback on what they want in the end product.

The benefits of using cross-disciplinary teams range from 30% time and cost reductions in the development of military training programs to 1,000% increases in productivity by JAD/RAD teams.

- Computers can help cluster tasks for individual workers or teams to handle more efficiently. Example: A utility developed a computer-aided radio dispatch system (CARDS) to cluster service requests (e.g., electricity out, no heat as these come in to the utilities customer service desk). The computer assembles polygons of five service requests using an algorithm that minimizes the geographical area within the polygon. Before reengineering, every time a request came in, a truck would go out. After reengineering, a truck— with all necessary parts, work orders, and instructions—was dispatched only when it had a critical mass of five service requests in an area. Cost per service call declined 50%—and response time to service requests improved. The computer system so speeded up the "setup time" needed to gather parts and work orders that average time to complete all five repairs decreased.

HR example: Computer monitoring of requests from management or employee customers for vended products and services (e.g., training materials or programs, new types of benefits, staffing requisitions) can identify opportunities to purchase large lots at volume discounts, start a recruiting campaign to serve customers worldwide, distinguish a "critical mass" of employees needing training—and address these needs more efficiently by dealing with them together rather than separately.

No Paper: Never Create, Touch, Move, or Store a Piece of Paper

Hammer & Champy[7] cautions against just "paving the cow paths" (i.e., computerizing existing inefficient pieces of paper or work flows), not least because onscreen automation by itself saves only 10% of time and costs. It is foolish to pave a cow path by automating an unnecessary paper-based system that should simply be eliminated.

I have found, however, that asking people to have a paperless mindset (i.e., "Do whatever you do without creating, touching, moving, or storing a piece of paper anywhere in the process") helps them think outside the box and see different ways to reengineer work flows:

These are some examples of paperless HR transactions:

- Direct-deposit payrolls
- On-line information status changes
- On-line benefits enrollment and changes. Mellon Bank found that 85% of employee benefit enrollments and changes could be handled by interactive voice response (IVR). IVR-prompted responses reduced errors from 12% to 2.5%. (The remaining 15% of employees didn't understand the IVR instructions, had to confirm a change in writing and/or needed to talk to the HR4YOU help desk.)[8]
- Voice-response surveys. HR can get any information it needs from employees by using automated voice-response survey systems. A PC calls a random sample of employees and asks them to respond to questions by pressing numbers on their touch-tone phone (e.g., "What do you think about the change in our benefits program? Press 1 for very dissatisfied, 2 for somewhat dissatisfied, 5 for very satisfied." At the end, an employee can add any comments by speaking to a voice mail tape recorder. Firms can very inexpensively query several hundred employees and have data to make policy decisions all in a day's time.
- All HR policy manuals, labor law advisories, benefits information, and so forth are on-line using a document database (e.g., Lotus Notes). (A firm I have worked for estimated it saved 8.5 *miles* of paper simply by putting all company policy manuals and routine reports to managers on a document database. Each morning when an employee starts his or her computer, an electronic newsletter summarizing any changes or additions appears as the first item on the e-mail screen. An employee can download any information from the corporate database—and even print it out on paper. (Employees realize a printout is unnecessary as soon as they are confident the data is on the database whenever they need it.)

No Travel: Substitute Communication for Transportation and Commuting

Core concepts include:

- *Sending electrons, not paper or people.* Obvious examples are telephones, voice mail, and voice-response systems. As voice-recognition technology improves, most queries for information can be made by phone. Responses can be recorded, obtained by touch-tone codes if numeric or relatively simple, or converted directly to text data by voice-recognition software.
- *Teleconferenced recruitment and selection interviews.* Innovative college placement offices and search firms are experimenting with recruitment

interviews by picture phone. Company recruiters can conduct interviews with job candidates without either of them having to travel.

- *Distance learning.* Training can be delivered on CD-ROM disks sent to remote locations, or via computer-assisted instruction on-line over telephone or fiber optic cable line to an employee's PC. The coming Information Superhighway will enable consumers to view any of tens of thousands of movies available in film companies' central archives. Similarly, computer-assisted training programs will be available from central firm or vendor server libraries (CD-ROM optical jukeboxes) to any employee, anywhere in the world.

- *Performance support systems.* "Living" help screens will train learners at their workstations (e.g., as illustrated by the Chapter 1 example of the manager who received coaching advice on how to handle a confrontation with an employee about a drug and alcohol program).

No Office

Employees work from home, from their cars or trucks, from airplanes, from client sites, from motels, virtually anywhere in the world via computer modem, wireless e-mail, and very soon, video conferencing. As noted in Chapter 2, PC teleconferencing packages (a plug-in video card and top-of-monitor video camera) costing around $1,000 are now available to connect anyone anywhere, using ordinary telephone wires.

- *Telecommuting.* An estimated one million Americans telecommute from home or remote locations, a number expected to reach 10 million as telecommunications improve and clean air environmental laws limit commuting by car. According to 13 studies summarized by Kugelmass,[9] telecommuting increased productivity 10% to 300%, an average of 25% to 30%, in a variety of business and government organizations. Telecommuting also has many HR benefits: 25% lower absenteeism, lower turnover, higher morale and job satisfaction, lower stress, improved employee safety (fewer accidents getting to and at work), and faster disaster recovery.

- *Hoteling.* Many firms are substituting "hoteling"—temporary offices reserved like hotel rooms—for permanent offices. An employee who needs to visit a central office calls the concierge to reserve a temporary office. If the employee does not have a computer, a PC loaded with the preferred software is set up in the office. Mobile file cabinets containing the employee's paper files are also wheeled into this office. Hoteling is particularly cost effective for consultants and legal and sales firms whose employees are frequently on the road.

Staff agreeing to telecommute and hotel might receive:

1. A *notebook computer* and *printer,* ideally with teleconferencing capability, and a dedicated phone line or credit for use of one's personal home phone.

2. *Software,* the standard word processing, spreadsheet, presentation, e-mail, document database, and connectivity used throughout the organization. Standardization of software is critical to ensure compatibility and efficient employee-to-employee communication.

3. A *fax modem* permitting remote access to the central office network using Lotus Notes or other remote mail access software. An employee working at a distance can be "virtually" present on the network as if in an office down the hall.

Benefits to telecommuters include reduction in commuting time, cost, and hassles, and greater freedom to set their own work schedules.

Logical candidates for telecommuting include:

- Professionals who are out of the office a lot.

- Staff whose work doesn't require their physical presence (e.g., programmers, desktop publishers, telephone salespeople who may be able to work at home with a virtual connection to one another and to central office clients through a dedicated phone line or the network).

- Staff whose work doesn't require access to equipment, inventory, or files not yet in digital form, and is accessible on the network from the server database.

- Staff whose work is easily measured by outcomes or results against objectives, for example data entered, sales, customer service calls made, claims processed, programming or writing tasks completed on time.

- Staff who know their jobs well, and have performed well with minimum supervision, are known to be able to solve problems without depending on managers or colleagues (although these may be only a phone call or e-mail away). Other traits used to select telecommuters are independence, self-motivation, self-discipline, low need for social interaction, and a preference for working alone uninterrupted—although at least one study has failed to confirm these factors.[10]

- Staff with lifestyle reasons to work at home (e.g., arduous commutes, dependent care issues).

Telecommuting probably does not make sense for:

- Staff who need physical access to colleagues, equipment, inventory, or files available only at the central office.
- Staff who need supervision, social contact, or the discipline of "having a place to go to" to get into a work mindset.
- Managers whose physical presence is necessary for supervisory or morale reasons.

A space and overhead alternative to hoteling is "hot bunking"—sharing a temporary office with one or several other people. Hot bunking is a Navy term used to describe the sleeping arrangements on submarines, which have one-third as many bunks as crew. Crew work rotating shifts: eight hours on, eight hours off, and eight hours sleeping in a bunk. The bunk is always hot when one gets into it because someone just left it. There is no bunk downtime: Physical assets are at a premium on submarines and cannot be left idle.

Office hot bunkers get their own space when in the central office. If hot bunkmates are in the central office at the same time, they use a conference room or other hoteled office. Each hot bunked office has a dedicated central office phone extension, a color monitor to which employees can connect their notebook computers, and sometimes a dedicated bookshelf, file cabinet, and locker. This arrangement requires only that office mates leave a clean work space for colleagues.

Cost savings in reduced rent and overhead from hoteling and hot bunking can be significant. The Boston office of Ernst and Young saves 12,000 square feet— $300,000 in annual rent—and plans to shed an additional 50,000 square feet to save an additional $1,250,000.[11]

Electronic filing offers additional cost savings. A four-drawer file and the space needed to open it occupy about nine square feet, which at $25 per square foot costs $225 a year in rent. Off-premise warehouse storage is available at $8 to $12 a square foot, or for much less on a hard drive or central server database.

No Controls

Eliminate Controls That Don't Control Anything or That Cost More Than the Thing Controlled

For 20 years I have signed stacks of employee time sheets and travel and expense statements each week. I have never disallowed one; in fact, I have never even *looked* at any of them. I sign them on automatic pilot concurrently while doing other value-added work. My step in this work flow is patently absurd. All of these forms are checked and signed off by two different accounting functions. The one transgression I know of (one of 104,000 time sheets and T&E forms: 2

× 50 employees × 52 weeks a year × 20 years) was caught by accounting when I was out of town. Every firm I have ever studied is full of control steps that don't control anything. Control only when control is cost–benefit justified. Never spend more to control something than the thing itself is worth.

A famous study[12] at Intel, a well-managed high-tech firm, found an engineer had to endure a 95-step work flow with 12 required paper approval forms to order a mechanical pencil. The pencil cost $2.79; the requisition/control work flow cost $43. Intel Corp. went to a stockless inventory system: It was much easier and cheaper to let engineers go get a pencil when they needed one (or even steal pencils by the handful) than to waste their own and other employees' time trying to control pencil-getting. Every company has countless examples of processes costing $20 to $40 to check and control $15 cab fares on employee T&Es, pennies-a-day copier and postage charges, and so on.

Build Error Trapping and Exception Control into the Information System

Computers can trap, prevent, or correct many errors (e.g., refuse to accept invalid employee codes, do arithmetic correctly, or flag and fix spelling and grammatical errors). Expert systems can help tellers decide which loans to approve. Computers can beep when employees try to enter out-of-range T&E charges ($125 meals).

State tax-collection agencies are considering selling or giving away tax preparation software (e.g., tax returns on disk or downloadable to your PC from the IRS's central database). On-screen tax preparation software could ensure that arithmetic is correct. The IRS could also build in exception controls. If, for example, you enter medical deductions, charitable donations of art, or any other figure outside the IRS's guidelines, your computer screen could turn red, beep, display the message, or warn with voice synthesis: "Check this. Submission of this figure will almost certainly result in an audit."

HR example: Computers can trap or control by exception any data entered into an HRIS: hirings, promotions, firings counter to EO/AA guidelines, salary increases that exceed budget.

Delegate Quality Control and Approval Decisions to the Person Who Performs the Task

Japanese managers criticized the American (pre-TQM) practice of one group doing the work, then another group of quality control inspectors checking the first group's work—not least because it doubles the work force (*halving* productivity). The "radical" Japanese TQM practice is that the employee who does the work is also responsible for quality control at the time the work is done (i.e., the doer and checker tasks are combined).

In reengineered systems, quality control and approval decisions are delegated to the front-line workers who come in direct contact with the customer. Bank tellers can approve loans; retail clerks can resolve customer complaints on the spot; employees and managers can enter their own HR data and confirm (approve) changes by signing with their electronic passwords.

A radical corollary to the delegation concept is the "let the fox guard the henhouse" principle. Examples include towns allowing (trained) utility workers to write their own building permits and insurance companies allowing (approved) auto body shops to handle claims adjustment.

Claims adjusters are insurance company controllers who estimate the damage and how much the insurance company will reimburse you to have it fixed. The fox-guarding-the-henhouse approach is one where an insurance company provides a list of approved auto shops. The insurance company controls by sample and exception; it checks periodically to see if the auto body repair shops are cheating or to flag expenses ($2,000 for a bent bumper?!) that exceed guidelines.

The American medical system essentially operates the same way, with specified payments approved for diagnostic review group treatments. For example, the no-questions-asked payment for a gallbladder operation might be $3,500. If the hospital can do the operation for less, it keeps the difference as profit; if its costs exceed the specified payment amount, it has to eat the difference. Hospitals that cheat are decertified by the government or insurance company paying the bills.

Control by Sample

Check only three out of a hundred forms rather than every single one. The IRS, for example, samples between 1% and 3% of taxpayers' returns to check for accuracy and keep taxpayers honest.

Control as a Byproduct of Some Other Task

In most states, citizens waste millions of hours each year standing in line to register motor vehicles in drafty 1930s-era registry offices. An obvious reengineering solution is to let citizens register their cars by touch-tone phone. Critics always respond, "But this would result in loss of control. People could register stolen vehicles." The fact is people can and do register stolen vehicles *anyway*, after standing in line for an hour. Meaningful control in this case could be provided by the police force as a byproduct of its regular duties when chasing speeders, drunks, and crooks. The real control point for the Registry of Motor Vehicles is, when you are stopped, whether you can show the police officer a piece of paper that says you own the vehicle you are sitting in.

No Wait

Parallel Versus Sequential Processing

Do as many tasks as possible concurrently to save overall cycle and customer waiting time. In product development efforts, this is called concurrent engineering. Kodak, Hallmark, and the Big 3 automakers have cut camera, greeting card, and automobile concept-to-market time by as much as 50% by creating cross-disciplinary teams of R&D, artists, inventors, manufacturing and usability engineers, marketers, and customer end-users.[13]

Parallel Processing Customer Orders

Gas furnace installation by a major East Coast utility offers a striking example of *before* versus *after* order-to-delivery cycle time with parallel processing. Before reengineering, it took nine months from the time a customer called in an order for a gas furnace to the time it was installed. The business impact of this slow customer-service cycle time became apparent to the utility during the Gulf War of 1991. Just before the war, Iraq was expected to invade Saudi Arabia, seize much of the world's oil-producing capacity, and send oil prices from $20 to anywhere from $80 to $160 a barrel. This situation was a marketing windfall for the gas utility (which is always trying to convince oil customers to switch to gas). Twenty-thousand customers called the gas utility asking to replace their oil furnaces with gas furnaces. Unfortunately, with a nine-month order-to-delivery time, long before the utility could install even one furnace, the Gulf War was over, oil prices had dropped back to $18 a barrel, and almost all orders for new gas furnaces had been canceled.

Figure 4.2 shows the sequential steps in the gas furnace order-to-delivery process.

1. A customer telephones an order for a furnace.

2. A technician comes to the customer's home, examines the customer's basement, plumbing, and so forth, and designs a furnace installation.

3. Engineers "load model" the installation—that is, see how much gas pressure in the area drops if additional demand is made on the system.

4. If installation proves feasible, the customer is invited to apply for a $2,000 loan to pay for the new furnace.

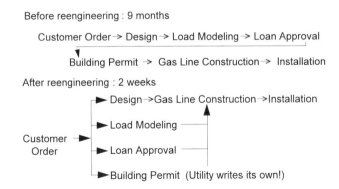

Figure 4.2 Parallel Versus Sequential Processing of a Customer Order

5. Once the loan is approved, the utility applies for a town building permit to dig a trench for new gasline service and the furnace installation.

6. Once the building permit is obtained, the utility backhoe arrives to dig the ditch for the gas pipe and install the piping.

7. After the pipe is in place, another installation team arrives to install the furnace.

After reengineering, this process was cut to two to three weeks. Now when a customer calls to order a furnace, the steps for design, load modeling, loan approval, and building permit are completed simultaneously. Designers design on clipboard computers and modem the data directly to the load modeling computer. The designer also helps customers complete and modem a loan approval form to the bank that holds their mortgage (most loans are automatic and pre-approved based on homeowner equity). Most ingeniously the utility persuaded towns to "deputize" their installers to write their own building permits (an example of the fox-guarding-the-henhouse control concept discussed earlier).

HR example: Parallel processing in hiring. Hiring requests, writing of job descriptions, compensation analysis and approvals, job vacancy announcements, review of resumes, reference checking, medical form completion, and competence assessment can be done concurrently by managers using shared databases to coordinate data gathering, analysis, and decision making with HR professionals. Lotus Development Corporation, using its own Notes™ software, cut requisition-to-hire time from 59 to 7 days, an 88% cycle time reduction (and estimated 50% cost reduction).

ENDNOTES

1. Meridian Bancorp. (1993, September). *TESS: The Employee Self-Service System.* Reading, PA: Meridian Bancorp Inc.

2. Ho, R. Mellon Bank: A Case Study. Paper presented at the Saratoga Institute Human Resources Effectiveness Conference, Scottsdale, AZ (May 23, 1994).

3. Meridian Bancorp, Ibid.

4. Handy, C. (1994). *The Empty Raincoat.* London, UK: Business Books.

5. Ho, Ibid.

6. Spencer, L. (1986). *Calculating Human Resource Cost and Benefits.* New York: John Wiley & Sons.

7. Hammer, M., and J. Champy. (1994). Reengineering the Corporation. New York: HarperCollins.

8. Ho, Ibid.

9. Kugelmass, J. (1995). *Telecommuting.* New York: Lexington Press/Free Press.

10. Sharp, B. J. (1988). "Telecommuter Personality Characteristics: A Comparison of Workers in the Home and Office." Unpublished Doctoral Dissertation. Los Angeles: California School of Professional Psychology.

11. Ackerman, J. (1993, May 22). The Incredible Shrinking Office. *The Boston Globe.*

12. Main, J. (1981, June 29). How to Battle Your Own Bureaucracy: Intel Has a Way to Measure Office-Worker Productivity—and Raise it 30%, *Fortune.*

13. Hammer and Champy, Ibid.

5

Reengineering Human Resources: Functions and Processes

WHAT'S TO BE REENGINEERED?

The very suggestion that HR *functions* need reengineering is anathema to any right-thinking reengineer. As discussed in Chapter 3, HR activities should be thought of as cross-functional *processes*, not functions. Most HR departments and professionals are, however, still organized in functional disciplines, so an examination of the existing content knowledge, functional cow paths is instructive. What exactly is HR?

The Society for Human Resource Management (SHRM) provides a comprehensive, 50-page map in its Certification Study Guide. SHRM's Human Resources Certification Institute (HRCI) is a nonprofit organization that "identifies and codifies the Human Resources body of knowledge" to develop examinations for certification as a Professional in Human Resources (PHR) and Senior Professional in Human Resources (SPHR).

Tables 5.1 through 5.6 summarize HRCI's HR body of knowledge, indicating (in columns 2 and 3 to a tenth of a percentage point) what a PHR and a SPHR should know or be able to do in each content area shown in column 1. The HRCT map of HR functions and processes, and options for reengineering, will be examined from two perspectives: methods (e.g., data retrieval or expert systems) and functions and processes (e.g., staffing or compensation and benefits).

Table 5.1 SHRM Findings Data for Management Practices

Function	HRP	SHRP	Data Retrieval				Decision Support		Training	Data Entry
			Text info %	doc db = e-mail (help screen navigation)	Data %	Database EIS	Spreadsheet Templates	Expert System Advice		
I. Management Practices	15.0%	35.0%							On-line	
A. Role of HR in Org.	1.4%	3.2%	100%	theory, policy procedures—by industry, organization form				x		
B. HR Planning	1.9%	5.2%	50%	policy, methods	50.0%	labor market forecasts, demographics	x	x		
C. Org. Design & Development	1.8%	4.6%	100%	theory, methods	0.0%	survey data on line	"what if" analyses	choice of org designs		
D. Budgeting, Controlling, Measurement	1.8%	4.1%	50%	policies, procedures, rules	50.0%	HR measures, audit, costs, budget	cost vs. budget variance analyses, budget templates	x		
E. Motivation	0.9%	2.1%	100%	theories		employee motivation (competency) scores		Motivation Advisor: If situation, person... then (prescription)		
F. Leadership	0.9%	2.1%	75%	theories	25.0%	employee leadership competency data		Leadership Advisor: If situation, people... then (prescription)	x	

G. Quality & Performance Measurement	1.6%	3.6%	60%	theory model forms	40.0%	employee performance results and competency data		analyzing performance problems—prescriptions	on-line: how to conduct	appraisal forms on-line
H. Employee Involvement Strategies	1.3%	2.3%	100%		0.0%	employee survey data; suggestion data (amount submitted, accepted)		when to use participative styles	on-line	survey data sugges-tions
I. HR Research	1.4%	2.8%	100%		0.0%		statistics	when to use which experimental designs, data gathering methods, statistical tests	on-line	data collection
J. International HR Manage-ment	1.0%	2.3%	90%		10.0%	compensation, benefits, cost of living data		selection	culture, language, adjustment	
K. Ethics	1.0%	2.7%	100%	policy, codes of ethics, procedures	0.0%			If X situation = ethical solution	on-line	

Legend: doc db = document database on-line, e.g., using Lotus Notes

EIS = Executive Information System

Table 5.2 SHRM Findings Data for Recruitment and Placement

Function	HRP	SHRP	Data Retrieval				Decision Support		Training	Data Entry
			Text info %	doc db = e-mail (help screen navigation)	Data %	Database EIS	Spreadsheet Templates	Expert System Advice		
II. Selection and Placement	20.0%	15.0%							On-line	
A. Legal & Regulatory	4.4%	3.2%	100%	laws						
B. Equal Opportunity/ Affirmative Action	4.0%	3.1%	75%	laws, model plans	25.0%	workforce, avail-ability data reporting: performance against plans		legal advice, plan advice	on-line	record keeping
C. Recruitment	4.0%	2.7%	75%	theory, policy	25.0%	internal & external sourcing via electronic job posting efficiency/ effectiveness measures time cost per hire	evaluation	selection criteria: job competency requirements analysis choice of sources media		applications: on-line resumes: electronic submission, scanning
D. Selection	4.1%	2.6%	20%	theory, policy	80.0%	candidate data efficiency/ effectiveness measures: validity statistics: performance turnover percentage	reliability, validity statistic calculations	choice of assessment methods, auto generation of interview guides; job/ person match fit scores	conducting interviews	on-line pre-employment testing, reference and background checking, medical exams
E. Career Planning & Development	3.5%	3.4%	75%	theory, procedures	25.0%	mobility data: promotions, demotions, transfers, relocations		auto counseling auto generated development plans	on-line	interest, self-assessment inventories, tests, mobility data

Table 5.3 SHRM Findings Data for Training and Development

Function	HRP	SHRP	Data Retrieval				Decision Support		Training	Data Entry
			Text info %	doc db = e-mail (help screen navigation)	Data %	Database EIS	Spreadsheet Templates	Expert System Advice		
III. Training and Development	20.0%	15.0%							On-line	
A. Legal & Regulatory	3.4%	1.8%	100%	legal policy						
B. HR Training and the Org	3.2%	3.2%	75%	theory policy	25.0%		cost-benefit analysis			
C. Training Needs Assessment	4.5%	3.3%	50%	process methods	50.0%	training needs by division, level, competency		choice of process, methods, prioritization of needs	perceived needs competencies	
D. Training and Development	4.8%	3.6%	75%	theory: design methods, etc. programs: course catalog on line: times schedules prerequisites vendor lists ratings costs	25.0%	materials inventories	cost-benefit analysis calculations re: alternative methods	choice of methods choice of programs for maximum value added trainer selection	on-line	data: enrollment, completion rates, change in employee competencies and business results
E. Evaluation of Effectiveness	4.1%	3.1%	100%	methods	0.0%	enrollments % completions change in employee competence—and business results—by division, level, etc.	cost-benefit calculations	choice of evaluation metrics, methods	on-line: how to	data: enrollment completion rates, change in employee competencies and business results

Table 5.4 SHRM Findings Data for Compensation and Benefits

Function	HRP	SHRP	Data Retrieval				Decision Support		Training	Data Entry
			Text Info%	doc db = e-mail (help screen navigation)	Data %	Database EIS	Spreadsheet Templates	Expert System Advice	On-line	
IV. Compensation and Benefits	20.0%	15.0%							On-line	
A. Legal & Regulatory	2.6%	1.5%	100%	legal	0.0%					
B. Tax and Accounting	1.0%	1.0%	100%	regulations	0.0%					
C. Economic Factors	1.0%	0.9%	100%	theory	0.0%	inflation, interest rates, competitive trends	what if, trend analyses			
D. Strategy & Policy	1.1%	1.5%	100%	theory, current policy	0.0%			choice of policies given org. strategy		
E. Programs	1.8%	1.2%	100%	theory, current programs	0.0%	pay data by program, level, employee type demographics, etc.	"what if" with different models	choice of models		

									how to develop	standard forms
F. Job Analysis, Description	1.9%	1.0%	100%	theory, methods model descriptions (DOT)	0.0%			auto construction from on-screen questionnaire	how to	
G. Job Evaluation	1.8%	0.9%	100%	theory, methods	0.0%			auto construction from on-screen questionnaire	how to (JET)	
H. Job Pricing, Administration	1.9%	1.1%	80%	theory, methods	20.0%	wage, salary survey data	"what if" senarios	auto construction from on-screen questionnaire		
I. Benefits	2.9%	2.6%	100%	legal programs	0.0%			choice of programs		
J. Benefits Management	1.7%	1.7%	90%	theory	10.0%	coverage, status by employee groups	what if	choice of programs		employee survey data re: benefit preferences, satisfaction
K. Communication	1.0%	0.9%	100%	employee queries about coverage, status	0.0%			choice of communcations programs, methods		employee survey data re: benefit preferences, satisfaction
L. Effectiveness Evaluation	1.2%	1.3%	100%	methods	0.0%	budget, cost management data utilization review	budget templates "what if" senarios	choice of methods		budget, cost data

Table 5.5 SHRM Findings Data for Employee and Labor Relations

Function	HRP	SHRP	Data Retrieval				Decision Support		Training	Data Entry
			Text Info %	doc db = e-mail (help screen navigation)	Data %	Database EIS	Spreadsheet Templates	Expert System Advice	On-line	
V. Employee and Labor Relations	20.0%	15.0%								
A. Legal & Regulatory	3.3%	1.8%	100%	legal	0.0%			auto advice		
B. Unions	1.9%	1.4%	100%	legal	0.0%			auto advice		
C. Employer Unfair Labor Practices	1.7%	1.3%	100%	legal	0.0%			auto advice		
D. Union Unfair Labor Practices	1.7%	1.1%	100%	legal	0.0%			auto advice		
E. Collective Bargaining	1.7%	1.3%	100%	theory, legal, model forms notice filing	0.0%		"what if" scenarios	negotiation strategy		
F. Managing Union Relations	1.7%	1.3%	100%	legal policy, procedures model grievance forms	0.0%	grievance rates by division, supervisor		grievance handling arbitration preparation	handling grievances	grievances arbitration data
G. Public Sector Union Relations	0.8%	0.6%	100%	legal regulations	0.0%			auto advice		

106

H. Employment Practices: discipline, etc.	2.4%	2.0%	100%	legal, policy	0.0%	disciplinary, absence, tardiness, termination, harrassment complaint data		auto advice	how to handle disciplinary confrontations, harrassment investigations, terminations (to avoid legal problems)	disciplinary incident data
I. Individual Employment Rights	1.0%	1.2%	100%	legal, policy				auto advice		
J. Performance Appraisals	2.6%	1.9%	100%	theory, legal, policy, types, methods	0.0%	employee business results against goals competencies, by division, level, location		auto advice: how to conduct	how to conduct	goals, appraisal forms on-line
K. Employee Attitudes	1.2%	1.1%	50%	methods, confidentiality	50.0%	survey data by division, location, supervisor	data analysis templates	IF (morale problem) = THEN (corrective action alternatives) advice		survey data collection on-line: voice response from phones, etc.

Table 5.6 SHRM Findings Data on Health, Safety, and Security

Function	HRP	SHRP	Data Retrieval				Decision Support		Training	Data Entry
			Text Info%	doc db = e-mail (help screen navigation)	Data %	Database EIS	Spreadsheet Templates	Expert System Advice		
VI. Health, Safety, and Security	5.0%	5.0%							On-line	
A. Legal and Regulatory	1.5%	1.5%	100%	legal	0.0%					
B. Health	1.2%	1.2%	100%	policies available programs referal, enrollment, e.g., employee wellness	0.0%	employee health data by division, level, demographics, location, etc. employee use of wellness programs		IF (health problem) = THEN (corrective action alternatives) advice		employee health, utilization of wellness program data
C. Safety	1.3%	1.3%	75%	legal, regulations accident report procedures safety inspection procedures	25%	accident rates accident investigation results inspection completions (mandatory) training completion		IF (safety problem) = THEN (corrective action alternatives) advice	training,job aids on line	accident, inspection, training completion, etc. forms and data entry on line
D. Security	1.0%	1.0%	100%	policy procedures for investigations model plans	0%	break-in, theft, fraud data by division, location, supervisor, etc.		IF (security problem) = THEN (prevention or corrective action alternatives) advice	how to conduct investigations	theft, fraud reports; investigation data

Analysis of SHRM findings suggests that Human Resources is primarily information and content knowledge, including:

- Laws, regulations, and rules
- Policies and procedures
- Theory, design principles, motivation, and leadership concepts
- Methods (e.g., for evaluation of training)
- Other data: labor market forecasts, demographics, HR audit costs, budgets, and the like

A central tenet of this book is that HR management—at least at the PHR level—is being decentralized to line managers and employees. The challenge for reengineering is how to "informate" or enable line managers and employees to function effectively as professional HR generalists themselves.

The data retrieval, decision support, training, and data entry columns in Table 5.1 summarize reengineering *process* ideas for each HR topic and function.

DATA RETRIEVAL

If most of HR practice is text content knowledge, the obvious reengineering step is to put all this text on a document database (e.g., Lotus Notes) and make it available to all managers and employees at kiosks or on their own PC screens. All lists of services, including catalogues of training courses, wellness programs, benefit coverage, and enrollment forms, can be put on this document database.

The simplest form of this document database has key word-search capabilities, so that when an employee interested in training searches the course catalogue on reengineering, the screen will pop up any reengineering training courses offered by the company.

A manager wondering "Can I terminate an eight-month-pregnant woman who has met her performance goals but has been accused of abusive behavior toward her subordinates?" can search on *termination, pregnant, performance,* and *abusive.* The manager can read whatever the database turns up but then make up his/her own mind about what to do.

A slightly higher level of service is to equip the document database with help screen navigation tools—cross-indexing or hypertext "drill down" links that enable a user to double-click on a word and see additional, more detailed information. Help screen navigation tools are familiar to users of Microsoft Windows products—and in fact can be easily developed for any text using Microsoft Help, the same software Windows developers use.

A still higher level of service is to provide model or template forms and plans (e.g., job descriptions, job application blanks, performance appraisal forms,

National Labor Relations Board filings) that managers and employees can use or edit to meet their unique needs.

Similarly all HR data that line managers and employees need for planning can be available on the server database, with appropriate security restrictions (e.g., so managers can see only their subordinates' but not their peers' or their bosses' performance appraisals). HR data on-line can include:

- Basic employee information: names, addresses, dependents, educational levels, work experience, technical skills, and competencies
- Economic, demographic census, and labor forecast data
- Survey information (e.g., wage and salary data by job category, benefit utilization rates)
- Suggestions: numbers submitted, accepted, cost saving, or revenue enhancements
- Training needs assessment: employee competencies and course completion rates by demographic characteristics, level, location, or function
- Indicators of the health of the organization's Human Resources: job offer acceptance rates, grievance rates, turnover rates, employee satisfaction, culture, and morale data

The lowest level of service is simply to have a database that users can navigate to identify the information they need. Databases' front ends increasingly are user-friendly, allowing users to simply click on search criteria but leaving the burden of finding and analyzing the information on the user.

A higher level of service is an Executive Information System, or EIS, a pre-programmed report generator that gathers, summarizes, and analyzes data from many databases to answer specific questions executives have (e.g., What are customer service satisfaction levels in Eastern Europe? How do these correlate with employee Customer Service Orientation competencies? Completion of core customer service training by country? Office?).

DECISION SUPPORT

Beyond simple retrieval of text and data information are spreadsheet analysis templates and expert systems that help managers and employees make HR decisions.

Spreadsheet templates for decision analysis developed by the HR staff can include:

- Work force planning and budgeting templates, with last year's data, which can be completed simply by filling cells with current data
- Templates for analyzing
  a. Alternative compensation plans

b. Cost versus budget variance analyses

c. Statistical tests of reliability and validity

d. Cost–benefit analyses for evaluating alternative methods of delivering services (e.g., stand-up versus computer-assisted delivery of training)

e. Trend analyses permitting tests of "what-if" scenarios using different model assumptions or data

Expert Systems

Much more powerful than simple provision of text information are expert systems that actually provide advice on how to handle difficult situations. A newly appointed 21-year-old supervisor is unlikely to have heard of or want to read the Norris LaGuardia Federal Anti-Injunction Act of 1932, or the Pregnancy Discrimination Employment Act of 1978. The supervisior wants to know whether he or she can fire a high-performing but abusive eight-month-pregnant employee, and is best guided through making this decision and completing all the necessary HR procedures by answering a series of questions on-screen:

Click on possible reasons for termination:

POOR PERFORMANCE

■ Has the employee met her performance goals?

If No: (additional questions on documenting performance shortfalls)

If Yes: (next question)

ABUSIVE BEHAVIOR

■ Has alleged abusive behavior been documented according to the following procedures?

If No: (sample documentation form appears on-screen, with text, voice, or talking head instructions on how to fill it out)

If Yes: Has she been given a formal warning about her behavior?

If No: (formal warning form appears on-screen)

If Yes: (next question), etc.

When all questions have been answered and forms completed, the computer can then advise:

1. No, you cannot terminate this person without violating company policy or labor law.

2. You may be able to terminate this person if you use the following procedures and document cause: contact your Senior Human Resources Professional labor lawyer or outside counsel for advice.

3. A recommended way of handling this situation is as follows:

- Let the employee go on maternity leave as provided for in the Family Leave Act of 1993.

- When she returns to work, confront her about her problem, give her a formal warning (form appears on-screen), set very specific behavioral goals for her, monitor and give her weekly feedback on her performance.

- Document any problem behaviors as they occur (form appears on-screen).

- Coach her in how to better deal with problem situations.

- Suggest she complete the following development activities:

  Tutorial on managing problem employees available on-line on her workstation.

  Training Courses (assertiveness training, conflict resolution, and stress management).

Management Advisor HR expert systems exist for:

Analyzing performance problems

Conducting performance appraisals, disciplinary sessions, and coaching sessions

Choosing leadership and managerial styles

Dealing with motivation and morale problems

Dealing with ethical and legal issues (e.g., InCompliance™, a labor and EO/AA expert system produced by Decisis™ Corp).

Selection advisor expert systems show which candidates are the best match and have the highest probability of success in a given job. Legal expert systems provide advice on developing equal affirmative action opportunity plans. Other HR expert systems:

Develop competency models from questions about job elements.

Suggest assessment methods for different competencies.

Generate development and career path plans.

Provide automated career counseling.

Suggest evaluation metrics and methods, experimental designs, and statistical tests of reliability and validity for various HR programs.

Advise on choice of compensation policies and models given organizational strategy and critical success factors.

Generate job descriptions, job evaluation points, and recommend compensation for specific jobs pricing

Help employees choose an optimum combination of benefits from "cafeteria plan" alternatives.

Help managers choose communications programs and methods.

Provide advice on negotiation strategy, grievance handling, and arbitration preparation.

Guide managers through the steps of developing health, safety, environmental, and security plans—and solving problems in any of these areas if they occur.

TRAINING

Reengineered levels of service in training include:

- On-line text information about available training and tuition reimbursement programs
- On-line registration for training courses
- Training administration systems for tracking enrollment, attendance, completion, test scores, certification of competence, travel and expense costs, availability of training rooms, equipment and materials
- Expert systems advice (e.g., autogeneration of development plans based on competency deficiencies: "IF your job requires Achievement Motivation Level 6 and you are at Level 4, THEN: Read these books, take these courses, work for these mentors, do these developmental assignments, etc.")
- Actual provision of training on-line at the employee's workstation, using management, leadership, motivation, grievance handling, or other expert system advisors; or by working through on-line computer-assisted instruction or interactive video tutorials downloaded from a central database

Employees can work through training programs at their own pace and have their proficiency tested on-line and reported back to a central database.

DATA ENTRY

For up-to-date text or data to be easily retrievable from on-line databases, it must be continually and efficiently entered on-line. As has been suggested throughout this book, virtually all personnel transactions should occur on-line, by phone or on-screen, by PCs or kiosks and be put directly into 's where data can be made accessible to any manager or employee formation. Examples include on-line:

- ʝʋʋ analysis and description forms, including expert system "job analyst" help in identifying skills and competencies employees need to do the job well.
- Resume submission via scanning or modem transmission to employment bulletin boards.
- Job applications.
- Pre-employment or in-service testing (e.g., typing, reading, numeracy, content knowledge, or more advanced skill testing via simulation). Pilots have long been tested in flight simulators before risking their lives, passenger lives, or a multimillion dollar plane. Apprentice welders can be tested using simulated on-screen welding exercises in which the student has to demonstrate eye–hand coordination, maintenance of flame color, management of molten pool of metal, and so forth, with a mouse instead of a torch.
- Reference and background checking.
- Medical examination data (protected by appropriate security clearances).
- Employee interest, self-assessment inventory, and perceived training-needs data.
- Performance appraisals.
- "360 degree" (boss, peers, subordinates, customers) assessments of employee competencies.
- Suggestions.
- Equal opportunity affirmative action demographic record keeping.
- Training course enrollment, completion rates, and change in employee competencies and business results following training.
- Employee benefits survey data regarding benefits preferences and satisfaction with benefits.
- Personnel service budget and cost data.
- Disciplinary incident reports and grievance filing.
- Employee survey data collection: satisfaction, morale, perception of organizational climate and culture (e.g., via voice response from phones or on PC screens).
- Accident safety inspection reports and forms.
- Theft and fraud investigations and reports.

Studies by Electronic Data Systems' Business Process Systems and Services (BPSS), IBM's Work Force Solutions (WFS) and the author's value analyses indicate most firms offer between 50 and 70 HR products and services, organized in 6 to 15 functions or processes. These services may have several hundred sub-services (e.g., training programs offered by a firm's Training and Development function). Table 5.7 shows a typical organization of HR functions/processes/services by the strategy, delivery, and categories discussed in Chapter 1.

Most HR services in practice are *processes* which cross functional silos. For example, a manager seeking to hire a new employee is likely to need a position requisition for Job and Organization Design, a job evaluation, salary guidelines and benefits information from Compensation and Benefits; help from Staffing in recruiting, assessing, and selecting candidates; a Performance Plan from Performance Management Systems; arrangements for orientation and new hire training from Training and Development. Indeed Staffing/Destaffing is better designed as a *process*, conducted by managers themselves with help from their PC HR expert system, by the HR Help Desk, and as a last resort by a cross-functional "Staffing Team" composed of Job Design, Staffing, Performance Management, Training and Development, and Compensation and Benefits specialists.

The categories of service shown in Table 5.7 provide an alternative way of summarizing reengineering ideas.

Organization and Job Design

Conduct market research on-line. Many government and research firm work force forecasts are available via the Internet or by subscription to on-line services like Compuserve. Managers' projected work force requirements can be queried by e-mail using spreadsheet templates, or saved to the HR server.

Designs should be done on PCs and organizational charts continually updated and made available to all managers and employees at kiosks or their workstations

Job descriptions and description templates for all jobs in the firm should be available on-line, so managers can access and edit existing job descriptions to create new positions. Knowledge Point Software's "Descriptions Write Now!" software includes job description templates for 6000 jobs.

Staffing/Destaffing

All new hire requisitions and requisition approvals should be done on-line. Use "Job Evaluation/Hiring Advisor" expert systems that ask questions to evaluate and price the job and identify the skills and competencies that predict superior performance in the target job. Hiring Advisors recommend questions to ask in hiring interviews, with scoring systems to interpret candidate responses, and tests, assessment center exercises, and other assessment methods to identify the best candidates. When data for a candidate are entered, the expert system will calculate a job-person-match fit score that predicts the applicant's probability of success in the job, and writes an evaluation report on the candidate.

Table 5.7 Human Resource Functions and Processes

	Org/Job Design	Staffing/Destaffing	Perf Mgmt	Training & Development	Comp & benefits	Employee Assistance	Employee/Labor Relations	Org Development
Strategic planning	–Market research –Work force planning –Org and Job design	–Work force planning for future –EO/AA, ADA legal, regulatory –Budget	–Firm HR prodecures manuals –Ethics –Leadership –Perf Mgmt Systems design	–Strategy –Firmwide needs assessment	–Market research, economics –Strategy –Package design –Budget	–Strategy –Firmwide needs assessment: health, safety, security	–Strategy, plans, legal procedures	–Strategy
Delivery	–Write job descriptions	–Recruit –Assess –Select –Place –Career Plan –Succession Planning –Terminate/outplace	–Per Mgmt System +Goal Setting +Coaching +Appraisal Reviews +Reward	–Training Delivery +Internal +Outsourced vendor sourcing, negotiations, management	–Write job descriptions –Job evaluation and pricing –Benefits vendor sourcing, negotiations, management –Benefits plan enrollment (with counseling)	–Delivery +Internal +Outsourced vendor sourcing, negotiations, management	–Union negotiations, relations: grievances, arbitration- Open door, ombudsman, dispute resolution	–Delivery of consulting services: +Survey guided development, team building, TQM, reengineering, change management –Employee involvement –Suggestion systems
Administration	–Record keeping	–Record keeping	–Record keeping	–Record keeping	–Payroll –Defined benefit plan, 401(k) –Claim processing –Record keeping	–Record keeping	–Paper trail processing, e.g., grievances	–Survey data collection and processing

Job or team role openings should be posted electronically—on the firm's internal bulletin board, to external recruiters, colleges and universities, professional associations, and the many job matching services (e.g., E-Span's "Job Search"™ and "On-Line Access"™ and Job Ads USA™ offered through Compuserve™, America On-line™, Prodigy™, and the Internet's On-line Career Center™, a non-profit association sponsored by 40 Fortune 500 firms). On-line service users are highly educated technical professionals; to get on-line, find and respond to electronic job postings screens candidates for computer proficiency.

Further candidate screening can be done by interactive voice response (IVR). Usually only 2 or 3 resumes out of 100 are from viable candidates. Screening the remaining 97 to 98 is best done by asking candidates to *call* an IVR system that asks them screening questions, for example, for a C++ programmer:

> "Do you have a MS in Computer Science? Press 1 for No, 2 for Yes."
>
> IF "1," THEN "Thank you very much for considering Stellar Software . . ." (polite brush off)
>
> IF "2," THEN "Please enter the number of years of experience you have in C++ programming by pressing the appropriate key on your touch-tone phone"
>
> IF "2" or less, THEN (polite brush off) . . .
>
> IF "3" or more, THEN (continue) . . .

Usually only five to ten questions are needed to window the 2 to 3 best candidates from each 100 who apply. At the end of the inquiry, the IVR system can ask screened candidates to *modem* or FAX their resumes, with samples of code or screens they have written, to the hiring manager's number.

Applications, resumes, and work samples should be submitted electronically if possible. Applications can be downloaded to candidates' PCs to be completed and faxed back. If applicants apply in person at a firm site, a number of Application PCs can be made available so that applicants can complete applications on screens. Aspen Tree Software's "Greentree Computer Assisted Employment Interview"™ and Dovetail Software's Dovetail™ present applicants with 50 to 100 questions about their candidates' job goals, work experience, and educational background.

On-screen "computer-assisted interviews" can include interactive questions similar to those shown for the IVR system above, automating "weighted application blank" (WAB) systems that screen and select candidates on the basis of their responses to application questions. These systems can also include many kinds of tests: reading, numeracy, typing, eye-hand coordination, listening and responding, IQ, programming aptitude, personality, honesty and integrity.

"Computer adaptive testing" systems quickly identify skill levels by asking very easy (fourth grade long division) to very hard (calculus) questions to "zero in" on an applicant's abilities.

An alternative is to use resume scanning expert systems (e.g., Resumix™ or Restrac™ to scan paper resumes received), "read" them using optical character recognition, and analyze them using key word search algorithms. For example, a person applying for a programming job whose resume reads

"Sept 85–June 94 High school math teacher"

"June 94–Sept 94 C++ programmer"

will be identified as having 9 years' teaching experience and 3 months' C++ programming experience. The system is smart enough to search for and interpret dates located near key words like "teacher" and "programmer." This person will not be shown as a viable candidate if "3 or more years C++ programming experience" is used as the database search criteria.

IVR and resume scanning systems are only as good as the algorithms built into them. For example, an MS in Computer Science (earned ten years ago) may not predict C++ programming ability, and many high school math teachers have become first-rate programmers. A more sophisticated screening device could download a C++ programming task or test to an applicant, measure how long it took the candidate to complete it, and whether it worked.

Hiring interviews should be conducted by phone or teleconference. Employment and education records verifications, medical and other records should be collected by phone, fax, or modem.

Enter and track all data in a candidate/hire electronic folder in the HR server database. NO PAPER: convert paper to electronic records as soon as possible—or better, insist that candidates submit information electronically.

Performance Management

Automate Performance Management Systems by doing all steps of the Performance Management cycle on-line (screen or phone):

1. Goal setting or performance contracting at the beginning of a performance period (agreement between manager and subordinate, or between team members) about expectations for work to be performed;

2. Coaching: manager help, advice, training, feedback, support, and encouragement during the performance period;

3. Appraisal/feedback; and

4. Reward (or discipline) at the end of the performance period.

Management by objectives, "tickler" e-mail reminders, praise and reprimand, performance appraisal, warning and discipline forms can all be completed on-line, signed with passwords, and stored in appropriate manager, employee, and system data bases. ManagePro™ by Avantos is PMS software that tracks goal accomplishment, prompts managers to give feedback and praise at regular intervals, and includes a "Management Advisor" that offers suggestions on how to motivate employees. Action Technology's Action Workflow software can track performance agreements and accomplishments among many team members involved in complex processes.

Training and Development

Conduct "JIT" training needs assessments on-line by querying data from Organization & Job Design, Staffing/Destaffing, Performance Management and Training & Development employee evaluation databases, or by random samples of customers by e-mail.

Provide employees with on-line career planning expert system software, such as Drake Beam Morin's "Career Navigator" or Career Design Software's "Career Design." These programs ask employees about their vocational interests, strengths and weaknesses, jobs they have liked and done well versus not liked and not done well. The expert system includes a "Development Advisor" which recommends books, education and training courses, and developmental assignments to help employees prepare for their ideal jobs. The software then helps employees summarize their data and develop and write a career plan.

Resume writing software may also help employees wanting to change jobs. Examples include LightingWord's "Instant Resume System," Spinaker's "PFS: Resume and Job Search Pro," and Individual Software's "ResumeMaker." Smart resume programs ask questions to highlight user strengths, such as "What was your biggest accomplishment in your last job? How much did you improve performance? Be specific: use time, dollars, productivity, or quality percentage change statistics."

Provide JIT "performance support" and training on-line via CAI/IV from libraries of courses on CDROM in optical jukeboxes (the firm's or vendors) and via teleconferencing.

Consider outsourcing generic (not-firm specific) training.

Build testing into all training programs to evaluate training effectiveness, assess employees' competence, and keep employee assessment databases current.

Consider "continuous learning" requirements with testing and recertification on-line; make data available for planning to Organization and Job Design, Performance Management, and Compensation (for skill-based pay).

Provide JIT updates of technical and process information on-line via e-mail, document data bases, bulletin boards and discussion forums, such as Lotus Notes. Solutions to many technical problems can be posted to colleagues and customers almost as they happen. Timely notes like "I've found a bug in the xyz module; here's the fix . . ." are far more useful to colleagues in the field than a revised training program or repair manual that may not appear for months or years.

Use "help desk" IVR systems, backed up by human experts and mentors on-line, to get customers help for DIY solutions to problems JIT.

Compensation and Benefits

Access compensation and benefit survey data on-line. Survey providers are developing methods that collect and disseminate information electronically. For example, a software "agent" can sample a firm's compensation practices for key jobs and job families each night and transmit these data to the survey firm's database, to be combined and analyzed with data from other firms subscribing to the survey service. A manager or compensation professional needing the current market price for a job can access this on-line database, much as subscribers to Dun & Bradstreet can access credit reports on-line.

Use on-line expert systems, such as Hay's HRXpert, for job evaluation, pricing, and salary administration. Managers and compensation panels can use these systems themselves, with results checked by exception on-line by compensation experts. Evaluations can be done in minutes, much faster, more accurately—and without paper—than by previous manual systems.

Outsource: 60 percent of major firms outsource 401(k) savings plan, 35 percent benefits administration, 15 percent payroll—and 80 percent are considering outsourcing these and related administrative record keeping activities.

Employee Assistance

Collect "market research" data by having employees complete Wellness Surveys on-line. These 300 item instruments can identify many physical and mental health, stress, work, and family problem and lifestyle issues. Expert systems analyze survey results and offer diagnoses and prescriptions, including referrals to health care and other professionals for help with problems related to drug and alcohol, weight reduction, smoking cessation, fitness, child care, compulsive gambling, and shopping.

Provide information on-line that employees can access DIT, using IVR, HR help desks (e.g., Mellon Bank's HR4YOU), kiosks (e.g., Meridian Bancorp's TESS™, The Employee Self-Service System™, or Merck's EASY™, Employee Access System™), or document databases.

Provide counseling services on-line. Employee Assistance vendor United HealthCare Corporation's Institute for Human Resources provides OPTUM, a "dial-a-shrink" counselor on-line 24 hours a day—a business version of the Samaritans suicide-prevention hotline. On-line counselors can help with mental health, drug and alcohol, stress, family, conflicts with co-workers, and other personal problems. Tele-conference counselors will doubtless be available when PCs with teleconferencing capabilities become more common. ("Eliza," the 1960s expert system shrink-in-the-PC, is not widely available, but there is no reason a more sophisticated version could not be offered on-line.) Teleconference counselors will doubtless be available when PCs with teleconferencing capabilities become more common.

EA help can be made available on CD-ROM or from the HR server by clicking an EA icon. Services could include everything from Jane Fonda aerobics videos to medical advice (already available on Home Medical Advisor CD-ROMs) to JIT relaxation/meditation tapes for stress. Software is available with exercises for relieving eye strain and carpal tunnel syndrome. As noted in Chapter 4, telemedicine will aid all employees' DIY health and wellness efforts.

High-tech security systems can help insure employee safety. Electronic sniffers and beepers—robot versions of the canaries miners carry to warn them of toxic fumes—alert employees to unsafe conditions.

Employee and Labor Relations

Employees can receive any information about the company, changes in policies, procedures or benefits, financial data, competitors' moves by voice mail, e-mail, or from the HR server's document database.

Grievances and complaints can now be filed by filling out templates on kiosk and PC screens, or even by IVR. All grievance process paperwork can be done, tracked, and filed on HR database, and available on-line to workers, union officials, and management.

Ombudsmen can receive complaints and conduct mediations and negotiations by phone or teleconference. "Letters to the editor" (management) and even "flame mail" (gripes) can be e-mailed.

Expert systems can provide on-line labor law, management coaching, and negotiation advice.

Organization Development

Employee attitude, culture, and climate surveys can be conducted by IVR or on-line on kiosk or PC screens, with data analyzed almost instantly, enabling managers to get continuously updated, JIT readings of employee morale.

Initiation or reinforcing bulletins on the progress of change programs—TQM, Reengineering can be communicated on-line.

Voice-mail, e-mail, IVR, and Help Desk "Rumor" or "Answer Lines" can help the firm communicate with employees, minimizing the harm done by false information.

"Groupware" software that lets every member of a group contribute ideas or vote anonymously on recommendations can facilitate team building and problem-solving sessions.

The next chapter describes how HR information and services delivery can be integrated by a smart Integrated Human Resource Management Information System (IHRMIS)

ENDNOTE

1. Kennedy, J.L. and T.J. Morrow. (1994). *Electronic Job Search Revolution*. New York: Wiley. Provides an excellent summary of dozens of job search services and software vendors with contact numbers and addresses.

6

Integrated Human Resource Management Information Systems

Human Resource Information Systems (HRIS) are evolving from databases, used primarily for salary, benefits, and administrative record keeping, to expert system knowledge bases that integrate Human Resource functions and help HR professionals make decisions. This chapter describes the architecture, applications, and benefits of emergent *Integrated Human Resource Management Information Systems* (IHRMIS)—shared databases of information about jobs, people, and the organization, with artificial intelligence decision-support capabilities that can improve HR management.

HISTORY

Computerized HRIS are used by most U.S. companies with more than a few hundred employees. More than 1,100 HR software packages are on the market. They range from simple spreadsheet templates and single-purpose HR software applications to large mainframe systems costing several hundred thousand dollars. Most are payroll, benefit, and government reporting systems.

HRIS evolved in the 1970s, spurred by information requirements of government regulation, decreasing computer costs, and the growth of the time-sharing for companies without computers. For employers of more than a thousand people, the costs of complying with government reporting requirements under the equal opportunity laws, ERISA, OSHA, and other legislation made computerized personnel systems economically feasible. For example, EEO compliance requires statistical data on past employment practices and continual monitoring of the status and progress of hiring, job activities, performance evaluation, promotion and career pathing, compensation, and benefits for various federally protected groups.

At minimum, HRIS systems include four elements:

1. A database of such variables as employee ID, job code, and salary level.
2. Data entry/edit—an efficient method for creating and updating data.
3. Data retrieval or report generation—rapid retrieval and formatting of data in useful reports.
4. An administrative system that supports maintenance and security, which protects against access to sensitive employee or organizational data.

IHRMIS is an HR decision-support program that includes:

- A common database of information on jobs, people, and organization variables that is shared by many (ideally all) HR functions and that provides a common language and integrates all HR services.
- A knowledge base of algorithms or decision rules that can assist management in making professional HR choices (e.g., whom to select for a job; the most cost-effective training available to improve an employee's productivity, etc.).

In addition, IHRMIS features usually include:

Automated Analysis/Assessment Methods.   IHRMIS data on people, jobs, and the organization are gathered by the system through diagnostic questionnaires that query human respondents and analyze the data into relevant metrics.

Decision Support.   IHRMIS supports specific HR decision making. System report formats are designed to act on specific questions (e.g., "Rank order candidates for job A in descending order of predicted performance in this job").

Multiple Applications.   IHRMIS supports many (ideally all) HR applications, not just one or two. Applications are integrated so that data generated or used by one HR function (e.g., selection) can be accessed and used in other functions (e.g., compensation or development).

Easy Access and User-Friendliness.   IHRMIS is designed for real-time use by HR practitioners, line managers, and employees in field settings. These systems typically are decentralized, are networked PC-based, and use graphical user interface (GUI) point-and-click or menu interfaces.

IHRMIS differs from the typical HRIS in that its primary purpose is *decision support* rather than information management and reporting. IHRMIS is often built on top of and linked to an HRIS that contains basic personnel data.

ISSUES DRIVING IHRMIS DEVELOPMENT

HR issues driving the development of IHRMIS include fragmentation of HR functions and programs; destaffing of HR departments with decentralization of HR functions to line managers and employees; and reengineering of HR functions.

Fragmentation

Since the 1960s, HR management has developed a number of disciplines or specialty areas, such as staffing, compensation, training and development, and information systems. Each discipline is supported by distinct professional organizations, the American Compensation Association (ACA), the American Society for Training and Development (ASTD), and the Human Resource System Professionals (HRSP), to name a few.

Disparate HR functions and services use different and often conflicting languages and systems.

- Recruiters recruit for one set of characteristics.
- Compensation specialists measure jobs and pay people on the basis of a different set of compensable factors and evaluation points.
- Performance appraisals assess another set of characteristics.
- The training department teaches yet another set of knowledge and skills.
- Separate HR functions often become warring political fiefdoms competing for resources and confusing their manager and employee customers.

HR Fragmentation Results in Inefficient Use of Resources.   Duplicate computers and databases, duplicate staffs, and excessive head count. Managers and employers who must master the several different languages receive conflicting messages about what is important. HR programs at best do not reinforce one another, and at worst, directly conflict. For example, a firm's incentive plans may reward employees for individual performance and independent work at the same time its training department is promoting teamwork and collaboration. Inconsistent signals from different programs reduce the effectiveness of the HR function.

HR Programs Should Be Mutually Reinforcing.   Efforts in one area should reinforce and be reinforced by all others. Selection, development, compensation, and performance management programs all should be linked to the values, strategy, and objectives of the organization. IHRMIS impose a common language and "wire together" HR applications to help ensure consistency, coordination, and focus of HR programs on the critical success factors of work and people that drive organizational effectiveness.

Destaffing and Decentralization

As described in Chapter 1, many firms are cutting HR staff and decentralizing, returning HR work and decision making to line managers and employees who may lack the information and expertise to handle these responsibilities effectively. An IHRMIS expert system can provide the information and advice needed to answer such questions as:

- What characteristics should I look for when hiring for job A?
- What criteria should I use in managing person B's performance?
- Who are succession candidates with the highest probability of succeeding in key jobs L, M, and N?
- What are the career development options for engineers with four years of experience who want to go into management?

Timely answers to these questions with data and advice from IHRMIS can help managers make more informed decisions.

Reengineering

Firms increasingly are looking to networked computer systems to simplify or eliminate paperwork by doing administrative work on screens and moving and storing data electronically, and enable managers and employees to use most HR services themselves with the help of expert systems.

IHRMIS Concept and Architecture

A database "nucleus" contains information about the organization's external and internal environment, its jobs, and its people. This common database is used by the eight HR processes shown in Figure 6.1 and Table 5.8 (see Chapter 5): organization and job design (HR Planning); staffing/destaffing; performance management; training and development; compensation; employee assistance, employee and labor relations. and organization development (culture management).

Organization.   "Organization" can be a database for the entire firm, for groups outside it, for example, "applicants," or for sub-organizations within it, for example, "Finance," Customer Service in Kiev, Ukraine; or temporary teams: "Release 2.01 Bug Fix Task Force June 1–August 31 1995." Suborganization database are "cuts" of the entire organization database that can speed up data queries and enforce security (users access is limited to databases for business

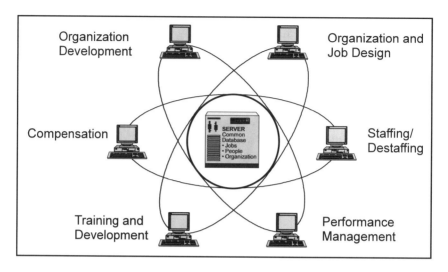

Figure 6.1 IHRMIS Architecture Showing HR Processes Linked
and Integrated by a Central Server

use). Organization data can include market or competitive information such as
the life cycle stages of its products; the organization's mission, values, and strategy; its structure and culture (managerial style and employee attitudes); and its
performance results (customer satisfaction, quality, productivity, and profits).
Table 6.1 shows the database structure detail.

Job/Role. A job or role is a generic description of a position in the organization a person can occupy—for example, Regional Sales Manager or "team database expert." Data can include the purpose, duties, responsibilities,
performance standards, compensable factors, and competency requirements
of the job/role.

Position. A position is a specific instance of an occupied or vacant job, for
example, Regional Sales Manager in St. Louis, presently held by Pat Exemplar
or "database expert on Task Force X" (vacant). Positions are "join" databases
that reference data (often "tailored") for the job/role and the person in the position.

Person. "Persons" can include full-time, part-time, contract, and candidate
employees. Data can include current (and potential) employees' demographic
information (age, sex, race), education, work history, training and development
history, compensation history, competency assessments, performance appraisal
data, development plans, and career path.

   Data are organized in hierarchical or logical order. For example, an organization's external environment influences its mission, values, and strategy, which in
turn drive its structure, managerial style, and culture. Job/role purpose, duties,

Table 6.1 Example Data Fields for Major IHRMS Data Categories

Organization/ Team	Job/Role	Position	Person
Environment	Title	Title	Demographics
Mission/Strategy	Purpose	Purpose	Personal health,
Structure	Duties and	Duties and	benefits
Workforce	Responsibilities	responsibilities	dependents' data
Planning:	Performance	Performance	Education
demand	goals and	goals and	Work History/
and supply	standards	standards	Experience
forecasts by	Compensable	Compensable	Compensation
job/role	factors and	factors	History
Managerial Style	compensation	Competency	Performance
Climate/Culture	Plan: fixed,	requirements	Appraisal:
Employee	variable/merit	Incumbent:	results
Attitudes:	ranges	Person data (left	competencies
morale	Competency	column)	Development
motivation	Requirements		Plan
Product and			Career Path
Service Quality			Potential
Customer			
Satisfaction			
Productivity			
Financial			
Measures: costs,			
revenues and profits			

and responsibilities drive performance standards and objectives as well as compensable factor evaluations, and are related to competencies of people who do the job/role well (competency requirements of the job). A person's education, work, and development history influences his or her competencies, which in turn drive his or her development plans and career path alternatives. All information in the database is linked and available to all HR applications.

IHRMIS is designed to interface with existing systems to extract key information for setup and update records. Typically, on initial setup the IHRMIS extracts employee and job information from an existing payroll or HRIS system. Data may include employee name, ID number, job classification, work unit, location, salary information, appraisal ratings, and other relevant information. Similarly, job data extracted can include job code, evaluation ratings, grade and classification data, and competency requirements.

The IHRMIS database serves as a platform on which users can add application modules as needs arise. Users usually begin with a few modules; once these are operational, users can add more functions.

ORGANIZATION AND JOB DESIGN (HR PLANNING)

Organization and job design sets organizational structures and the nature of the work in these structures. HR planning addresses present and projected staffing of the organization: how many people with what types of skills will be needed to do future work. These planning activities are supported by the following modules.

Organization Charting.   Modules produce graphic charts of the organization's structure. These can begin with the head of the organization and his or her direct reports, and cascade down through the organization so that all positions are addressed. Organizational charting modules usually allow users to define the nature and extent of information displayed for each job on the chart. Charts can include just a job title or show additional data such as the jobholder's name, job location, promotability, and other desired information.

Organization structure modules also can address organizational design, calculating such variables as span of control to identify potential problems such as redundant positions. These analyses also allow the user to experiment with alternative organizational structures that may contribute to reducing costs or enhancing productivity.

Workforce Planning.   Modules forecast demand for key jobs as well as employee turnover and patterns of interorganizational mobility. Using historical trends and business strategy, spreadsheet and statistical analyses help project employee and competency needs as well as objectives for staffing and employee development activities.

Job Description.   Modules produce printouts that describe jobs according to user specifications and information input into the system. At minimum, job descriptions include job title, purpose, and duties and responsibilities. Additional data on compensable factors, salary grade, and competency requirements for the job usually are included.

Job Description modules should allow authorized users to update and reformat job descriptions and extract job data sorted by level, organizational unit, and other dimensions of interest.

Job Competency Requirements Analysis.   Modules analyze job duties and responsibilities to identify competencies that predict effective job performance. Competencies can include general education and experience (or equivalent) requirements, knowledge, skills, or personality variables (self-concept, traits, and motives). Algorithms based on an extensive competency study database can infer employee characteristics that predict doing specific job tasks well. For example: "IF the job requires continuous improvement in performance AND repeated innovation AND accomplishment of challenging goals, THEN successful candidates should show achievement motivation at Level 4 or above." Competencies identified should meet "legal defensibility" content and criterion validity. Figure 6.2 shows a competency model developed by an expert system for a managerial job.

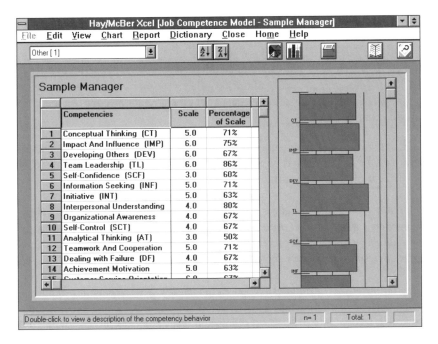

Figure 6.2 An Expert System Generated Competency Model for a Manager Job

Staffing/Destaffing

Staffing applications address recruitment, selection, and placement functions and can include the following modules.

Job Posting.   Modules list job openings within the organization. Typically, the list identifies the job title, job location, primary responsibilities, and job requirements. Employees may browse through the job posting, identify jobs that fit their interest and capabilities, and apply for these jobs on-line. Increasingly, WANs link internal job posting systems to external job/person-matching bulletin boards.

Hiring Advisor.   Is an interview protocol generator that creates questions that help interviewers assess applicants on competencies (identified by the Job Competency Requirements Analysis) that are required to perform well in the job. For example, if achievement motivation is required, the Hiring Advisor generates focused Behavioral Event Interview questions, such as:

"Tell me about your biggest accomplishment in your last job" and a checklist for recording statements that code for specific levels of the competency:

Applicant mentioned doing something new to improve productivity or quality (Ach 4): _____

Applicant provided quantitative data about the amount of improvement (15%, saved $xxxx, etc.; Ach 6): _____

Hiring Advisors can include Assessment Advisors, which recommend specific tests or assessment center exercises to evaluate candidates, with recommended cut-off scores for hiring.

Applicant Tracking.   Modules are databases of key information on job applicants: résumé; education; work experience; interview data; competency assessments (e.g., test and/or assessment center scores); background, reference, and credit checks; medical exam results; and other relevant selection process information.

Selection Advisor.   Modules compare competency assessments of candidates to job competency requirements. The Selection Advisor calculates job/person goodness-of-fit (probability of success) scores and lists candidates in descending order of fitness for a job. Figure 6.3 shows an expert system candidate selection screen.

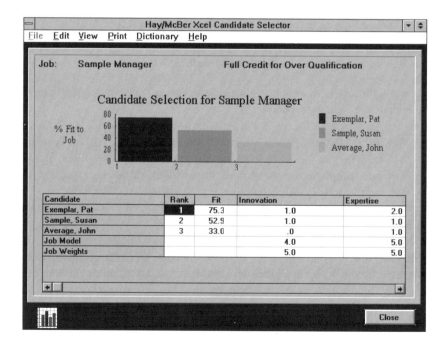

Figure 6.3 Expert System Candidate Selection Screen

Job/person-matching.   Modules can be used for efficient candidate screening, selection, job placement, succession planning, and career pathing. Information about the gaps between an employee and his or her current job—or a job he or she might seek in the future—can be used to prescribe development options for the employee. (See Development Advisor later in this chapter.)

Succession Planning.   Modules track and report information on the availability of competent candidates for key positions (using, for example, the job/person-matching module described later in this chapter). Reports include replacement tables identifying candidates for each key position, and the development needs of candidates where they fall short of the requirements for a target job.

PERFORMANCE MANAGEMENT

Performance management applications help managers direct and motivate employees to achieve organizational goals, and to develop their competencies. Performance management modules generate performance appraisal forms based on the goals, standards, and competencies required by a job, and record appraisal ratings for employees on goal accomplishment and competency assessment.

Results against Accountability Goals and Objectives modules record goals set for employees at the beginning of a performance period and track employee performance against these goals. Figure 6.4 shows a IHRMIS Goals

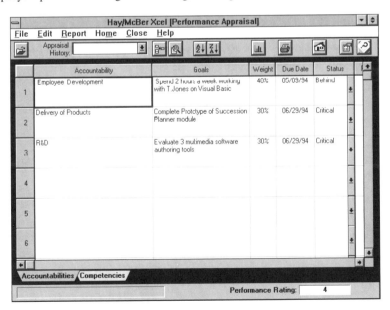

Figure 6.4   An IHRMIS Goals and Results Performance
Management Screen

and Results tracking screen. Goals set and accomplished can be aggregated and reported by organizational unit. The purpose here is to see whether unit managers are helping subordinates focus on appropriate behaviors in order to accomplish organizational objectives and to track organizational progress toward strategic goals.

IHRMIS Performance Management modules can also track competency development objectives, as shown in Figure 6.5.

Competency (Re)assessment. Ratings of employee competencies may be entered by an employee's manager or in "360 degree" approaches by multiple raters: manager, peers, subordinates, external observers, and even clients or customers. Network-based IHRMIS permit very rapid reassessment of employee competencies, for example, to answer a staffing question: "Does John Average have the right stuff to fill a job in Jakarta starting next Monday?" A line or HR manager can e-mail John's boss, peers, subordinates, and customers and ask them to complete an on-line competency assessment for John using a point-and-click screen similar to one shown in Figure 6.6.

IHRMIS can automate the entire performance management cycle shown in Figure 6.7 of (1) performance contracting (goal and objective setting) at the beginning of the performance period; (2) performance coaching during the performance period; (3) performance appraisal at the end of the performance period; and (4) reward (or sanction) consequences.

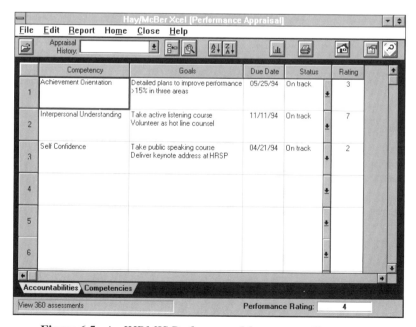

Figure 6.5   An IHRMIS Performance Management Competency
Development Objectives Screen

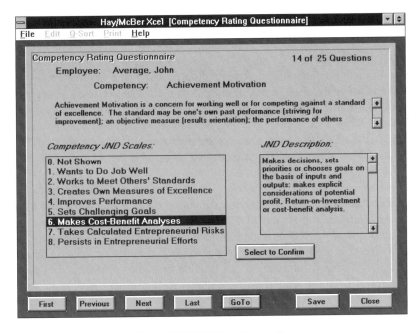

Figure 6.6 An IHRMIS Employee Competency
Assessor Screen

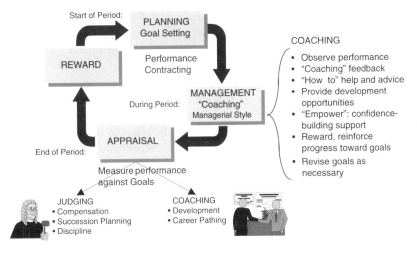

Figure 6.7 Performance Management Cycle Automated
by IHRMIS

Managers and employees can revise and track progress against goals and competency development objectives and record notes on coaching feedback. They can also conduct virtual performance appraisal sessions, for example, a manager in Helsinki and an employee in Kuala Lumpur can look at the same screen using white-boarding software, discuss and agree on the employee's results against goals, competency development against objectives, and aggregate performance rating. Upon agreement, they sign the form with their password, click on "Confirm" or "Send," and the perormance appraisal is instantly communicated to the IHRMIS server. Data on the employee's competencies is immediately available to line and HR management worldwide for strategic HR assets assessment and staffing/destaffing decisions.

Performance appraisal information can be used in many IHRMIS applications. Appraisals keep employee competency data up-to-date for use in HR Succession Planning, Staffing, Job-Person Matching, and Development Needs Assessment and Advisor modules. Goal accomplishment and competency assessment information may be used in Reward Management modules for salary planning. Aggregated appraisal information can provide moment-to-moment data on the competence of various employee populations in the organization as shown in Figures 6.9, 6.10, and 6.11.

Training and Development

Training and development applications support the effective implementation of training and development activities, and can include the following modules:

Training and Development Record Keeping. Modules track recommended training for skill levels, training site availability, course schedules, enrollments, attendance and completion, and course trainer and trainee evaluation results. Employee data (e.g., educational achievements and degrees, certifications, courses, and training recommendations for career development) may be updated by training and development modules.

Career Planning and Pathing. Modules provide information on alternative job options and help employees compare their competencies with the competency requirements for these jobs. Job opportunities can be listed by a goodness-of-fit index or by development value—a job's potential to help an employee develop a competency he or she needs. Career planning modules can summarize and print employees' career targets and plans to achieve these goals, as shown in Figure 6.8.

Development Needs Analysis. Modules identify employees and employee groups that may best benefit from training and development. They can answer queries like "How many of our salespeople demonstrate Customer Service Orientation competencies at Level 5 or above?"

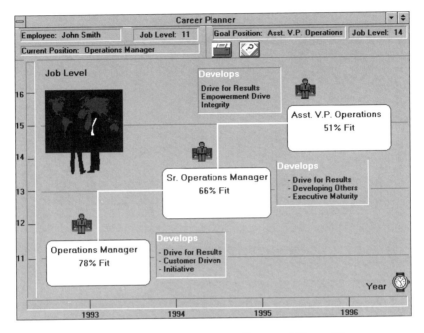

Figure 6.8 An Expert-System-Generated Career Plan

Competencies	10	11	12	13	14	15	16	17	18	19	20	21	22
	(30)	(24)	(25)	(15)	(16)	(32)	(5)	(32)	(34)	(30)	(7)	(19)	(35)
Drive for Results	37%	25%	17%	62%	7%	46%	36%	85%	74%	54%	50%	60%	46
Executive Maturity	52%	53%	17%	62%	25%	74%	16%	73%	90%	90%	24%	76%	73
Optimism	75%	12%	63%	43%	95%	59%	69%	28%	33%	53%	61%	17%	73
Self-Confidence	7%	97%	41%	11%	8%	81%	90%	66%	54%	41%	49%	79%	40
Respect for Others	58%	66%	41%	55%	39%	4%	52%	26%	10%	82%	67%	21%	88
Thinking Outside the Box	47%	3%	70%	68%	37%	22%	11%	11%	62%	80%	86%	93%	73
Analytical Smarts	30%	57%	33%	89%	49%	9%	74%	5%	41%	66%	37%	8%	10
Customer Driven	26%	12%	62%	81%	17%	12%	40%	33%	93%	71%	31%	8%	62
Organizational Impact	64%	12%	22%	4%	47%	34%	46%	77%	13%	97%	30%	77%	70
People & Organizational Savvy	27%	78%	20%	54%	26%	14%	49%	30%	90%	34%	16%	38%	3%
Relationship Building	29%	29%	57%	89%	62%	2%	22%	24%	61%	49%	52%	46%	43
Developing Others	81%	6%	10%	43%	53%	53%	33%	48%	35%	41%	23%	13%	40
	80%	30%	46%	66%	17%	64%	11%	26%	16%	68%	58%	13%	28

Division: East. Europe N = 576 Division Fit Score: 71%

Competencies (Percentage of Scale) by Job Level

Figure 6.9 An HR "Executive Information System (EIS)" Showing
Competency Fit Scores by Salary Grade

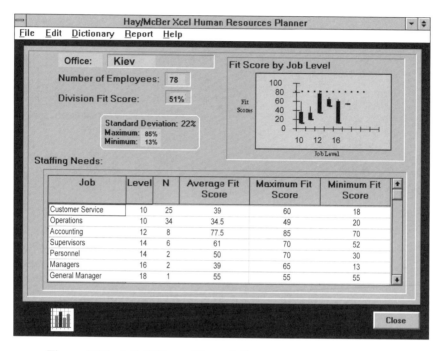

Figure 6.10   A Drill Down View of Competency Fit Scores by Job
and Job Level in a Specific Office

For example, in Chapter 1, Fiona Prokofiev was alerted by her HRMIS Executive
Information System (EIS) that sales were down in Eastern Europe—and that
likely causes included low customer service competencies, as shown in Figure 6.8.

Fiona can "drill down" on specific offices in Eastern Europe (e.g., Kiev, as
shown in Figure 6.10) and even get data on specific individuals (as shown in Figure 6.11) to see more precisely where development needs are.

Training Needs Assessment focuses on development actions (e.g., by identifying which of several course topics available to an organization meet its greatest
needs). Similarly, if limited training is available, it can identify those individuals
with the greatest development need.

Development Needs			
Employee	Employee ID	Current Job	Fit Score
Ivan Poorski	EU953-162	Office Manager	13%
Svetlana Malikov	EU190-324	Customer Service Rep	23%
Yosef Iridichev	EU285-972	Training Director	34%

Figure 6.11   A Further Drill Down to See the Development Needs
of Specific Individuals

Development Advisor. Modules provide development recommendations to employees by identifying gaps between an employee's competencies and job competency requirements of his or her current (or desired) job.

For example, if John Average decides he wants a managerial job, he can assess himself against a generic competency model for managers, as shown in Figure 6.12. The expert system will identify those competencies most important for John to develop (competencies rated most important to success in the job with the largest job/person gap).

Figure 6.12 indicates that Impact and Influence competence at Level 7 is critical (weighted 5) for success as a manager. John's current level of competence is 4, so the weighted gap between the job's requirements and John's current ability is $5 \times (-4) = -20$. Impact and Influence is John's highest development priority.

Suggestions are provided to help guide the employee, for example, "IF you score Level 2 in Achievement Motivation, AND the job requires Level 4, THEN read these books; take these training courses; do these development activities; work for these mentors," and so on. These modules can construct and print complete development plans for employees, as shown in Figure 6.13.

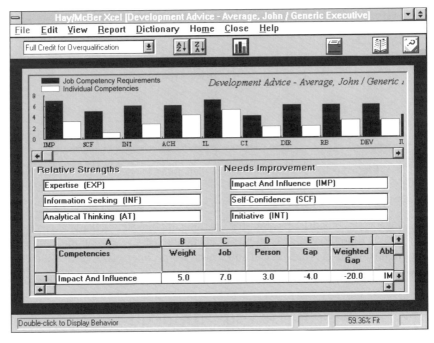

Figure 6.12 An Expert System Screen Showing Weighted Gaps Between Job Competency Requirements and an Individual's Competence—Hence Priorities for Development

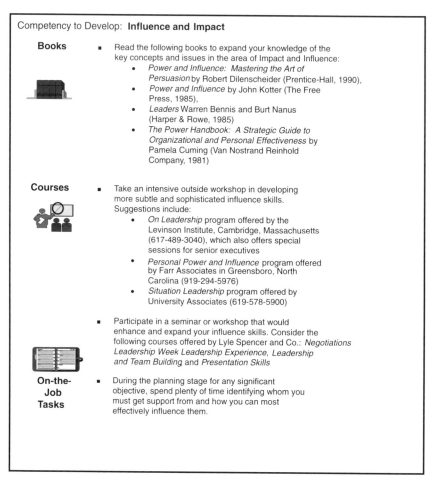

Figure 6.13 An Expert-System-Generated Development Plan

As discussed in Chapter 1, the step beyond expert system-generated advice is just-in-time training available on-line at the employee's work station. John need only double-click on "Impact and Influence" for an interactive video course on how to win friends and influence people.

COMPENSATION MANAGEMENT

Reward Management applications support compensation and benefits administration, ensuring that internal and external pay equity is maintained and that pay effectively motivates employees toward appropriate goals.

Job Evaluation.   Modules called Computer Assisted Job Evaluation (CAJE) systems help managers determine job evaluation points, salary grades or classifications levels, and job hierarchies. CAJE modules administer and record responses to questionnaires that measure compensable factors in a wide range of an organization's jobs. CAJE algorithms translate questionnaire responses into evaluation points, using any of several point-factor job evaluation methods (e.g., the Hay or the National Metal Trades Association (NMTA) systems), and calculate recommended salaries for specific jobs. Figure 6.14 shows an IHRMIS expert system-generated job evaluation.

Job evaluation modules usually include quality assurance reports that assess the integrity and consistency of evaluation results and help ensure that the evaluation process is being accurately and equitably applied.

Compensation Administration.   Modules track, analyze, and report compensation information on pay-grade structure and provide merit increase guidelines and amounts, Fair Labor Standards Act (FLSA) classification (i.e., exemption status), salary administration, and incentive allocations.

These data help support salary budgeting (e.g., by allocating increases according to alternative criteria and tracking results in terms of comp-ratio and other statistics).

Equity Analysis modules assess the relative equity of an organization's pay practices. These modules produce scattergrams (see Figure 6.15) that compare evaluation point totals for jobs to employees' actual pay. Employees receiving pay markedly different from the general organizational trend (i.e., outliers) can be identified and corrective action taken where appropriate to ensure internal equity.

Title	Code	Know How	Problem Solving	PS %	Account-ability	Total Points	Grade
PRESIDENT/COO		528	304	57%	528	1360	9
PERSONNEL MGR	1103	350	175	50%	230	755	6
SALES MGR	6005	350	152	43%	230	732	7
CONTROLLER I	1043	304	152	50%	175	631	7
SUPPORT SERVICES MGR	1076	264	100	38%	132	496	4
PURCHASING MGR	1074	230	87	38%	115	496	4
ENGINEER I	1067	200	76	38%	76	432	3
DATABASE ANALYST II	1048	230	87	38%	87	404	4
LOGISTICIAN II	1095	200	76	38%	76	352	2
SALES REP	6003	200	57	29%	87	344	4
ACCOUNTANT	1011	175	50	25%	57	282	4

Figure 6.14   An Expert-System-Generated Job Evaluation Screen

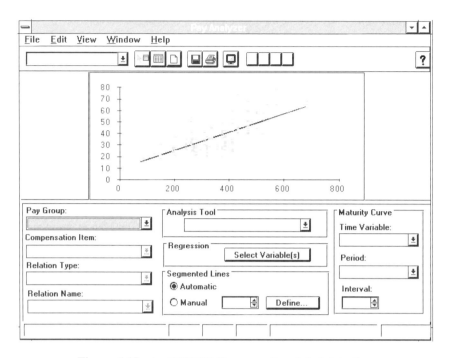

Figure 6.15 An IHRMIS Compensation Administration
Job Evaluation Point Factor x Compensation
Scattergram Screen

Scattergram analyses also may be conducted for groups of employees, for example, by gender or location. Pay equity initiatives in various states may require gender comparisons of actual versus predicted pay using regression lines of salary against point values of jobs.

Employee Assistance.   Modules collect and track data on employee physical and mental health, stress, work and family problem and lifestyle concerns. Expert systems analyze survey results and offer diagnoses and prescriptions, including referrals to health care and other professionals for help regarding drug and alcohol, weight reduction, smoking cessation, fitness, child care, compulsive gambling, and shopping. Advanced systems may provide help information and counseling on-line. As noted in Chapter 4, telemedicine will aid all employees' DIY health and wellness efforts.

Employee and Labor Relations modules can track grievances and employee concern data, facilitate complaint mediations and negotiations by phone or tele-conference. Expert systems can provide on-line labor law, management coaching, and negotiation advice.

ORGANIZATION DEVELOPMENT

Employee attitude, culture, and climate surveys can be conducted by IVR or on-line on kiosk or PC screens, with data analyzed almost instantly, enabling managers to get continuously updated, JIT readings of employee morale.

Organization development (or culture management) applications support the effective implementation of management practices and can include the following modules:

Managerial Style Analysis.   Modules use on-line questionnaires completed by employees to identify behaviors of their immediate management. Data are aggregated and reported for individual managers, departments, and the total organization. This information helps management determine its effectiveness and identify, for example, whether training is needed to teach management methods more likely to motivate employees. Appendix A shows examples of team competency, managerial style, organizational climate, and culture graphs that can be generated by on-line surveys of employees.

Organizational Culture/Climate Analysis.   Modules analyze employee attitude survey data, which help managers identify employee concerns and appropriate management actions. IHRMIS expert systems can include Management Advisors (e.g., "IF Organizational Clarity (a survey variable) is below the 25th percentile, THEN give a vision speech followed by an all-employees meeting to determine whether people understand the organization's three most important goals").

SUMMARY

Advantages/Benefits of IHRMIS

- Timely information and expert advice on HR decisions can be provided to line managers on-line and inexpensively, reducing dependence on HR staff and minimizing administrative paperwork.
- "Wired together" HR programs and processes share information in a common language, send a consistent message to employees, and reinforce one another to help managers achieve organizational objectives.
- Every "Administrative" and "Delivery" level HR transaction generates data which, captured by the central IHRMIS server, provides information for HR strategic planning. Routine staffing, performance management, training, and employee assistance requests and evaluations provide a by-product of up-to-date data about the firm's HR assets which can be used for strategic HR planning.

Disadvantages/Obstacles to the Implementation of IHRMIS

- Considerable investment in data collection is required to make IHRMIS work. For example, job/person-matching works only when competency requirements have been analyzed, employees' competencies assessed, and these data entered into the system.

- Users may lack access to computers or need to be trained to use decision-support information.

- HR specialists may resist giving up their single function systems or their professional power to a machine or line manager and employee customers.

- Data security for certain types of confidential information may be difficult to maintain.

The Future of IHRMIS Systems

True IHRMIS systems are in their infancy. It is only very recently that computer hardware and software and conceptual designs have advanced sufficiently to support IHRMIS. Nevertheless, rapid growth of IHRMIS is inevitable. Current standalone HR applications will be integrated into IHRMIS. Competitive pressure will force HRIS vendors to add IHRMIS features or reengineer HRIS systems to interface with IHRMIS applications provided by other vendors. Technical advancements in computer hardware and software will make IHRMIS systems still more attractive.

- Each year PC computers double in power (Moore's Law, see Chapter 2) while declining in cost. Soon all knowledgeable workers will have access to PCs capable of running IHRMIS.

- User interfaces are becoming more friendly, with graphic point-and-click navigation through applications.

- Database managers are becoming more powerful in terms of size, speed, and information networking.

- Data entry is becoming easier with the optical scanning of documents and the use of optical character (i.e., text) and voice recognition software.

- Increasingly sophisticated artificial intelligence algorithms will make the "expert systems" embedded in IHRMIS smarter and easier to use.

- Multimedia voice and video on inexpensive CD-ROM disks will make the HR services that can be delivered by computer nearly limitless. Performance support systems (PSS) will provide training on-line.

- Because increasing use of IHRMIS is likely to change the roles of HR professionals, they will need to be more computer literate and understand complex information systems and networks. At minimum, they will need to know how to use IHRMIS program modules. HR experts increasingly will work as knowledge engineers, designing and storing their expertise into expert systems. As fifth-generation computer languages make computer programming accessible to everyone, more HR professionals will become programmers.

- HR staff will become expert (systems) consultants to and partners with line managers in the management of people—and as such, may be more highly valued by line management.

- Quicker access to more and better information about organization problems and opportunities will enable HR staff to become more effective and more influential strategic planning business partners with top management.

IHRMIS, if properly implemented and used, can be a powerful tool for HR management. As a decision-support system, it can improve HR practices by specialists and line managers, while simultaneously increasing productivity and reducing administrative costs. By integrating an organization's HR efforts, IHRMIS can increase HR support of individual and organizational effectiveness.

7

People

An axiom of sociotechnology is that when work (organizations, technology, or work flow processes) changes, people need to change. This chapter discusses the HR and employee changes most likely to result from reengineering.

COMPETENCE

A competency is a "relatively enduring characteristic of a person causally related to effective or superior performance in a job." In other words, a person's competence predicts whether he or she will be able to do a job at all (effective performance) or will do it *well* (*superior* performance, defined as the one standard deviation above average performance achieved by the top 14% (roughly best one out of 10) people doing the job.

I prefer the *superior* criteria definition of competence because:

1. It has significant economic value.
2. It drives Human Resources to add value, that is, do *better* than its present average performance.

Figure 7.1 shows the economic value of superior performance one standard deviation above average:

+19% productivity in low-complexity jobs

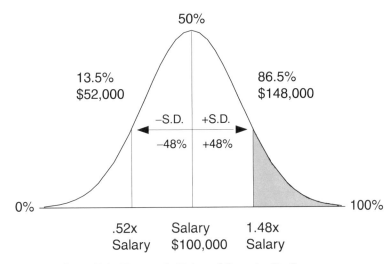

Figure 7.1 Economic Value of Superior Performance

+32% productivity in moderate-complexity jobs

+48% productivity in high-complexity jobs

+48%–120% productivity in sales jobs

A superior performer in a job where the average salary is 100,000 currency units (CU) is worth 148,000 CUs, half again as much as an average employee. Put another way, the superior performer does the job of one-and-a-half average performers.

Figure 7.2 shows the distribution of programmer productivity in Albrecht function points per programmer month (AFPPM). An Albrecht function point is a common denominator measure of computer programming productivity (e.g., a screen with a certain number of inputs, processes, file queries, and outputs).

An average programmer produces five AFPPMs per month. A top-one-out-of-ten star programmer produces 16 AFPPMs, 320 percent greater productivity. Superstar programmers (the top 2%, two standard deviations above the mean) produce 64 AFPPMs, 12.7 × or 1272 percent more than an average performer. If an average programmer's salary is $50,000/year, a superstar doing the work of 12.7 people is worth $635,000/year.

This economic value severely understates the case for jobs that leverage any kind of economic assets. Superior performance in sales jobs is 48 to 120 percent above average: The familiar rule of thumb is that star salespeople sell twice what average salespeople sell. As shown in Figure 7.3, average salespeople in a study of 44 U.S. Fortune 500 firms, earning a mean salary of $41,777, sold an average $3 million per year. Superior performers sold an average of $6.7 million. The difference between average and superior performance is 123 percent, but the value-added by a superior performer is $3.7 million, 88 × or 8,800 percent of salary.

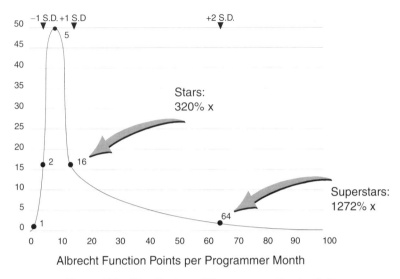

Figure 7.2   Distribution of Programmer Productivity

The bottom line is obvious: superior performers are highly valuable. Most firms have adequate numbers of adequate performers, but they need more stars to improve performance and gain competitive advantage. Any firm not using superior as opposed to average performance as its benchmark or template for

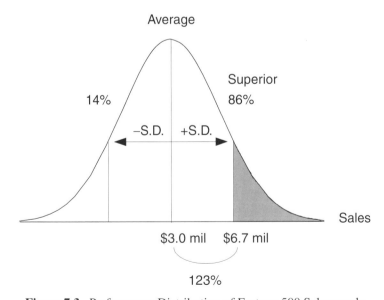

Figure 7.3   Performance Distribution of Fortune 500 Salespeople

recruitment, selection, succession planning and development, is selecting and training to mediocrity— its current average level of performance.

EXAMPLE OF A COMPETENCY

The best researched competency is *achievement motivation,* a strong, almost obsessive concern with doing better against a standard of excellence, or unique accomplishment, inventing new ways to do things (very often the way one does something better is to figure out a new way to do it). As shown in Figure 7.4, achievement motivation predicts:

- Setting challenging goals above one's current performance or the performance the organization is requesting.
- Using feedback to continually improve performance.
- Taking personal responsibility for goal attainment (i.e., *owning* the goal rather than blaming others for one's failure to achieve it).
- Calculated risk taking, because trying to do something new or better than before usually involves risk.

People high in achievement motivation in their jobs demonstrate continuous improvement in quality, productivity, and hard economic outcomes; sales and

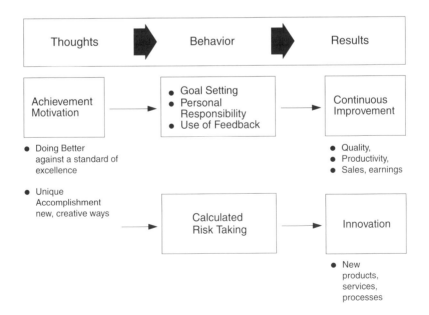

Figure 7.4 Achievement Motivation

earnings; and innovation such as introducing new products and services to market and new work flow processes adopted by the company.

Companies that can identify, select, and train for the competencies that predict superior performance in reengineered work can gain significant competitive advantage. As shown in Figure 7.5, effective training has a good statistical chance of significantly improving bottom-line performance. Training can shift the bell curve to the right by as much as .67 of a standard deviation worth .67 × 48% = 32% increased productivity.

COMPETENCIES FOR REENGINEERING

In two studies of reengineering efforts in high-tech, financial, military, and government organizations, individual competencies, leadership style, and team climate variables distinguished successful reengineering efforts from those that were not successful. Appendix A contains a Reengineering Team Readiness Questionnaire you can use to assess yourself or your colleagues on these variables.

The studies revealed that individual competencies predicting success in reengineering were:

1. **Achievement Orientation:** thinking about doing better against a measurable standard of excellence.
2. **Analytical Thinking:** the ability to break complex problems (e.g., work flows) into their constituent parts and arrange them in hierarchical, time sequential, and causal order. Analysis of hierarchical order requires the ability to prioritize (A is more important than B is more important than C). Analysis of time sequential order requires the ability to lay out work

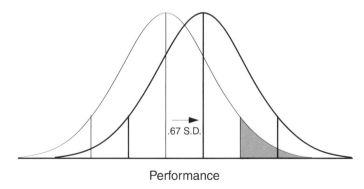

Performance

Figure 7.5 Bell Curve Shift as a Result of Training

flow process steps in sequence (Do step A before doing step B before doing step C). Analysis of causal order requires the ability to recognize If = Then relationships (If A happens, then B is likely to happen; or if X happened, it probably was caused by U and V).

3. **Customer Service Orientation:** proactively going out and asking downstream customers how you can serve them better (e.g., change your process or outputs, get customers better inputs just-in-time). In the studies mentioned above, less successful reengineering leaders *reacted* to downstream customers' requests for better service or inputs, while superior reengineering leaders *initiated* customer contact to find out how they could help.

4. **Influence and Persuasion:** Superior reengineers persuaded people (over whom they had no direct authority) to cooperate with the reengineering effort by emphasizing the benefits. They created compelling visions that motivated multidisciplinary team members to align their interests and work for shared project goals. They also built political coalitions of process workers and customers to lobby for the funds, computer equipment, and other resources necessary for success.

5. **Initiative:** Superior reengineers took action. They pushed, wheedled, and cajoled to get colleagues, employees, suppliers, and customers to adopt new methods.

6. **Team Orientation:** Superior reengineers exhibited many team-building behaviors. For example, one described the importance of building a team not only among his own consulting colleagues but with vendors of competing computer equipment and software and with employees in the client organization. He initiated various team-building activities. For example, he began coming in an hour early each morning with coffee and donuts bought out-of-pocket, and invited team members to drop in and chat. At the end of each week he devised ways to celebrate any advances the team had made.

7. **Discontinuous Thinking:** Superior reengineers really do think "outside the ox." They continually act as devil's advocate, proposing radical alternatives to the way work is done and challenging colleagues to eliminate work that doesn't need to be done.

8. **Technology Know-How:** Superior reengineers cited many more examples of cutting-edge management techniques and technologies; read management and computer journals; and enthusiastically promoted the benefits that the latest techniques and gadgets offer.

Team Leadership Styles

Statistically, four team leadership styles distinguish successful from unsuccessful reengineering team leaders.

1. **Authoritative.** The authoritative leader continually communicates a vision of what the reengineering effort is trying to achieve and why it is critically important to the firm that it succeed. "Whys" tend to be either a great opportunity ("If we pull this off, we'll be number one in the world!") or a great threat ("If we don't make this work, in six months we will be out of business."). By contrast, unsuccessful reengineering leaders never made their vision clear—as measured by the clarity dimension of team members' organizational climate.

2. **Affiliation.** Superior reengineers cared about their people, supported them, and expressed personal concern and sympathy with the changes they were going through.

3. **Democratic Participative.** Superior reengineers welcomed input from all team members regardless of their position in the organization as well as from top executives and end-user customers. No good idea was ignored.

4. **Coaching.** Superior reengineers made many development opportunities available to their colleagues, including formal training in both hard and soft reengineering techniques and technologies (e.g., team building and LAN administration); they also provided advice and feedback to individual members to help them improve their performance.

Reengineering Team Climate

Organizational climate, usually measured by a survey, is employees' perception of organizational factors that predict performance. Successful reengineering efforts were predicated on four team climate dimensions:

1. **Standards.** Successful teams felt that the objectives for the reengineering effort were clear and challenging, and improvement against standards was continually encouraged.

2. **Clarity.** All members of successful teams, including executive sponsors and customer end users, were clear about the vision, importance, specific objectives, methods of the reengineering effort, and their roles and responsibilities.

3. **Rewards.** Successful teams believed that the team members who contributed the most to the team's success (by offering new ideas, working long hours, championing changes) received the most rewards by way of training opportunities, additional responsibility, celebration parties, and so forth.

4. **Team Commitment.** Members of successful reengineering teams expressed considerably higher levels of pride, loyalty, commitment, and discretionary effort exhibited by their willingness—over and above what was necessary to keep their jobs and collect their paychecks—to help the team succeed.

These competency research findings can be used for:

- Selection of managers to lead reengineering efforts.
- Training and development of reengineering team leaders and members to increase their likelihood of success.
- Competency-based performance management. Team leaders and members can be assessed and given feedback on which competencies and managerial styles make the difference between success and failure. Assessment data can be collected using 360-degree surveys (e.g., The Reengineering Team Readiness Questionnaire provided in Appendix A).
- Organization development. Instrumented feedback and problem solving based on survey data can be used to reintroduce, revitalize, or reinforce reengineering efforts.

COMPETENCIES FOR REENGINEERED FUTURE JOBS

Firms undergoing reengineering efforts must identify those employees who have the competencies to be successful in the future. Firms that are downsizing must identify the employees they will keep.

With reengineering, organizations change from:

- Hierarchical to flat.
- Functional to team processes.
- Command and control (bosses dictate, see Figure 7.6) to right-side-up (see Figure 7.7). Front-line workers are line self-managing work groups working for customers; bosses are supporting staff.
- Stable, fixed, and staffed mostly with full-time employees to temporary part- and full-time employees—along with vendors, customers, consultants, and contractors—who work together for a time on a specific project and then disperse (see Figure 7.8).
- Local and homogeneous to global and diverse.
- Slow, consistent, and regulated to fast, constantly changing, entrepreneurial, and innovative.

Jobs in these new organizations change dramatically for front-line employees, technical professional knowledge worker supervisors and middle managers, and executives.

Workers' Jobs Change from Simple to Complex.   Simple, narrow, task-oriented, single-function jobs are replaced by complex multidisciplinary, interpersonal skills-intensive "do the whole job for the customer" jobs. Reengineering results in jobs that involve significantly more initiative, problem solving, customer service

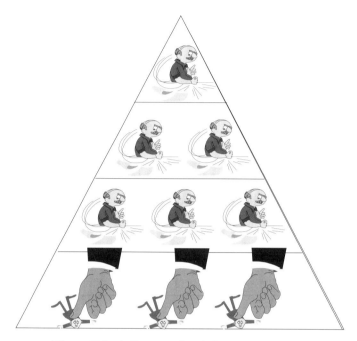

Figure 7.6   A Command and Control Hierarchy

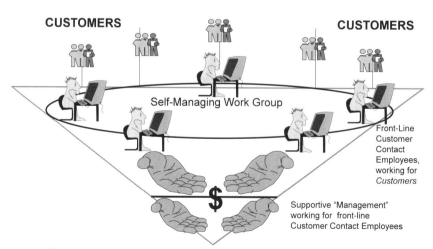

Figure 7.7   "Right-Side-Up" Bosses Are Supporting Staff

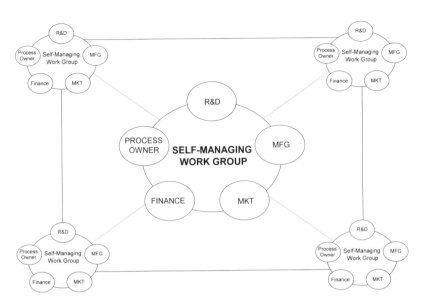

Figure 7.8 "Pepperonis" of Self-Managing Work Groups

orientation, interpersonal skills, selling skills, and data analysis skills. Customer Service Orientation implies a genuine desire to help others, a willingness to hear and understand customers' needs and take initiative to overcome obstacles in one's own firm to solve customer problems. Here are some examples.

From Furnace Fixers to Customer Service Reps

Utilities realized that blue-collar furnace-repair technicians call on numerous customers every day, and that a fixer's role could be reengineered to that of customer service representative. While fixing an ancient furnace a customer service rep could also sell to a homeowner:

"You know, this furnace is 30 years old and only about 40% efficient. Sixty cents of every dollar you spend fueling it is wasted. We now offer a small, clean porcelain furnace/heat pump that is 99+% efficient, and will not only heat you in winter but cool you in summer. We offer complete financing at a low 8.6% interest rate, and, because you own your home, you are already approved for a loan to buy the new heat pump/furnace. Your money will be repaid in less than three years—a 33% return on investment. This is probably the best financial investment you can make: You will earn a much higher rate of return than you can get from the bank—much more than the loan will cost you. And you'll be cool in the summer. Would you like to sign up?"

The obvious question for the utility: Which of its furnace fixers has the right stuff: motivation, interpersonal and selling skills, and ability to understand and communicate business and financial aspects of selling an investment?

From Computer Hardware Salespeople to Consultants

A major computer company realized that it could no longer compete in selling computer hardware, and that it was making more money selling services than selling "boxes." So the company repositioned itself to become a process reengineering consulting firm. Reegineering consulting competencies included higher levels of business analysis and conceptual thinking, team building, long-sales-cycle relationship and project management skills, and willingness to defer rewards. The firm found that only about a third of its salespeople—used to pushing hardware and getting an immediate commission payoff—had the conceptual, business, or interpersonal skills or the motivation to become consultants and "customer *relationship* managers."

From Managed to Self-Managing

Employees increasingly are working in self-managing work groups that hire their own members; choose their own suppliers; set their own goals for production, quantity, and quality; discipline one another; and determine one another's compensation and bonuses.

Competencies required of effective self-managing work group members include collaboration, team leadership skills, and commitment to the organization.

Collaborativeness is the ability to work cooperatively with diverse coworkers in multidisciplinary teams while exhibiting positive expectations of others and interpersonal understanding. For example, Saturn Motor Corporation's primary selection criteria for assembly line workers is not sensory motor skills or technical knowledge of car assembly but team collaborativeness.

Applicants are assessed in leaderless group exercises that simulate the kinds of decision making their self-managing work groups are expected to perform (selecting a supplier, disciplining a nonperforming teammate, solving a complex production problem). Saturn employees are trained and coached in interpersonal skills and team-building skills and are "performance appraised" by their teammates on the extent to which they help "produce a world-class car at a competitive price."

From Local and Homogeneous to Global and Diverse

Workers at every level will need to work effectively with colleagues regardless of gender, cultural background, or ethnicity. Multidisciplinary process teams developing products for sale in Asia, Eastern Europe, and Latin America will need members high in cross-cultural interpersonal sensitivity.

From Slow to Fast

Stable, regulated environments and long product life cycles are being replaced by ever faster, more competitive, more rapidly changing environments, technologies, products, services, organizational forms, and job demands.

Competencies that predict success in dealing with constant change include achievement motivation, flexibility, early adoption (feeling excited rather than intimidated by change), innovation, ability and motivation to learn, and entrepreneurial initiative.

Achievement motivation is the impetus for innovation and *kaizen*, the desire to continuously improve quality and productivity so as to meet, or even lead the ever increasing competition.

Flexibility/willingness to change is the predisposition to see change as an exciting opportunity rather than a threat (e.g., adoption of the new technology as "getting to play with the new gadgets"). A flexibility scale I have found useful has the following levels:

-2 Active resistance to change; cites union work rules or job description to justify flat refusal to change or adopt new technology.

-1 Passive resistance to change; when asked to change or use a new technology, does nothing, quietly refuses, waits for them or it to go away.

0 Neutral; neither positive nor negative toward changes or new technology; does what is told.

+1 Interest, receptivity; when hears a new change is coming, says: "Sounds great. When do I get to try it out?"

+2 Proactive learning or initiative to adopt; says, "If you'll give me a copy of the software, I'll take it home and play with it over the weekend." Does so, and on Monday morning uses the new software to produce the next report.

+3 Advocate for change; a missionary who leads or introduces colleagues to technologies new to the organization; says, "Boss, the program you want us to adopt is neat, but I saw even better software at a computer show I attended last weekend, which I want you to try. Let me show you this demo disk. I suggest we use this instead because it will increase our productivity even more. I've given demo disks to everybody in the work group."

+4 Invents new technology.

The degree of innovation at levels three and four of flexibility also can be scaled:

- New to the individual: Finding and adopting new software, for example, to help better maintain client or sales prospect contact lists.

- New to the work group: Champions an innovation, technology, or managerial method that changes how the entire group works.

- New to the organization: Introduces a change that impacts the entire organization.

- New to the industry: Identifies or develops a concept new to the industry, which gives the firm a competitive advantage.

Figure 7.9 shows these levels on a diffusion of innovations curve called a normal ogive (a bell-shaped curve with its right side flipped up). In this case, people likely to be superior performers in the future are the innovators—the inventors, discoverers, and advocates of new methods to improve productivity at the bottom left of the curve. They are the first 13.5% to lead or get to where the firm needs to go in the future.

Information Seeking/Ability and Motivation to Learn.   An obvious predictor of flexibility is genuine enthusiasm for opportunities to learn new technical and interpersonal skills. An example is the secretary, who when asked to learn a spreadsheet program and take on budget data analysis, welcomes this request as job enrichment rather than seeing it as an additional burden. This competency transcends computer literacy and other specific technical skills future workers are likely to need—it is the impetus for lifelong learning of any new knowledge or skill demanded by the changing requirements of future jobs.

Work Motivation.   Under time pressure, work motivation requires some combination of achievement motivation, flexibility, stress resistance, and organizational commitment that enables individuals to work under increasing demands for (new) products and services in ever shorter periods of time. Often expressed as "I work best under pressure; the challenge really gets my juices flowing."

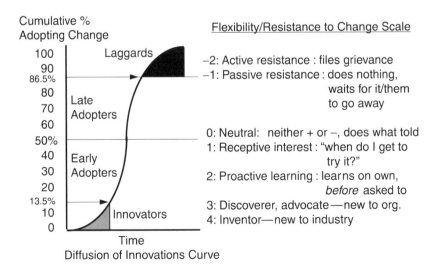

Figure 7.9 Diffusion of Innovations Curve

TECHNICAL PROFESSIONALS

From Individual Contributors to Team Players and Leaders

Reengineered work in process teams requires a much higher degree of teamwork and cooperation. A major example of this transition is in health care. Dr. Mark Bard, Chief of Medicine at Harvard Community Health has observed that the problem with reengineering in his field is that health care is a team activity filled with professionals trained as individual contributors. As discussed in Chapter 4, health care reengineering often requires physicians to reconceptualize their role from pure individual contributor to team leader 80% of the time, individual contributor only 20% percent of the time, and reallocate their efforts to coaching nurses and health care technicians in front-line delivery of service to patients. New competencies needed by physicians and nurses are interpersonal sensitivity, developing others, and team leadership.

From Individual Contributors to Consultants

HR legal, corporate planning, and marketing research staff who now work as individual contributors, will increasingly become consultants to line managers and employees. As part of their consultant role, technical professionals will become consumer guide compilers, purchasing agents, and resource brokers. No longer will corporate training/legal/marketing act as direct providers. Rather these functions and their professionals will advise line division groups as to which vendors to hire to meet their needs.

Competencies required to make this transition include consulting help desk skills and teaching and training competencies.

Knowledge Engineers

Technical professional practitioners also will increasingly become "knowledge engineers" who build expert systems or consult to those who do. Competencies to become expert system developers—for example, developers of interactive, multimedia training programs on CD-ROM to support distance learning—include a much greater degree of information technology knowhow, information seeking, conceptual thinking, and computer-programming skills.

Supervisors and Middle Managers

Perhaps the biggest change will come for managers and executives. Supervisors and middle managers traditionally plan, organize, motivate, control (check up on and reward or punish), and coordinate. In reengineered jobs and process teams empowered workers will perform all of these functions for themselves. What then is the role for managers in the future? First, they will be fewer.

From Dictators to Trainers, Coaches, and Consultants

Supervisors will change from directors and controllers to trainers, coaches, and consultants on the latest technologies and work flow methods.

This is the right-side-up organization and management concept described above. A manager's job is to support front-line workers and teams, who in turn provide service to customers. Good managers get resources for their teams, take care of team members, and shield the member from *administrivia* so they are not distracted by it. Competencies needed by supervisors and managers in reengineered organizations include:

Empowering.   Sharing information, soliciting coworkers' ideas, fostering employee development, delegating meaningful responsibility, providing coaching feedback, expressing positive expectations of subordinates irrespective of diversity differences, and rewarding performance improvement. Such managerial behaviors make employees feel more capable and motivate them to assume greater responsibility.

Team Facilitation.   Group process skills needed to get diverse groups of people to work together effectively to achieve a common goal: establishing goal and role clarity, designing effective work flow processes, controlling excessive talkers, inviting silent members to participate, resolving conflicts.

Flexibility.   As always, the willingness and ability to change managerial structures and processes to implement organization change strategies.

Change Implementation.   The ability to communicate to coworkers the need for change in the organization and facilitate training process to implement change in work groups.

Entrepreneurial Innovation.   The motivation to champion new products, services, and work flow processes.

Interpersonal Understanding.   The ability to understand and value the inputs of diverse workers.

Portability.   The ability to adapt rapidly and function effectively in foreign countries. Research indicates this competency is correlated with a liking for travel and novelty, resistance to stress, and cross-cultural interpersonal understanding.

Executives

Top management will change from controllers to leaders. The three most important competencies identified for executives of the future are:

Anticipatory Strategic Thinking. The ability to understand rapidly changing environmental trends, market opportunities, competitive threats, technological advances, and the strengths and weaknesses of their own firms in order to identify the optimum strategic response. The best executives have long time horizons—they see farther into the future and are capable of handling greater cognitive complexity.

Change Leadership. The ability to communicate a compelling vision of the firm's strategy, which arouses the motivation and commitment of its many stakeholders and makes adaptive responses appear both feasible and desirable. Executives must sponsor innovation and entrepreneurship and allocate company resources optimally to implement frequent changes.

Relationship Management. The ability to establish relationships with and influence complex networks of others whose cooperation is needed for the organization to succeed, and over whom the executive has no formal authority. These include product champions, customers, stockholders, labor representatives, government regulators at all levels, legislators, and interest groups in all countries around the world. Kotter has called this ability "spider web" management of a "dependency matrix," meaning all the competing individuals and groups the executive is dependent on to achieve his or her objectives.

WHAT PERCENTAGE OF THE EXISTING WORKFORCE CAN ADAPT TO REENGINEERED WORK?

A question I always put to my classes and clients is "What percentage of your employees can make the transition to do the reengineered work of the future?" Almost always the guesstimate is "about 50%."

My own experience coupled with reports in the business press of workers laid off as a result of reengineering, suggests a slightly more hopeful ratio, one that is analogous to findings on the outcomes of psychotherapy: One-third are cured, one-third are helped, and one-third show no change or get worse.

In the aftermath of reengineering, about one-third of existing employees are found to have the ability to learn and become fully effective—even superior—performers in the new work environment. Another third have sufficient competence to be effective enough to keep their jobs until retirement. A final third do not have the motivation or competencies to adapt and are candidates for early retirement or outplacement.

SUMMARY

They copied all they could, but they couldn't copy my mind;
And I left them sweating and stealing, a year and a half behind.
                                        — *Rudyard Kipling*

As Peter Drucker has repeatedly observed, in a fast-changing technological and business environment, the only sustainable competitive advantage is *people*. Every other competitive advantage—information technology, financial leverage, marketing methods—quickly will become obsolete or can be reverse-engineered if the competition is smart enough.

The only way a company stays ahead in the world of the future is to innovate faster than its competitors—and its core competence in being able to do so lies in the core competencies of its people. As emphasized in Chapter 1, reengineering HR is not just about cutting costs or heads in the HR function—it is about doing HR *better* to shift the competence curve of all of a firm's human assets to the right toward superior performance. The most important competitive advantage HR can offer is the ability to reliably select employees with competencies that predict superior performance, and continually (re)skill, motivate, and reward them to sustain performance at their highest level of competence.

PART
IV

Implementation

8

Implementing Reengineering Change Programs and Projects

Implementation of reengineering efforts is a play within a play. The larger play is of managing change: implementation of the *overall* or "macro" reengineering program including the effort's vision, plan, communication, implementation, dealing with resistance, sorting out, institutionalization, and acculturation.

The smaller play within is the implementation of *specific* reengineering projects, which involve visioning and scoping, planning, assessing, designing, developing, implementing, and improving a specific work flow process.

The relationships between the macro and micro reengineering change efforts are shown in Figure 8.1.

MACRO REENGINEERING STEPS

Vision

Top management must have a clear and compelling vision of what it wants the reengineering effort to achieve: the great opportunity—"if we succeed we'll be number one in the world," or the great threat—"if we don't succeed we'll be out of business in six months."

The vision must be feasible, desirable, and different from the status quo so that it energizes people to change. An effective vision is ambitious. It has

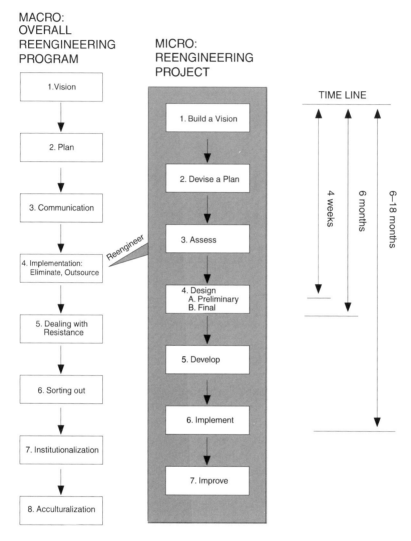

Figure 8.1 Macro and Micro Steps in Reengineering Change Programs

challenging if not radical goals (for example, to cut costs and cycle time to market by 50%). Vision can include consideration of the following:

- How the firm will interface with clients in the future.
- How employees will work with one another.
- The products or services the company wants to provide in the future, compared with the products or services the company offers now.
- Opportunities and threats in the environment.

- Strengths and weaknesses of the firm in human resources, technology, sales and marketing, manufacturing, and inbound and outbound logistics.[1]
- Critical Success Factors: the three to six things the firm must do well to succeed.

The vision statement should include the scope and priorities of the reengineering effort: which processes it will address first, and why, or processes with most impact on customer satisfaction.

Development of this vision typically takes about four months. Frequently outsiders—consultants and top executives who can provide perspective on how other companies have achieved success—help a firm develop its reengineering vision.

Plan

Good planning involves assessing the organization's readiness for change as well as determining the direction (top-down versus bottom-up participative) and pace (all at once versus incremental) of change. Good planning also allows for development of the reengineering organization (team selection and training) and development of the implementation plan itself (communications and provision of human, technology, finance, and other business resources).

Assessment of Organization Readiness

Planners are advised to do some market research. Most important is assessment of top management support: Are the CEO, president, and strategic vice presidents of key line and staff organizations truly committed to the reengineering effort?

Planners can conduct group sessions with employee end-users, customers, and other stakeholders likely to be affected by the reengineering effort. Planners can identify threats and opportunities to employees, union representatives, vendors, customers, and even political representatives of the local community. The sessions would provide a forum to minimize threats and emphasize opportunities, which may help gain stakeholder support as shown in Table 8.1.

Choice of Direction and Pace of Change

Change can be top-down, that is, driven by high-level management dictates and imposed by (external) consultants, or bottom-up participative, in which employees are invited to submit ideas for reengineering their own jobs and processes.

Reengineering usually is conducted as a top-down change process, dependent on top management vision, communication, and support and led by "SWAT" teams of dedicated work analysts because employees are considered unable to see radical alternatives to their present ways of working.

Current change theory agrees that both approaches are needed: Change is most likely when end-users are consulted (bottom-up), but meaningful change rarely succeeds without top management leadership and support.

Table 8.1 Stakeholder Threats and Opportunities

Stakeholder	Threats	Appeals to Minimize Threats	Opportunities	Appeals to Maximize Opportunities
Employees	Job loss	Re-skilling and placement in growing part of company	Better jobs	Higher wages; more interesting work; new skills, which increase chances of employment anywhere

The pace of change can be very rapid or phased in incrementally over a learning period.

The case for a big bang approach is that the disruption in processes, technology, and people are over with quickly rather than prolonging the uncertainty. Two examples of successful big bang change are Price Waterhouse and Holiday Inn.

Price Waterhouse moved abruptly over a weekend to place 10,000 computers on employees' desks. All paper supports were withdrawn. Everyone from the most senior partner to the lowest-level secretary had to go paperless and use a computer to do all their work. Employees who asked for their paper telephone directories found there were none. Computer-phobic managers who asked their secretaries to fill out time sheets or invoices found there were none. All employees were essentially asked to sink or swim—to learn to use the new technology on their own (a very rapid learning curve). Those who chose not to, resigned.

When British brewer Bass bought Holiday Inn, it appraised the Holiday Inn headquarters culture in Memphis as incapable of the radical change needed to improve productivity and customer service. Bass abruptly announced it was moving Holiday Inn's headquarters 900 miles to Atlanta—and declared all 2,500 headquarters jobs, from CEO to janitor, vacant. Any employee who wished to continue working for the firm had to compete for a new job at the Atlanta headquarters. Bass hired back 200 of those employees on the basis of achievement motivation and customer service orientation competencies, effectively laying off 92 percent of the firm's former staff.

The danger of big bang change is that it is high risk. During the disruptive period of change and learning, customer commitments can be missed and valuable employees lost.

A more conservative (and perhaps humane) change strategy is the incremental approach described earlier. Employees are consulted and change objectives communicated clearly by management. New processes and technology are phased in: run in parallel with the old processes while being debugged and while employees are being trained to do the new work. Transition from the old to the new system occurs only when everyone is confident that the new system will work as expected. Applicable to reengineering is the cautionary systems managers' rule: Don't unplug the mainframe until you are absolutely sure the client–server system works!

Reengineering Organization Development and Team Selection and Training

Research indicates that five roles are critical to the success of a reengineering effort.[2]

1. *Executive Sponsor:* A respected senior executive with the organizational influence to get resources for the reengineering team, convince other top managers to cooperate enthusiastically with the effort, and protect the reengineering program against inevitable attacks when it begins to bite.

2. *Champion or Entrepreneur:* The fanatic who leads the reengineering charge, works 16 hours a day to make it happen, and is a tireless missionary for technology and organizational change.

3. *Technical Experts:* Those who support the reengineering team. HR often supplies trainers, team-building facilitators, and organization development consultants. Other valuable help can come from Information Systems (network developers, administrators, and programmers), Finance (financial analysts to do activity-based costing, cost-benefit analyses, and return-on-investment analyses), Public Relations (development of employee communications strategy and materials), and if unionized employees will be affected, Legal and Labor Relations.

4. *Creative Innovators:* Discontinuous thinkers who provide an outside "radical" perspective and continually challenge reengineering team members to think outside the box about how work can be changed.

5. *Administrators:* People who keep the paperwork filled out correctly and keep the entrepreneur out of trouble. Administrators come in two flavors: nurturant and toxic. Nurturant administrators take care of all administrative functions and paperwork, figure out how to get needed resources no matter what, and to keep their teams from being distracted by administrivia. A nurturant administrator is invaluable.

   Toxic administrators get in the way. They burden the team with administrivia, pile on rather than cut through red tape, and blame others when they can't get needed resources. A toxic administrator is worse than none at all.

The Reengineering Team Readiness Index in Appendix A can be used to select team members with the competencies to succeed. Figure 8.2 shows the organization of a typical reengineering effort.

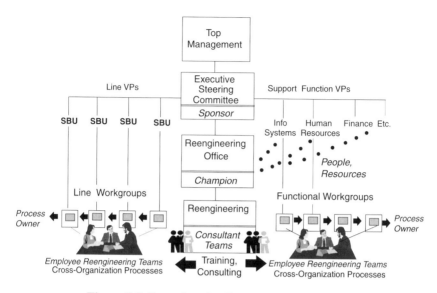

Figure 8.2 Reengineering Program Organizations

A top management steering committee chaired by the executive sponsor coordinates the effort. This committee includes key line and staff function vice presidents to ensure they support the effort and put the word out to their organizations that reengineering is coming and to enlist enthusiastic cooperation.

The reengineering office, headed by the champion, recruits a core staff of permanent reengineering consultants (often from external reengineering consulting firms). A minimum core staff of four is recommended to provide a self-sustaining critical mass. The core staff is supplemented by technical experts from line and staff functions (trainers from HR, LAN administrators from IS, financial analysts from Finance). Fast-track employees (up and coming MBAs) often do a one- to two-year development assignment in the reengineering office to give them wide exposure to the problems and opportunities in the firm, to introduce them to the cutting-edge technologies and management methods used in reengineering, and to develop their consulting interpersonal skills.

The reengineering office finds or develops tools and methods, deploys consultant teams to train and work with line and staff work group customers, and keeps score—evaluates and documents the adoption of new work flows and the time and cost savings these achieve. Evaluation helps reengineering consultants accumulate lessons learned and identify solutions that are transferable to other work group processes.

Reengineering consultant teams (usually teams of two) go out to work with line and function work groups or cross-organizational and cross-functional process teams charged with breaking down the organizational walls between steps in work flows. Reengineering consultants usually begin by conducting a "Reengineering Basics" seminar for the process owner and work group employees.

These awareness seminars are very useful for identifying employees for the employee reengineering teams who will do the actual reengineering work. I look for live ones: seminar participants who are excited by the ideas and rush up at the breaks exclaiming, "We could change to do it this way! And this! And this!" These enthusiasts are the work group's innovators and early adopters. Unless they are utter pariahs (the process owner will know which employees have peer credibility), their motivated self-selection should be recognized and used.

A process owner—a manager or team leader responsible for seeing that the work flow works and that line and function "silo" loyalties don't get in the way—is the reengineering consulting team's client. Process owners should combine the competencies of the executive sponsor and the champion; be respected by peers in other functional groups (whom they will have to coordinate); and be enthusiastic champions of the reengineering process. The Reengineering Team Readiness Index in Appendix A can be used to select process owners and employee reengineering team members.

Implementation Plan

The reengineering implementation plan includes:

Communications Planning.   The development of all communications methods and materials the firm will use to tell its employees about the reengineering effort, maximizing the opportunities and minimizing the threats.

HR Planning.   Figure 8.3 shows the principal levers HR can bring to bear on any organizational change: organization and job design, staffing/destaffing (recruitment, selection, succession planning, redeployment, and outplacement), performance management systems, training and development, compensation, employee assistance, employee and labor relations, and organization development interventions, and IHRMIS.[3]

Systems theory suggests that change is most likely to occur when all inputs are changed concurrently, reinforcing the change message sent by one another.

Figure 8.3 shows this principle using the analogy of tugboats (HR levers) trying to change the course of an organization oil tanker with great inertia. Tugs pushing and pulling in different directions exert no effective force for change. Tugs aligned, so their force vectors push in the same direction, exert considerable force. HR support for the reengineering effort using these levers includes:

- *Organization and job design:* As discussed in the previous chapter, reorganization into small, cross-disciplinary, cross-functional process workgroups and individuals empowered to "do it all" for a customer at the first point of contact.
- *Staffing/destaffing:* Recruitment, selection, succession planning, redeployment, and outplacement on the basis of competencies that predict superior

performance in reengineered jobs in the future—and contingency planning for those who do not. When downsizing is likely, organizations should develop very specific plans for how layoffs, severance, early retirement, and outplacement will be handled. Highly visible selection and advancement of persons who demonstrate competencies and lead (or at least support) the reengineering effort—and outplacement of those who resist—can send a powerful message.

- *Training and development:* Course development and delivery of reengineering awareness training (one hour, half day, one day) with briefings on the objectives and methods used in reengineering; and more technical training in activity-based costing, value, and work flow analysis for reengineering team members. Plans also should be developed for training employees in technical skills and competencies needed to do reengineered work in the future, for example in networking and software tools or selling and customer service skills.

- *Performance management:* Goal setting for radical improvements in productivity, quality, and cost reduction using reengineering methods, along with coaching feedback in support of these goals and performance reviews against results and competencies needed to be successful in reengineered work or jobs in the future.

- *Compensation:* Gain sharing for those who get reengineering results—and more radically, for competencies the firm will need in the future—and sanctions for those who actively or passively resist change.

- *Employee assistance:* Reengineering changes and the demands of new, more responsible jobs can cause employee stress. EA stress management,

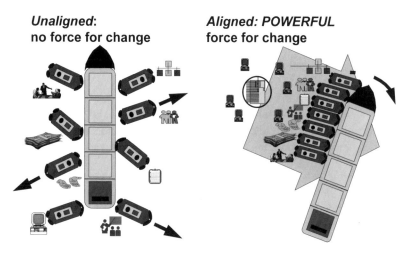

Figure 8.3 Alignment of HR Levers for Change

career and life planning, overcoming computer-phobia, and other programs can help employees adapt to new roles and ways of working.

- *Employee and labor relations:* Unions and other employee groups should be involved in reegineering planning from the beginning. Union support for the reengineering effort, often in return for guarantees against layoffs and (retraining for better future jobs, obviously increases the chances of success.

- *Organization development:* Team-building, survey-guided development and process consultation to help reengineering teams succeed and turn resistance to problem solving.

- *IHRMIS:* The "glue" and coordinating mechanism to ensure all HR activities use the same concepts and data, and to monitor employee development of competencies that predict economic outcomes and growth in competitive advantage.

Tables 8.2 and 8.3 provide an example of a professional service firm's incremental plan to use aligned HR levers to re-skill employees for computer literacy needed to reengineer its operations. This particular firm decided all its employees, from secretaries to managing partners, needed to be computer literate in the

Table 8.2 Computer Literacy Re-Skilling Objectives for Reengineering

IS APPLICATION	BASIC	INDEPENDENT	LEAD	ADVANCED
	-Use in simulated exercise, simple internal application	-Use in complex business application, client project -Demo, sell	-Train, install, support as mentor	-Program, develop
MS Office Word, [Excel, Powerpoint, Access, Mail, Notes, Network, etc.]	-Create business letter, memo	-Create multi-page proposal with graphics	-Train three employees to independent competence	-Program VBA macros to assemble compound documents
Firm Software Products	-Use internally	-Demo product to potential clients	-Train colleagues to use, demo -Train clients -Install on client systems	-Configure for client systems program interfaces, SQL calls to client mainframe or client/server

Table 8.3 HR Levers Aligned to Promote Employee Changes in Computer Literacy

HR LEVER	HR SERVICE	COMPUTER LITERACY CRITERIA
Organization & Job Design	Job and role descriptions; criteria for team membership	—Basic or independent level of computer literacy a stated requirement of job or role
Staffing/Destaffing	Recruit/Select/Hire	—Require basic computer literacy; select for enthusiasm, motivation for technology (professionals who are computer hobbyists, who write programs for fun) — Outplace employees who refuse to learn
	Promote/Succession Plan	—Not eligible unless have passed independent level of competence "Bonus points" for championing technology, mentoring others, leading reengineering innovation, IS stars clearly on fast track for promotion
Performance Management System	Development Objectives	—Goals for level of computer literacy (minimum: basic or independent) in *all* employees' performance objectives
Training & Development	Self-paced instruction	—Self-instruction materials available to all employees (e.g., excellent CAI tutorials included with MS Office applications)
	Seminars (used sparingly due to expense—and only when CAI programs aren't available)	—Advanced topics
	Designated mentors, tutors, PC gurus	—Role play demonstrations of software to clients before lead or advanced colleagues
Compensation/Reward	Carrot	—Pay for competence: bonus when attain higher level of computer competency
	Stick (deferred carrot)	—New hires: 80% salary until pass basic level of computer literacy —No bonus until pass computer competency objective level in Performance Plan
Org Development	Market research—ask consultant and support staff "customers": What is highest value to customer? What is highest value to firm? Venting/problem-solving sessions	—Percentage of employees at each level reaching computer literacy objectives —Qualified turnover (loss of employees the firm wants to keep)
HRMIS	Data collection at hiring, performance appraisal, after training	—Tracking of computer literacy competency level of all employees from all HR functions

application software the firm used in its daily operations (Microsoft Office, plus internal network and accounting programs) and the software it sold to its clients. Table 8.2 shows four levels of competence: basic, independent, lead, and advanced.

All employees were expected to achieve basic competence in four months and independent competence in one year, using the tutorials that came with the application software for on-line self-instruction, with coaching help from lead and advanced colleague mentors. Higher-level lead (install, train, mentor) and advanced (programmer) competence were optional extra credit levels of expertise rewarded but not required. CAI/IV tutorials and formal training courses were developed for the firm's software products.

Certification of competence was done by instructors and lead or advanced colleagues who observed professionals' demonstrations and use of software with clients.

Table 8.3 shows the HR Change Levers used to support and reinforce reskilling. As might be expected, employee resistance was greatest to the succession planning and compensation "sticks"—no promotion or bonus until computer literacy objectives were met. The "united front" and consistent message sent by all the HR levers prevailed in motivating most of the firm's employees to become computer literate.

Business Resources Planning.   The final HR support for the reengineering effort involves the development of budgets for computer equipment, networks, software, consultants, and other resources.

Communication.   Typical methods of announcing the reengineering effort include:

- Briefings for top executives, ideally by the CEO, the sponsor, and the champion who will lead the effort, to emphasize top management support and introduce key customers to the champion who will be working with them.

- Brochures, posters, and announcements by memo, in company media, and via e-mail.

- Training awareness workshops (e.g., one-hour, half-day, one-day introductions to reengineering concepts and methods).

- Videos, including the CEO's statement of commitment, an overview of the reegineering effort, and if possible, success stories of other firms.

The objective is to allay employee concerns about the reengineering effort, or more positively, to build a receptive, even enthusiastic audience for it, and market the services of the reengineering office and consultants. Evidence of communication campaign success is a large backlog of line and service groups clamoring for help from the reengineering office.

Implementation

Implementation begins with identification of key processes and process owners who will reengineer selection and training (perhaps simultaneously if training is used as a selection method) of employees who will participate in Employee Reengineering Teams (ERT).

Once the work flow process, process owner, and ERT members have been selected, the action moves to the play within the play: the seven steps in a specific reengineering project.

MICRO REENGINEERING

Project Implementation Steps

1. **Vision and Scope.** The reengineering consultants, process owner, and ERT begin by developing a vision for the specific work flow that will be reengineered. For example, the vision might involve reducing process time from two weeks to two days by having one empowered case manager handle the entire task on a PC.

2. **Plan.** The ERT identifies the roles and tasks of each of its members, decides on its work process, meeting times, and timeline of due dates and responsibilities.

3. **Assess.** This can be approached in one of two ways; predictably, reengineering experts differ on which is most effective. The first method involves flow charting and activity-based costing the existing work flow process, as described in Chapter 3. The advantage of this approach is that it gives all ERT members an in-depth knowledge of the work flow. It also frequently results in a motivating shock of recognition at the number of ridiculous, nonvalue-added steps; the amount of delay time in the present process; and the cost of the present process.

   The disadvantage of analyzing the existing work flow is that it may remind members of the existing constraints and so mire them in the existing cow path that they are blinded to seeing radically different ways to do the work. Close examination of a cow path inevitably leads to repaving it.

   The alternative is to start by asking what the ideal end state is for the customer (e.g., instantaneous, perfect service wherever the customer is), then brainstorming (assuming no constraints, a "magic wand") how this ideal end state could be provided. To stimulate discontinuous thinking, it is helpful to keep checking radical reengineering concepts: no work (customer DIY self-service); no paper (everything on-line on PC screens); no office (everyone has everything they need to work anywhere); no wait (instantaneous service); no travel (telecommunicating versus commuting or transport); and one person or team doing the entire task for the customer.

It is helpful to illustrate radical concepts with numerous succe~ amples from other work groups in the firm, other firms in the client ~ try, or world class firms in other industries who have been spectacula~ successful in employing one of the radical concepts under consideration. Success stories empower ERTs, giving people a sense that it can be done.

A useful aid for capturing creative ideas is to hang an "idea parking lot" flip chart in the ERTs work room to capture all improvement ideas as they arise. Anyone can add short statements to the flip chart at any time. Reengineering teams typically generate 50 to 100 improvement ideas during the first week.

Ideas for an ideal work flow should assume no constraints—or more positively, should assume all imaginable tools and permission:

- Any technology you can think of; an unlimited capital budget for computer gadgets and software.

- Enthusiastic acceptance by everyone: an organization, bosses, colleagues, workers, the union, and government regulators.

- Waiver of all rules, standard operating procedures, union contract provisions, laws, and constraints.

Only after the ideal work flow is charted and estimated for cost is the existing work flow charted and estimated for cost in order to compare proposed versus present cost–benefit and return on investment data. (An alternative is to have different teams brainstorm the ideal work flow and analyze the existing work flow.)

4. **Design.** After assessment, a detailed design is prepared for the reengineered work flow: charts of the proposed new work flow, descriptions of new jobs it will involve, and specifications for the new information systems—networks, hardware, and software it will use. The design document includes specific recommendations for both interim and final steps to achieve the desired new work flow.

Change recommendations are ranked on an Impact Changeability Analysis Report as shown in Table 8.4.

Table 8.4 An Impact Changeability Analysis Report

#	Change Recommendation	Reason	Impact Rating	Changeability Rating	Priority	Investment	Return
1	All management reports on screens	1,100 duplicate sets of paper reports/week @ $10/ea. × 50 weeks = $550,000 cost	1	2.5	1	Hardware: $100,000 Software: (Lotus Notes): $220,000 $320,000	$230K savings 72% ROI in Year 1
2							
3							

Impact is value-added to customers or to the business on a scale:

1 = considerable

2 = some

3 = little or none

Changeability rates how easy or difficult it is to make the change on a scale.

1 = Little or no effort: The existing team can make the changes themselves without higher-level approvals or additional capital investment in a relatively short period of time.

2 = Moderate difficulty: Some high-level approvals, organizational change, or approval and expenditure of capital investment budgets will be required; new hardware and software must be bought or developed; and/or employees will require training.

3 = Difficult: Major organization change will be required; several levels of higher-up approval will be needed; significant capital expenditures must be made in hardware and software; and/or extensive training or selection of workers with new competencies will be needed for the change to be successful.

As with activity value analysis, high priority recommendations are those with high impact and easy changeability.

Identification and implementation of interim steps are extremely important to maintain momentum. Managers and employees whose expectations have been raised by announcement of the reengineering effort expect to see change. The design team should ask: "What can we do *now* to begin improving things and start us moving toward the desired future system?"

Interim steps can include:

- Elimination of unnecessary, low value-added steps.
- Assessment of employees to see who has the competencies needed to do future jobs.
- Training in new software and hardware and work methods.
- Organizational changes to eliminate active and passive resisters or persons who lack the competencies to adapt to new reengineered jobs and work processes.
- Paper "low-fidelity" prototyping of forms and processes to be put on computer screens.
- Prototyping of forms processing on screens using fourth and fifth generation rapid application (RAD) software (Visual Basic, Power Builder,

or spreadsheets). These prototypes can be tested on small groups of end-users to refine the screen design user-friendliness.

■ Appropriate as opposed to high-tech electronic methods that do not require additional capital investments or budgets, for example, use of fax machines to move paper or enter survey data (a software program called Teleform turns any fax into an opscan, enabling users to turn paper survey forms into electronic data that can be entered directly into a computer for analysis).

■ Change in job designs (e.g., delegation of approvals down to teams and front-line workers).

■ Reassignment of tasks to less expensive workers (clerks and runners rather than professionals to get information or parts).

Typical timelines for these processes are shown in Figure 8.1. Steps 1, 2, and 3, and preliminary design can be accomplished in four weeks. It takes about six months to complete design specifications for new organizations and jobs; selection and training requirements for people who will do the reengineered work; reengineered work flows; technology (hardware, software development, etc.); and communications.

Final implementation of all HR and technology systems, including selection and training of employees, programming, testing, and validation of the new reengineered work flow(s) takes between six and eighteen months.

5. **Develop.** In the development phase, the human, technology, political, and organizational infrastructure is created to support the new work flow process.

Human Resources tasks include job/team design, staffing, development of education and training programs and employee training in whatever new competencies, interpersonal skills, and technology (e.g., use of new software programs) they will need to work in the reengineered process.

Information Systems tasks include purchasing equipment (PCs and servers); developing and testing networks; installing software purchased or developed using rapid application development (RAD) cycles of quick prototyping; usability testing, development, and final testing.

Finance tasks include developing budgets and getting approvals for needed investments. Other final implementation supports developed can include:

■ Interactive video/computer-assisted instruction programs for training employees at remote sites (a process that increasingly involves translating software and training materials into foreign languages).

■ Development of complete competency-based HR systems: staffing/destaffing, performance management, compensation IHRMIS.

■ Expert performance support systems to support front-line workers.

- Organizational changes to create self-managing, multidisciplinary process teams.

- Decentralization to front-line customer service organizations.

- Technical transfer to clients of routine delivery of HR services and advice.

6. **Implement.** In the implementation stage, the new work flow process is piloted and adjusted as described in Chapter 3. Often the new process is run in tandem with the old work flow process until management is confident the new system works. When this confidence level is reached, formal "cutover" of all work to the new system occurs, and the old work flow process is abandoned.

7. **Improve.** The new process is evaluated and progressively refined, using customer and end-user feedback as well as incremental TQM methods such as statistical process control and kaizen problem-solving groups). These groups may include members of the ERT. Improvement phases are driven, reinforced, and celebrated by measurement and feedback systems (for example, large trend graphs hanging on walls in public spaces) seen by every employee every day, which track how cycle time or costs have been reduced or how customer satisfaction has improved.

With the completion of these seven steps, specific reengineering projects—the smaller plays—rejoin the larger play, the implementation of the firm's (or HR functions') reengineering program.

Continuous evaluation of hard data—reduction in costs and cycle time as well as improvements in productivity and customer satisfaction resulting from reengineering projects—is a critical part of the larger reengineering program. The reengineering office should keep score by tallying average and total time, cost savings, and other benefits from all reengineering projects implemented. These results should be reported to top management regularly to sustain support for the reengineering program.

Dealing with Resistance

A new work flow process is announced, the new technology appears on everybody's desk—and nothing happens. Employees sit on their hands or other parts of their anatomy and wait for it all to blow over, assuming that reengineering is just one more fad and that if waited out, like all its predecessors, it will go away.

The basic way to deal with resistance is to train (convert) or replace. Training can take the form of problem-solving workshops followed by specific technical training, and the managerial, team-building, goal and role clarification, and conflict resolution sessions described later in Step 6.

Problem-solving workshops provide an opportunity for venting, participation, recommunicating the objectives of the reengineering effort, and dealing with implementation problems. The workshop can begin with open-ended questions to employees: What do you like about the new work flow or technology? What don't you like about it? What additional information do you need? Employees are encouraged to state their objections, which are recorded on a flip chart in an open, supportive, and accepting way. The workshop facilitator can then ask employees to recommend ways to overcome each of their obstacles—thus putting the energy of resistance into problem-solving.

Problem-solving workshops can be followed by more in-depth technical training such as computer or interpersonal skills needed to perform new reengineered jobs.

Sorting Out

For employees, the sorting-out phase means finding a new place in the new work organization—or leaving. HR services can facilitate this process.

Goal and role clarification workshops, team building, and conflict resolution sessions help people identify what they like and do well, what they don't like and don't do well, and how they will work with colleagues. Tough-minded role negotiation exercises help team members tell their colleagues what they can begin to do, do more of or do better, continue doing, do less of, or stop doing to help them and the team accomplish the new work objectives.

Statement of clear goals for performance and competence development and change, either by colleagues in the self-managing work group (preferred) or by management. Career and life planning seminars, either organization- or employee-driven, can help employees consider their career path options using competency-based job/person matching systems. And finally, outplacement services and early retirement assistance can be made available to help those whose competencies don't fit the firm's future find employment elsewhere (see Chapter 10).

Institutionalization

Institutionalization involves "formalization" of process, technology, and HR systems to support the new reengineered workplace.

Processes and technology can be documented in standard operating procedure manuals (ideally on-line, as just-in-time training or performance support systems job aids instantly available to employees as they work). Reengineering usually is so grounded in technology changes that institutionalization of new processes is built into the hardware and software itself. Employees may be able to maintain shadow paper systems and files, but for the most part they'll have to use the new systems because there is no other way to do the work.

Human resources levers (discussed earlier) are institutionalized to support, measure, reward, and reinforce employees doing the reengineered work.

Organization and Job Design

New job (or role) descriptions and career paths are developed and documented to reflect the flattening of the firm; reorganization of work into small, cross-disciplinary, cross-functional process teams; and increased responsibility of individual employees empowered to "do it all" for customers.

Staffing/Destaffing

Recruitment, selection, succession planning, redeployment, and outplacement systems are developed to continuously select (and deselect) for competencies that predict superior performance in reengineered future work. Staffing may simply be outsourced. If done internally, HR staffs and line managers are trained in competency assessment and HR management methods. Highly visible advancement of persons who demonstrate these competencies and lead (or at least support) the reengineering effort. Downsizing methods—layoffs, severance, early retirement, and outplacement—are formalized and implemented.

Performance Management

Systems and forms are changed to include employee goals for *radical* improvements in productivity, quality, and cost reduction using reengineering methods. Managers provide coaching feedback in support of these goals. Performance reviews measure employees against results and competencies needed to be successful in reengineered work or jobs in the future.

Training and Development

In an environment of ever faster technological and business change, firms must become continuous-learning organizations; training also must become a continual task. Firms need to develop procedures for ongoing training needs assessment, design and development of just-in-time on-line CAI/IV training, and identification of outsourcing vendors of these services. Continuous learning becomes every employee's responsibility, aided by on-line and outsourced providers of up-to-the-minute training.

Compensation and Benefit Systems

These are changed to reward employees who get reengineering results, for example, by gain sharing or, more radically, by putting employees in business for themselves. One food and beverage distributer turned its delivery employees, who formerly restocked supermarket shelves for a fixed wage, into entrepreneurial salespeople by selling their trucks and routes to them, wholesaling products to them, and making them proprietors of their own businesses, responsible for marketing, sales, customer relations, accounting, vehicle maintenance, and so on. The compensation plan became whatever profits they could make as sole proprietors.

Increasingly, forward-looking companies are adopting competency-based pay—pay for the skills and characteristics of people that predict performance in future roles, rather than a salary for a specific job—which in a highly volatile environment may not exist in six months. Pay for demonstrated achievement motivation or customer service orientation is almost certainly an HR trend for the future.

Employee Assistance

Stress management and adaption to change counseling services are maintained to help employees cope with on-going change.

Employee and Labor Relations

New work rules, "bumping" rights, and re-skilling training agreements are written into union contracts; grievance and ombudsman processes are established for workers displaced by reengineering.

Organization Development

Team-building, survey-guided development and process consultation are institutionalized as services available to process and reengineer teams to help them adapt—or better, proactively see the need for, plan and initiate—change, turn resistance to problem solving, and collaborate effectively.

IHRMIS

The institutionalization of an IHRMIS as part of a reengineering effort helps coordinate the HR levers discussed above to ensure that all provide maximum and aligned influence to help people change in the ways necessary for successful reengineering. The IHRMIS provides the coordinating "glue" which insures that all HR activities use the same concepts and data, and monitors employee development of competencies that predict economic outcomes and growth in competitive advantage.

Acculturation

In the final phase of the reengineering effort, new organizations, reengineered work flows, competencies, compensation, and reward systems all become an ingrained part of the firm's culture. "We are reengineered, innovative, high-tech, state-of-the-art, lean, and mean" is the self-image shared by the firm and its employees. Acculturation is facilitated by communications programs that provide:

- *Symbols.* Insignia on T-shirts, badges, caps, buttons (e.g., "Radical improvements accomplished here!").
- *Celebrations.* Reward ceremonies with gifts, especially high-tech toys: new software, the latest and fastest computers for successful team members and teams.
- *Heroes and heroines.* Acknowledgment of successful process owners (astute reengineers always let the process owner/customer take the credit),

champions, technical experts, and creators who have contributed significantly to reengineering efforts; extolled in e-mail, company publications, and videos.

ENDNOTES

1. Porter, M. (1985). *Competitive Advantage*, New York: Free Press/MacMillan, p.46.

2. Dalziel, M. And Schoonover, S. (1988). *Changing Ways*, New York: American Management Association.

3. Spencer, L. (1994). The right stuff for the new dynamic. In Berger, L and M. Sikora. (1994). *The Change Management Handbook: A Roadmap to Corporate Transformation*. New York: Irwin.

9

Making the Business Case for Human Resources Reengineering

Making the business case means providing management with cost benefit and return on investment data in hard economic terms: dollars made or saved to justify costs of reengineering. Costs include capital investment in computers and networks as well as human investment in programming, software development, and training.

There are two ways to make more money in business. One is to cut costs, either by reducing the expense of producing products and services or the costs of (poor) quality. The other is to increase revenues, either by increasing sales or increasing prices. The ability to get a higher price in the market also depends on product or service quality.

Of the two options, reengineering is most often justified by cutting costs and improving productivity. Does it work? Studies reported in Personnel Journal[1] found reengineering resulted in an average of 67% headcount and 58% cost savings. Typical results included:

Firm	Headcount Reductions	Cost Reductions
Florida Power & Light	50%	NA
IBM	78% (573 to 125)	75%
Sears	73% (3,300 to 900)	40%

Firms eliminated 27 percent (12 of an average 55) HR processes cut process cycle times from 50 percent to 99.9 percent.

Table 9.1 provides a fairly comprehensive example of a reengineering cost–benefit analysis in a major Fortune 500 corporation. Data are normalized to an employee population of 100,000. This focus of the firm's reengineering effort was replacement of separate legacy mainframe databases, all using different hardware and software, for payroll, retiree benefits, general employee data, training, educational assistance, union and grievance data, plus a separate database in Europe for international employees, with World-Wide IHRMIS, or WWIHRMIS (pronounced "We Hermes").

Four categories of savings from reengineering are indicated by the column heading across the top of Table 9.1. There are:

1. Productivity savings from reengineering:
   - Elimination of no- or low-value-added products or services.
   - Improved quality and reduced rework.
   - Reengineering process improvements (e.g., do-it-yourself, on-screen data entry by manager and employee "customers").
   - Other.

2. Sourcing Savings:
   - Outsourcing HR services provision.
   - Insourcing—provision of HR services previously outsourced because the reengineered WWIHRMIS actually enabled the firm to provide or make services more cheaply and at higher quality than it could buy them from vendors

3. Information Systems Savings:
   - Reduced maintenance of existing legacy systems, the most frequent cost saving from reengineering information technology and organizations.

The objective of the WWIHRMIS was to develop a single HR database that served all HR and management reporting needs worldwide. Problems with the legacy HR system included:

- separate HR payroll systems resulting in redundant data and inconsistent reporting.
- old technologies.
- incompatible data files.
- inefficient batch processing—all data was submitted on paper and no services were interactive on-line or in real time.
- centralized input and output.
- incompatibility between U.S. and international data.

The organization realized its future HR environment would be dynamic, with increasing client demands for service under severe time pressure (i.e., managers and employees needed on-line, instantaneous access to current HR data everywhere in the world). Consolidation and downsizing the many duplicated mainframe legacy systems into a network client–server system was expected to enable the firm to cut annual payments to vendors for maintenance of aging hardware and software.

4. Other savings:

■ Materials costs of paper, sextuplicate forms, computer printouts, and mail handling and postage (physical transport of paper within the firm or among its sites using national postal services).

Potential savings were classified by finance as either cash savings ("real money") from reduced payments to vendors for services, supplies, and computer maintenance contracts, or non-cash savings from reduced full-time equivalent (FTE) labor involved in low productivity HR paperwork processing and error correction.

The firm anticipated a five-year investment and payback cycle starting in 1994, with benefits accruing over four years, as shown in Table 9.2.

The rows in Table 9.1 show the savings from implementation of the WWIHRMIS system. These numbers were developed by employee teams of HRIS professionals from each HR function or service office coordinated by a central HR data advisory panel, supplemented by internal and external reengineering consultants. Each employee team was charged with doing a before-versus-after work flow analysis and activity-based costing cost–benefit analysis of how reengineering would change how the firm delivered services, and the time, cost, and full-time equivalent labor savings expected.

Examples in the benefit rows include savings from

1. HRIS data input and output:

■ Customer do-it-yourself (DIY), on-screen versus manual paper data entry.

■ Reduced duplicate data entry. Because any data entry updates the entire system, no function or department ever has to enter data twice.

■ Reduced reconciliation by HRIS, payroll, managers, and employees checking duplicate data that don't match, identifying which data are accurate, and bringing all systems into agreement.

■ Reduced rework and lost productivity due to data entry errors and delays: paychecks going to old addresses and incorrect termination numbers entered.

■ DIY on-screen and voice-response versus manual data inquiries by managers and employees, including on-screen versus manual report and organizational chart generation. Note: *$11+ million savings*, almost half the annual savings from the entire reengineering effort, is achieved by letting managers and employees get HR data at their own workstations.

Table 9.1 Reengineering HR Business Case

BENEFIT DESCRIPTION	Productivity Reengineering Savings				Sourcing Savings		Information Systems Savings		Other Savings		TOTAL SAVINGS						
	Product/Service Elimination	Quality: Reduced Rework	Process Improvement	Other	Outsource	Insource	Reduced Maintenance	Other	Materials	Other	Cash Savings	FTE Positions Saved	Average Annual Salary + Benefits per FTE	Non-cash Savings	Total Annual Savings	Years	Total Savings (Years × Annual Saving)
1. HRIS DATA INPUT/OUTPUT																	
A. DIY on-screen vs. manual paper data entry			$267									6.7	$40	$267	$267	4	$1,069
B. Reduced duplicate data entry			$501									12.5	$40	$501	$501	4	$2,004
C. Reduced reconciliation by HRIS, payroll, managers, employees		$209										3.5	$60	$209	$209	4	$835
D. Reduced rework, lost productivity due to data entry errors and delays		$1,253										20.9	$60	$1,253	$1,253	4	$5,010
E. DIY on-screen, VR vs. manual response to data inquiries by managers, employees (all policy, employee manuals, directories, advisories, etc., on line			$6,012						$250		$250	100.2	$60	$6,012	$6,262	4	$25,048
F. DIY on-screen/auto vs. manual report generation			$5,010									83.5	$60	$5,010	$5,010	4	$20,040

E. DIY on-screen/auto vs. manual organization chart generation	$225				3.8	$60	$225	$225	4	$902
F. Consolidation of US and International HRIS		$1,670		$1,670					4	$6,680
2. EMPLOYMENT										
A. Work force planning: data on-line vs. manual retrieval	$100				1.7	$60	$100	$100	4	$401
B. Employee tracking: data on-line vs. manual retrieval	$150				3.8	$40	$150	$150	4	$601
C. INTERNAL SEARCH: Reduce costs of external search by better identification of internal candidates		$300		$300			$0	$300	4	$1,200
D. PROMOTION REVIEWS: All data, approval paperwork on-line; exception controls in system	$501				8.4	$60	$501	$501	4	$2,004
E. Transaction Paperwork: Reduced document handling by secretaries	$301				7.5	$40	$301	$301	4	$1,202
Reduced mailing and filing of forms	$200		$10		5.0	$40	$200	$200	4	$802
F. Position Control: Elimination of redundant data on positions	$100				2.5	$40	$100	$100	4	$401
Improved budgetary control: matching employees vs. authorized headcount	$752				18.8	$40	$752	$752	4	$3,006
Reduced reconciliation of job analysis and evaluation data	$209				5.2	$40	$209	$209	4	$835

Table 9.1 (Continued)

BENEFIT DESCRIPTION	Productivity Reengineering Savings				Sourcing Savings		Information Systems Savings		Other Savings		TOTAL SAVINGS						
	Product/Service Elimination	Quality: Reduced Rework	Process Improvement	Other	Outsource	Insource	Reduced Maintenance	Other	Materials	Other	Cash Savings	FTE Positions Saved	Average Annual Salary + Benefits per FTE	Non-cash Savings	Total Annual Savings	Years	Total Savings (Years × Annual Saving)
3. PAYROLL																	
A. Consolidation of Payroll reporting: reduced manual preparation by managers			$134									3.3	$40	$134	$134	4	$534
4. OTHER EMPLOYEE DATA																	
A. EXECUTIVE DATA: On-line resumes and reports			$25									0.6	$40	$25	$25	4	$100
B. RETIREE DATA: DIY on-line, VR access of information			$150									3.8	$40	$150	$150	4	$601
Automated maintenance of name & address files, mailings			$27									0.7	$40	$27	$27	4	$107
Automated reporting			$25									0.6	$40	$25	$25	4	$100
5. BENEFITS ADMINISTRATION																	
A. Eliminate 3rd Party Benefits Administrator						$2,625					$2,625			$0	$2,625	4	$10,500

Item				Ratio				Qty	Total
B. AUTOMATE: On-screen data entry, reporting Consolidated, automated reporting (vs. manual)	$50			1.3	$40	$50	$50	4	$200
Automated notifications of changes	$60			1.5	$40	$60	$60	4	$240
DIY on-screen, VR response to employee inquiries	$501			8.4	$60	$501	$501	4	$2,004
Reduced errors→fewer disputes		$63		1.6	$40	$63	$63	4	$251
C. HEALTH INSURANCE Timely, accurate carrier data reporting→reduced data reconciliation, benefit payments to ineligible employees		$251		6.3	$40	$251	$251	4	$1,002
6. COMPENSATION									
A. CONSOLIDATED NON-EXEMPT SALARY PLANNING AND IMPLE-MENTATION Automated salary planning and reporting (vs. manual)	$200			5.0	$40	$200	$200	4	$802
Automated salary imple-mentation (direct link to payroll system)	$126			3.2	$40	$126	$126	4	$504
B.INCENTIVE COMPENSA-TION SYSTEM Report consolidation and automation	$38			1.0	$40	$38	$38	4	$154
Reduced (duplicate) systems maintenance			$38			$0	$38	4	$150

189

Table 9.1 (*Continued*)

BENEFIT DESCRIPTION	Productivity Reengineering Savings				Sourcing Savings		Information Systems Savings		Other Savings		TOTAL SAVINGS						
	Product/Service Elimination	Quality: Reduced Rework	Process Improvement	Other	Outsource	Insource	Reduced Maintenance	Other	Materials	Other	Cash Savings	FTE Positions Saved	Average Annual Salary+Benefits per FTE	Non-cash Savings	Total Annual Savings	Years	Total Savings (Years × Annual Saving)
7. UNION RELATIONS																	
A. Grievance/Disciplinary Action Tracking			$104									2.6	$40	$104	$104	4	$418
B. BID-BUMP Job Posting Automation			$501									12.5	$40	$501	$501	4	$2,004
8. HOURLY ATTENDANCE TRACKING Automate tracking system			$752									18.8	$40	$752	$752	4	$3,006
Improved attendance (due to timely identification and correction of attendance abuses)		$334										8.4	$40	$334	$334	4	$1,336
9. INTEGRATED TRAINING DATA: PROGRAM REGISTRATION & COMPLETION							$55				$55						
A. Reduction in (duplicate) systems maintenance														$0	$55	4	$220

B. Automated vs. manual registration of trainees			$1,825									45.6	$40	$1,825	$1,825	4	$7,300
C. Auto (vs. manual) report preparation			$80									2.0	$40	$80	$80	4	$320
10. SECURITY ADMINISTRATION																	
A. Assign, track employee security clearances, passwords			$301									7.5	$40	$301	$301	4	$1,202
B. Site Security: inspection data, reports on-line			$106									2.6	$40	$106	$106	4	$422
TOTALS	$0	$3,069	$18,373	$0	$0	2,925	$1,763	$0	$260	$0	$4,938	421.0		$21,442	$26,379	4	$105,517
%	0%	12%	70%	0%	0%	11%	7%	0%	1%	0%	19%			81%	100%		
Saving/Employee/Year											$49			$214	$264		

Table 9.2 Reengineering HR Business Case Return on Investment (ROI) Analysis

Capital	1994	1995	1996	1997	1998	Total
Central IS Hardware	$ 775					$ 1,150
PCs (@$3K/employee × 1000)	$ 3,000					$ 3,000
Total Capital	$ 3,775	$ 125	$ 125	$ 125	$ 125	$ 4,150
Depreciation Tax Benefit (10%)	$ (378)	$ (13)	$ (13)	$ (13)	$ —	$ (415)
Total Capital Cash Outlay	$ 3,398	$ 113	$ 113	$ 113	$ —	$ 3,735
Expenses						$ —
Software & Programming	$ 2,393	$ 685	$ 720	$ 755		$ 4,553
HR and Finance (Payroll)	$ 5,458	$ 2,363	$ 2,305	$ 2,605		$ 12,730
Total Expenses	$ 7,850	$ 3,048	$ 3,025	$ 3,360		$ 17,283
Total Cash Outlay	$ 11,248	$ 3,160	$ 3,138	$ 3,473	$ —	$ 21,018
Cost Per Employee/Year	$ 112	$ 32	$ 31	$ 35	$ —	$ 210
Total Cost Employee (94–98)						
Ratio: Soft Costs:Total Costs	30%	4%	4%	3%		18%
Ratio: Capital:Total Costs	70%	96%	96%	97%		82%
Total Cash Benefits		$ 4,938	$ 4,938	$ 4,938	$ 4,938	$ 19,752
Total Cash Savings	$(11,248)	$ 1,778	$ 1,801	$ 1,466	$ 4,938	$ (1,266)
Discount Factor (10%)	1.00	0.91	0.83	0.75	0.68	
Net Present Value	$(11,248)	$ 1,616	$ 1,488	$ 1,101	$ 3,373	$ (3,669)
NPV 1994–1998	$ (3,669)					
Return On Investment (ROI)	–33%					
Total Cash & Non-Cash Benefits	$ —	$26,379	$26,379	$26,379	$26,379	$105,516
Net Total Savings	$(11,248)	$23,219	$23,242	$22,907	$26,379	$ 84,499
Discount Factor at (10%)	1.00	0.91	0.83	0.75	0.68	
Net Present Value	$(11,248)	$21,108	$19,208	$17,210	$18,017	$ 64,296
NPV 1994–1998	$ 64,296					
Return On Investment (ROI)	572%					

- Consolidation of U.S. and international HRIS saves $1.67 million in reduced cost of maintaining duplicated mainframe systems.

2. Employment:
   - Work-force planning: data on-line versus manual retrieval.
   - Employee tracking: data on-line versus manual retrieval.
   - Internal search: reduced external head hunter fees by better identification of internal candidates using the WWIHRMIS, an insourcing cash, real-money benefit.
   - Promotion reviews: all data and approvals on-line, replacing manual paperwork with exception controls built into the systems so that human review and approval is triggered only 5% of the time when a promotion clearly violates a HR or business rule.
   - Transaction paperwork reduction. Document handling by secretaries and reduced mailing and filing of forms, including mail and form paper and printing cash savings.
   - Position control. Elimination of redundant data on positions and improved budgetary control. Matching employees to authorized head count and reduced reconciliation of job analysis and evaluation data.

3. Payroll:
   - Consolidation of payroll and HRIS reporting and reduced manual preparation of reports by managers.

4. Other employee data:
   - Executive data, on-line resumes, and reports for succession planning versus manual retrieval.
   - Retiree data: DIY on-line and voice-response access of information. Automated maintenance of retiree name and address files and mailings.
   - Automated reporting on benefit use by retirees.

5. Benefits:
   - Elimination of a third-party benefits administration vendor by insourcing the service, saving $2.625 million cash annually because the WWIHRMIS provides benefits administration more cheaply than the vendor can.
   - The automated benefits administration capabilities of the WWIHRMIS enabled the firm to consolidate and automate reports and notification of changes; provide DIY on-screen and voice-response answers to employee inquiries; and by improving quality, reduce errors and disputes.
   - Health insurance. More timely and accurate data reporting reduced data reconciliation time and costs and benefit payments to ineligible employees, former employees, and dependents.

6. Compensation:

- Consolidation of nonexempt salary planning and implementation using automated versus manual report generation for salary planning and automated salary implementation via direct link to the payroll system.

- Report consolidation and automation of incentive compensation, and reduced duplicate systems maintenance.

7. Union relations:

- Automation of grievance and disciplinary action tracking with on-screen, on-line entry of grievances.

- On-line "bid-bump" job posting (displaced union employees with seniority's right to "bid" for and "bump" less senior employees' out of jobs), reducing grievances caused by poor administration of the bid-bump process.

8. Hourly attendance tracking:

- Automation of the tracking system and improved attendance due to timely identification and correction of attendance abuses.

9. Integrated training data—on-line program registration and completion tracking:

- Reduction in duplicate systems maintenance and automated versus manual registration of trainees and report preparation.

10. Security administration:

- Assignment and tracking of employees' security clearances and passwords, on-screen and on-line; and on-screen versus paper recording of site security inspection and reporting data.

Table 9.1 contains interesting data about HR reengineering benefits. Notice that:

- No products or services were eliminated—no existing HR services were found to be of low or no value.

  "Quality is free." Reduced rework accounted for 12% of savings, roughly $3 million a year.

  Reengineering improvements accounted for $18 million, 70% of total benefits, mostly from enabling DIY customer data entry and retrieval.

  There were no benefits from outsourcing; in fact, no services were outsourced! Eleven percent of benefits, almost $3 million in cash savings (real money) came from *insourcing* services previously outsourced.

  Information systems savings from moving off antiquated mainframes to client–server systems accounted for $1.7 million, 7% of total savings.

  Material and other out-of-pocket cost savings (e.g., mail and postage) provided only 1% of total savings.

Cash (real money) savings were $4.9 million, 19% of total savings.

Noncash savings, $21.4 million, accounted for 81% of total savings.

Implications

Head Count Implications. At an average annual salary of $50,831, noncash savings of $21.4 million translate into 421 full-time equivalent (FTE) positions saved.

HR Head Count Implications. The firm had employed about 1,000 HR staff (the usual ratio of HR staff to total employees of about 1 to 100). The potential of saving 421 FTE positions implies the firm could cut its HR staff by 42% —if one assumes that all positions saved by reengineering are HR employees. In fact, as shown in Chapter 1, many of the "middle people" who go away when HR is reengineered are secretaries and middle managers: typers of forms and checkers and approvers. Although some HR generalists and data entry clerks will go away, 67% of positions saved are likely to be line and support personnel. Only 33% of the 421 FTEs, 139 heads, or 14% of the firm's HR staff, are likely to be redeployed or let go—a far lower percentage than the 50% across-the-board head count reductions usually cited as in store for HR.

Span of Control. Coordination, or service implications: The $67\% \times 421 = 282$ FTE line and support positions savings offer the opportunity for increased managerial spans of control (or coordination and service). With less HR administrivia to worry about, a manager who previously had ten employees reporting to him or her, can now have 15. Secretaries can similarly increase their spans of service (e.g., serve five managers instead of one or two, or 30 departmental employees instead of 15 or 20).

As comprehensive as this business case appears (it took the firm several person-years of effort with the assistance of various internal and external consultants), most members of the advisory committee suspected it understated the potential cost savings of HR reengineering. Numerous HR functions were not included (e.g., medical services).

Table 9.2 shows a return on investment analysis for the HR reengineering. The firm assumed an $11 million investment in hardware and software (software programming, HR and Finance personnel training) costs in 1994, with additional investments spread out over 1995 to 1998, and benefits accruing in 1995 to 1998.

Capital investments in central IS hardware (servers, network cabling, communications equipment, routers, and the like) were estimated to cost $1.125 million. Like most organizations, the firm had many employees, including almost all managers, who already had PCs—albeit PCs of various incompatible types and ages (old IBM XTs, ATs, and Apple Macintoshes). The firm's plan was to standardize on IBM-compatible PCs, costing approximately $3,000 per person for a Windows-capable 486 with communications hardware, Ethernet cards and software (Microsoft Office™ and Novell Netware 3.11™). The firm assumed that it would need to buy 1,000 additional PCs to be sure that every department had at least one PC that could serve as a public HR workstation or kiosk. Investment in PCs in 1994 was estimated to be $3 million. Total capital investment was $4.150 million, although depreciation tax benefits (estimated at about 10 percent, assuming straight line depreciation over three years, 33 percent per year multiplied by a 33 percent effective corporate tax rate) reduced this net cash investment $415,000. Net estimated capital cash outlay investment in the reengineering effort was $3.735 million.

The firm estimated it would incur significantly greater software programming and training expenses in HR and Finance over the four years. Note that the ratio of software and soft personnel costs (70%) to hardware costs (30%) is more than 2 to 1 in 1994. In later years, hardware capital investment drops to 4 percent to 5 percent of total investment each year. Total cost per employee for the reengineered HR system, 1994 to 1998, is approximately $210.

Benefits are divided into cash savings benefits and total cash and noncash benefits. Cash benefits from insourcing of services currently contracted out, reduced costs of maintaining legacy mainframe information systems, and materials and postage savings, are $4.938 million a year. A discounted cash flow analysis gives a negative net present value of ($3.669 million), a negative return on investment of 33 percent, if just cash real-money savings are considered. The HR reengineering effort clearly is not justified purely by out-of-pocket cash savings alone.

When total cash and noncash benefits are included, however, the net present value for 1994 to 1998 is a $64.296 million return on the $11.248 million initial investment, a whopping 572 percent return. This return assumes that the 421 FTE head count salaries plus benefits are saved, a reasonable assumption given an employee population of 100,000. (In fact, the firm has since laid off several thousand employees, although not just as a result of HR reengineering).

The business case for the HR reengineering is clearly made just by cost savings. Note that virtually all the savings in Table 9.1 are "bottom of the pyramid" savings in administration: reduced time and effort spent shuffling paper, correcting errors, and generating reports. No benefits are assumed from doing HR better, adding value at the delivery, or strategic planning levels of the pyramid.

Benefits from Value-Added

Increased Revenues

How might value-added benefits be calculated? As shown in my previous book, *Calculating Human Resource Costs and Benefits* and in Chapter 7, the possibilities include:

Hiring Better Employees.   A company can get the best and the brightest, above the organization's current mean level of competence, by:

- Better recruiting through use of IVR and on-line electronic accessing of resumes, and responding more quickly (before the competition does) to desirable candidates.

- Better selection, through use of on-line, competency-based assessment methods and job–person matching algorithms in expert systems, of an increased percentage of employees above the median level of the corporation's existing employees—and offering them jobs before the competition does.

The benefits of shifting the performance curves shown in Chapter 7 even a small amount are very significant. For example, if average pay plus benefits per an employee is $58,000 a year, a 10% shift in the productivity of an average employee in a 100,000 employee firm is worth $10\% \times \$58,000 = \$5,800/$ employee/year $\times$ 100,000 employees = $580 million.

As discussed in Chapter 7, this value often greatly *under*states the case: Star salespeople, executives, or R&D scientists who leverage economic values greater than their salaries are worth far more. Prevention of turnover of superior employees, or rather management of "qualified turnover" so that the best employees stay and the worst leave, can also shift the performance curve to the right toward better performance.

Development of Employees.   Technical and managerial training can increase employee productivity .67 of a standard deviation, or approximately $.67 \times 32\% = 21\%$ in a moderately complex job. This means effective, just-in-time training keyed to business performance results could increase productivity $21\% \times \$58,000$ (the average employees salary plus benefits)/year = $12,180. Increased productivity per employee per year $\times$ 100,000 employees = $1.2 billion.

Motivation, Morale, and Performance Maintenance.   Studies of "discretionary effort" have asked American workers to rate the average productivity of their work groups on a scale of zero—no useful work is being done—to 100+ percent, where 100 percent is the most employees could do on a sustained basis if highly motivated. (See Figure 9.1.) Employees rate the minimum required to get by just enough to keep their jobs at about 50 percent productivity and the most they could give if truly motivated at 95 percent productivity. The distance between the minimum required to get by and the most an employee has to give is defined as discretionary effort because the employee does not have to work any harder or produce any more to keep his or her job. Anything additional he or she contributes is voluntary or discretionary. I call this the sleeping bag indicator: If one walks through highly productive software or pharmaceutical R&D labs, one sees sleeping bags in close to half the offices or laboratory spaces. This indicates that professionals (who are not being paid overtime) are living there, working 16 to 18 hours a day because they're so excited by the work they are doing.

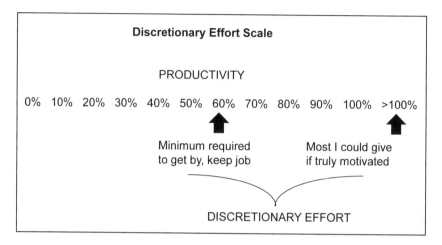

Figure 9.1 Discretionary Effort Scale

The bad news: 44 percent of U.S. employees say they do the absolute minimum required to get by. Only 19 percent say they are giving the maximum they could give.

The good news: 76 percent of U.S. employees say they would be willing to give more discretionary effort if they or their organizations were better managed. The economic value of discretionary effort is easily calculated: 95 percent (what employees could give)—minus what employees say they are giving times the payroll. Better HR management—better managerial training or organization development—that increases employee discretionary effort by a few percentage points can be worth thousands of dollars per year in increased productivity per average employee doing a job of moderate complexity.

Benefits from value-added by Human Resources are rarely calculated and even more rarely used to justify reengineering HR efforts, despite the fact that University of Michigan OASIS data clearly shows that focus on strategic HR activities adds value—produces better-than-industry performance in return on investment and growth in shareholder equity.

HR reengineering efforts need not be justified by cost savings only, although the data show they can amply demonstrate their value from bottom-of-the-pyramid administrative cost savings alone. The real challenge is to demonstrate delivery and strategic value-added by improved HR services and planning that shift a firm's entire human organization toward greater performance.

ENDNOTE

1. Greengard, S. (July 1994). "New Technology is HR's Route to Reengineering." Personnel Journal. 32C-32M.

Summary

10

A National Human Resources System for the Future

Reengineering has the potential to eliminate 30 percent of all jobs in the U.S. economy (see Figure 10.1). This restructuring, well under way, is causing massive and wrenching changes.

As shown in Figure 10.2, agriculture, manufacturing, mining, transportation, utility, and other employment is falling rapidly. In the year 2000 agriculture and other sector employment will employ fewer than 2 percent of the U.S. population. Manufacturing employment, now about 19 percent, by some estimates, will decline to 4 percent. Services/knowledge worker employment is expected to peak at about 92 percent. The history of humankind suggests that Homo Sapiens Habilis always invents tools to take the labor out of labor-intensive activities. McCormick reapers, and later huge combines, replaced millions of human harvesters of crops. Automated looms, assembly lines, and robots replaced manufacturing labor. When service and information work come to dominate employment and labor costs, the computer and reengineering appear to automate and reduce this labor.

Obvious questions for the future include:

■ What will replace today's information economy?

■ What will society do with employees displaced by reengineering?

Price of Progress
'Re-engineering' Gives Firms New Efficiency, Workers the Pink Slip

Re-engineering (by some estimates) will wipe out as many as 25 million jobs (of) roughly 90 million public sector jobs today....

Re-engineering of work could prove as massive and wrenching as the Industrial Revolution

Wall Street Journal, March 16, 1993

Figure 10.1   Price of Progress

THE NEXT ECONOMY

Guesses about what comes next for human workers include:

- *Entertainment:* "Software" extension of the current information services economy. Tens of thousands of computer channels and tens, even hundreds of millions of fiber optic pathways will create an ever-expanding need for entertainment/information software to be transmitted along the Information Superhighway. The question is whether the millennia of increased leisure time will ever arrive. Despite dishwashers, washing machines, telephones, automobiles, and computers, the percentage of human time spent in work has steadily increased since the Middle Ages. People now work about ten hours more than they did 40 years ago. Increased leisure time seems to be an ever-receding mirage, at least for those knowledge workers who remain employed. It is possible that the only people able to enjoy the increase in entertainment will be an increasingly alienated underclass unable to afford it.

- *Health Care:* Another extension of an existing knowledge/service economy component. Whatever the prospects for health care reform, ever advancing medical technology, and an aging population all but guarantee that health care's share of employment and economy will continue to grow.

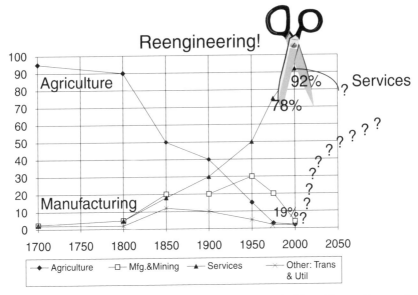

Figure 10.2 Replacement of Labor by Technology in Three Human Economies

Instead of flipping one another's hamburgers, we will be taking care of one another's aging selves.

- *Biotechnology:* Genetic engineering advances that will (further) revolutionize agriculture, medicine, even computers, based on molecular or biological transistors—artificial brain cells connected in neural nets that may change our very definition of life.

- *The environment:* Massive redeployment of human effort and resources to clean up and maintain the earth—initially in the industrialized countries, increasingly in developing countries.

- *Entrepreneurship:* The laissez-faire notion that human beings left to their own devices in an economy steadily growing richer from the increased productivity offered by the information knowledge economy will create employment in serving markets for as yet unthought of products and services.

- *Science, art, literature, culture:* A variant of the entertainment idea. Human beings will have the discretionary time to study, discover, and create.

- *Space:* Colonization of the moon and Mars.

Whatever the future, society's immediate problem is redeployment and reemployment of workers reengineered out of their jobs or laid off due to changes in the political economy, for example, the shrinking of defense industries with the

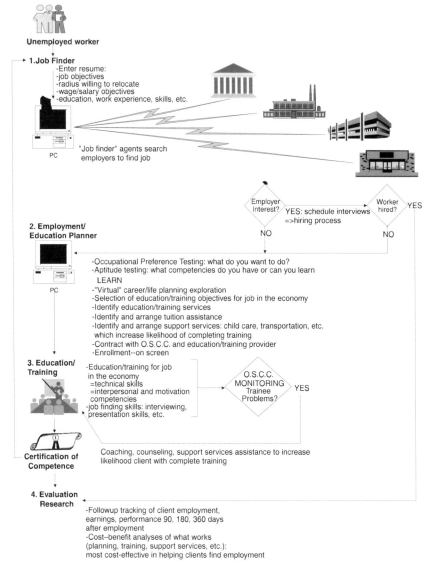

Figure 10.3   Work Flow for a National Reemployment System

end of the Cold War. Equally urgent is employment for youth who do not have the skills to participate in the knowledge/service economy. Societal Human Resources management faces massive needs for (re)training before it can redeploy its underutilized human assets.

At present the Clinton administration, through the U.S. Department of Labor, is launching a massive reemployment initiative based on the concept of one-stop

Career Centers (CCs). These CCs will offer two services not currently provided by most publicly-funded employment systems:

■ Computerized matching of unemployed workers with available jobs.

■ Computer-assisted self-directed skill and competency assessment, career planning, and education and (re)training for displaced workers in skills needed to find jobs in the new economy. Numerous consortia of public and private agencies and firms are working on CC prototypes.

Ideally, CCs are a *technology* not a place. Decentralized branches of a national HR system integrated by a national IHRMIS (which inevitably will become a worldwide IHRMIS) can be wherever there is a PC with a modem connection to the IHRMIS network. Out-of-work technical, professional, and managerial workers will have CC services as close as their own home computer and modem. For others, CC kiosks can be made available in any convenient public building: local police stations, fire stations, post offices, town halls, general stores, elementary and secondary schools, hospital waiting rooms.

Human CC counselors will assist clients who need support or guidance in using the reemployment computer system. For example, a counselor may sit next to a client, entering data for him or her, as he/she learns to use the system. (Best evidence of learning: when the client grabs the mouse and says, "Hey, I can do this myself!") .

Maine's Training Development Center (TDC) has developed a CC on-line automated (reemployment) case management system (ACMS) which computerizes the work flow steps shown in Figure 10.3 (opposite page).

Step 1: Registration

A job seeker registers with the system by filling in an on-screen resume/job application form, providing data on his/her background, education, work experience, knowledge, skills and competencies, and job objectives—desired location (commuting distance within x miles of any U.S. zip code), salary, and benefits.

Step 2: Job Search/Job-Person Matching

Job seekers' resumes, dates of availability, location preferences, and wage/salary and benefit objectives are posted on the CC and other "public" electronic candidate pool bulletin boards, and modemed to hiring firms' internal IHRMISs.

Job-Person Matching software developed by Career Search system can extend job searches nationwide. The Career Search system immediately shows on-screen information on 220,000 U.S. employers with job openings nationwide. A job seeker can click San Diego on a map, enter how many miles he/she is willing to commute from the downtown San Diego 91206 area code, and ask the system to identify all firms that employ welders, HR specialists, or COBOL computer programmers within 30 miles of Ocean Beach. The Career Search system provides information on firms meeting the search criteria, complete with the name and number of the prospective employer's hiring manager to contact. With a click of a mouse, the job seeker can modem his/her resume directly to this person.

Worldwide job-person matching systems described in Chapters 1 and 4 already exist on the Internet and Compuserve. Advanced Job Search systems can send software "job finder agents" out to search all databases of job openings for positions that meet a job seeker's criteria.

The CC helps job seekers arrange interviews and provides (on-line or human) coaching and counseling debriefing sessions after employment interviews to maintain job seekers' confidence and help them improve their interviewing skills.

Step 3: Individual Employment Plan

If the system cannot find a job matching a job seeker's existing skills, it guides him/her through development of an "employability plan" to prepare him or her for a job in the economy. Demographic data collected by the registration screen is analyzed by an expert system to identify which of several hundred local, state, or federal government tuition reimbursement, financial assistance, training, and social service programs (e.g., Defense Conversion and Job Training Partnership Act (JTPA) programs for economically disadvantaged, youth, dislocated workers, migrant, and seasonal farm workers, etc.) a job seeker may be eligible for.

ACMS uses computer-assisted testing (APTICOM and TABE—Test for Adult Basic Education) to assess reading, numeracy (first to twelfth grade), and clerical, sensory-motor, and manual dexterity aptitudes. A person unclear about his or her career objectives can take vocational interest tests (e.g., the USES, Strong-Campbell, Kuder Preference, or APTICOM Interest Inventory) on-screen and receive immediate feedback on jobs, careers, and industries that match his/her competencies and interests. Job seekers can then explore "virtual" job fairs, by matching themselves against any of 30,000 jobs in the database. Job fair data include videos of work on the job, career ladders and pay, travel requirements, and many other details. Anyone can "play an adventure game" with his or her life, changing jobs, careers, and lives with a mouse click until finding one that fits his or her preferences.

ACMS also diagnose job seekers' needs for prevocational services (e.g., medical care, including enrollment in Medicare or Medicaid or a private health insurance plan) if a job seeker needs a medical problem fixed to become employable.

At present Social Services clients in Maine have to register as many as 72 separate times with 72 different agencies to receive services, filling in the same information on 72 separate forms. With ACMS, a person need register only once:

As soon as his/her data are in the database, they are available on-line to all other service providers.

ACMS next helps job seekers develop an Individual Employment Plan. If a job seeker needs additional education or training in basic or specific vocational skills, the system matches him or her with training providers: local junior colleges, union apprenticeship programs, or even individual apprentice arrangements. If, for example, a laid off lawyer wants to learn to repair boots (a job in demand in Maine), the CC contacts all bootmakers in the radius the job seeker is able to travel and finds a master bootmaker willing to accept him or her as an apprentice. The CC helps job seekers register with public or private training providers and arranges tuition payment directly from eligibility programs. The CC also helps job seekers arrange other social services support such as child care and reimbursement, which can increase their chances of completing training.

CC client training requests provide instantaneous market research to all training and education vendors. Junior colleges and private education vendors can immediately find out what training programs are being requested by displaced workers and develop courses in skills most in demand.

The completed individual employment plan becomes a contract between the career center and the job seeker, with specified goals and due dates for completion of training and certification of competence. This contract becomes an on-line performance management tracking system, constantly updated as potential employees complete training milestones and are certified in employment skills. These data can be made available to prospective employers on-line.

Step 4: Education/Training

The job seeker completes the training he or she has contracted for and is certified competent in the skills required for his/her job objective. CC training includes a job search workshop, which teaches resume writing, how to present oneself in an employment interview, and job hunting techniques—for example, calling friends and associates to expand the network of contacts who know one is looking for a job.

[Return to Step 2: Job Search/Job–Person Matching]

As soon as a job seeker enters training to prepare for a job for which there is demand in the local economy, the ACMS begins marketing him or her to hiring firms using the Job Search/Job–Person Matching system described above.

Step 5: Follow-up and Evaluation

When a job seeker is hired, the CC collects information: the name of his or her employer, his/her starting wages/salary, and any on-job competency certifications or license exams he or she completes. The CC follows up 90, 120, and 360 days after placement to see if the new employee is still employed and how successful he or she has been in the job. If for any reason an employee loses his/her job, he or she can reenter the CC process simply by updating his/her registration records.

The reemployment system uses these data to evaluate and continually improve its own effectiveness, providing reports on:

- Total dollars allocated by training program and location.
- Client lists by program: how many clients are served by various demographic categories.
- Learning gains by individuals: basic skills, competency, and vocational certifications.
- Outcomes of placements: how many complete and how many drop out of training, how many become employed, and how many remain unemployed.
- Cost-benefit and return on investment analyses to identify costs per effective placement (person still employed a year later), the most cost-effective training programs leading to employment, and what works and what does not.

The ideal reemployment system can be entered from any place at any point in the labor market process. A firm laying off workers can have on-line CC workstations in its outplacement office. Every high school can have CC PCs that students can play with to help them develop individual employment plans, focus their education objectives on marketable skills, develop job hunting skills, and begin their employment search. ACMS in schools may become a potent force for school reform. As student (and parent) "customers" get better data about skills and competencies required for employment, they will become more discriminating consumers of educational services, demanding programs that lead to employment.

Juvenile justice organizations and prisons also can have CC services. Each prisoner's cell could contain a PC providing on-line training in basic literacy, numeracy, social skills, vocational skills, even ethics, and begin a job search well before release. Release could be conditional upon completion of training, certification of competence, and employment. Prisoners and other displaced workers could be hired and telecommute from wherever they are, for example, as computer programmers, claims processors, or voice data transcribers (until direct voice data entry reengineers these jobs out of existence)—with appropriate controls (successful computer wire fraud scams have been run out of prisons by computer-literate inmates).

SUMMARY

An effective national reemployment system creates an instantaneous perfect market for labor. Any employer needing help can identify potential employees with the competencies he/she needs on-line and instantaneously. Any potential employee can instantaneously access any available job opening anywhere that matches his or her interests and competencies. If a person does not have the competencies to be employed in his or her location, job, and firm of choice, he or she can instantaneously be enrolled in the training needed to provide these skills.

Initially this training is likely to be available through schools, unions, firms, apprenticeships to masters, and the like, but as communications improve, as computers in homes become as common as telephones and linked to the Information Superhighway, most instruction will be instantaneously available at the person's own home computer. Just as anyone able to view any movie in any film company's library simply by clicking on a menu, training will be similarly available from optical jukeboxes of thousands of training programs. Anyone wanting to learn anything anywhere will be able to download a training program on any topic just-in-time, on demand. Schools at all levels will become increasingly "virtual": learning will occur on computers and by teleconference, from Sesame Street for preschoolers to "electronic campuses without walls" for college and graduate school.

This continuous (re)education, (re)training, and (re)employment system offers the best hope for:

- Redeploying workers displaced by reengineering.
- Welfare reform, moving underclass left-outs into mainstream jobs and economic participation.
- Continual optimizing of the national economy, via up-to-the-minute information about value-added jobs, labor needs, labor availability, and education/training needs.

Immediate employment of workers able to fill available jobs—and immediate diagnosis and prescription of training to make people employable—will minimize unemployment waiting time underutilized human capacity. A mind is a terrible thing to waste. A national IHRMIS can greatly reduce that waste and help all citizens fulfill their economic and personal potential. And reengineering tools will help workers affected by reengineered programs.

$\mathscr{A}$

Reengineering Team Readiness

INSTRUCTIONS FOR COMPLETING REENGINEERING TEAM READINESS (RTR) QUESTIONNAIRE

Self-Assessment

For each item on this index, rate yourself according to the frequency with which you feel you have displayed that particular behavior within the past six months. Assign a "1" to those behaviors that you are unsure of having demonstrated, or thought you should have used.

Assessing Others

For each item on this index, rate the person you are assessing according to the frequency with which you have seen him/her demonstrate that particular behavior, or have heard it reliably described by someone else within the past six months. Assign a "1" to those behaviors that you have not definitely seen demonstrated or only assumed were used.

Rating Scale

4 = Often	3 = Sometimes	2 = Rarely	1 = Not Seen

It is important to remember that individuals do not demonstrate all these behaviors all the time. Therefore, in order to provide the most effective feedback, be sure to carefully consider the frequency with which you or the person you are rating uses these behaviors.

Rating Scale

4 = Often	3 = Sometimes	2 = Rarely	1 = Not Seen

The Person You Are Rating:

1. Finds better, faster, less expensive or more efficient ways to do things.

2. Understands a complex task by breaking it down into manageable parts, in a systematic, detailed way.

3. Works to add measurable value to customers (internal and external).

4. Does things to make others feel ownership of one's own solutions or proposals.

5. Does far more than is minimally required in the assignment or task.

6. Uses positive feedback and support to encourage and empower others.

7. Suggests genuinely new ways to organize work.

8. Sees ways to use information systems technology to improve work flow, e.g., networked (LAN, WAN) computers, client-server shared databases, e-mail, expert systems.

Column Subtotals (Items 1–8):

A	B	C	D	E	F	G	H
__	__	__	__	__	__	__	__

4 = Often	3 = Sometimes	2 = Rarely	1 = Not Seen

The Person You Are Rating:

9. States quality or productivity improvements in economic terms: dollars, cost–benefit ratios, ROI, etc.

10. Prepares detailed flow diagram to organize or describe a complex process or sequence of events.

11. Pushes customer (internal and external) to adopt new methods in the customer's best interest.

12. Identifies the most important concerns and issues of others.

13. Pushes or champions new ideas or technology.

14. Creates "common vision," motivation, morale among subordinates and colleagues from different organizations, technical specialties.

15. Proposes highly creative alternatives to present practices.

16. Keeps up with latest ideas in technology, e.g., by reading professional publications, computer magazines, attending conferences, keeping current with new management theories/concepts, "playing" with new hardware and software.

Column Subtotals (Items 9–16):

A	B	C	D	E	F	G	H
—	—	—	—	—	—	—	—

Column Subtotals (Items 1–8):

A	B	C	D	E	F	G	H
—	—	—	—	—	—	—	—

Column Totals:

A	B	C	D	E	F	G	H
—	—	—	—	—	—	—	—

Rating Scale

4 = Often	3 = Sometimes	2 = Rarely	1 = Not Seen

The Person You Are Rating:

17. Makes a special effort to explain to colleagues the purpose of their work.

18. Feels customer's (internal and external) feelings are as important as the task at hand.

19. Holds meetings to share information and ideas with colleagues.

20. Spends time looking for opportunities for colleagues' professional development.

21. Takes time to explain the reasons for decisions in terms of the best interests of the organization.

22. Demonstrates concern for others.

23. Gives capable colleagues the freedom to make decisions and mistakes without close supervision.

24. Helps colleagues think through the "who, what, why, when, and how" of completing tasks.

Column Totals:

I	J	K	L

Rating Scale

4 = Often	3 = Sometimes	2 = Rarely	1 = Not Seen

The Person You are Rating Encourages Colleagues To:

25. Take steps to improve work group performance.

26. Explain policies and procedures to subordinates.

27. Recognize people for doing good work.

28. Go out of their way to make the work group successful.

29. Set very high standards for performance.

30. Communicate a clear vision.

31. Recognize people in proportion to the excellence of their performance.

32. Cooperate with all members of the team.

Column Totals:

M	N	O	P

214

SCORING INSTRUCTIONS AND INTERPRETIVE NOTES

Three dimensions help predict successful reengineering initiatives:

- Competencies—personal characteristics that have been proven to predict outstanding performance;
- Team Leadership Style—a person's typical behavior when leading or managing people in various situations; and
- Climate—the atmosphere of the workplace or how people feel about the workplace.

The RTR provides both detailed and overall measurements of reengineering readiness at three levels. The first level assesses a manager's use of eight competencies and four team leadership styles. The second level measures four team climate dimensions. The third level represents the intersection between the manager's use of competencies and styles and the climate he or she has created. This score predicts:

- "Go"—all three variables are at an optimal level for reengineering.
- "Team Development"—reexamine the scores for each variable and identify the elements that need development. Train and include people on the team who can provide the missing elements.
- "Caution"—examine the scores and identify whether the difficulty lies in team climate, competencies, styles, or all three. Consider implementing an organizational improvement program that addresses the most critical issues. If scores for competencies and styles are low, it may be beneficial to undergo training to strengthen the applicable skills.

The following pages provide scoring instructions, descriptions, and development suggestions pertaining to the three variables.

The results of this survey can be applied to selecting people to lead reengineering, as a basis for training and development, performance management, and organizational development (feedback and problem solving issues based on survey data can be used as a foundation to revitalize, or reinforce reengineering efforts).

Instructions for Scoring Reengineering Team Readiness (RTR)

Scoring the RTR:

1. Total the ratings in the columns on each page of the questionnaire to obtain individual sums for columns A through P.

2. Transfer these scores to the scoring worksheet (and divide each by 2 as indicated). These are your individual scale scores.

3. Transfer your scores to the corresponding dimensions and letters on the graphs, found on page 218.

4. Connect the points that you have plotted on each scale.

To obtain the results of your overall RTR, add the score totals from *Team Leadership Style* and *Competencies*, and divide the total by 12. This is the raw score for your *Management Readiness Index*. Next, add the total scale scores for each team climate dimension and divide by 4 to get the raw score for your overall *Team Climate Index*. To plot the results, follow the RTR Profile directions on page 222.

Colleague Feedback

It is important, when possible, to solicit feedback from your boss, peers, and employees. Feedback from colleagues can provide team leaders with a practical basis for improving their organizational performance.

Distribute the RTR to several colleagues (a minimum of three is recommended). To encourage honest answers, ask them to write the name of the person they are rating, rather than their own names, on the questionnaire.

After scoring the employee data as above, the results can be averaged to create a composite profile. Are there significant gaps between your assessment of your team's readiness to implement reengineering and your colleagues'?

SCORING WORKSHEET

Competencies

Achievement Orientation	_____ ÷ 2 = _____ A
Analytical Thinking	_____ ÷ 2 = _____ B
Customer Service Orientation	_____ ÷ 2 = _____ C
Influence/Persuasion	_____ ÷ 2 = _____ D
Initiative	_____ ÷ 2 = _____ E
Team Orientation	_____ ÷ 2 = _____ F
Discontinuous Thinking	_____ ÷ 2 = _____ G
Technology "Know How"	_____ ÷ 2 = _____ H

Team Leadership Style

Authoritative	_____ ÷ 2 = _____ I
Affiliative	_____ ÷ 2 = _____ J
Democratic	_____ ÷ 2 = _____ K
Coaching	_____ ÷ 2 = _____ L

Total the scores, then divide by 12 to get your **Management Readiness Index**

TOTAL: _____ ÷ 12 = [ ]

Climate

Standards	_____ ÷ 2 = _____ M
Clarity	_____ ÷ 2 = _____ N
Rewards	_____ ÷ 2 = _____ O
Team Commitment	_____ ÷ 2 = _____ P

Total these scores, then divide by 4 to get your **Team Climate Index**

TOTAL: _____ ÷ 4 = [ ]

Competencies

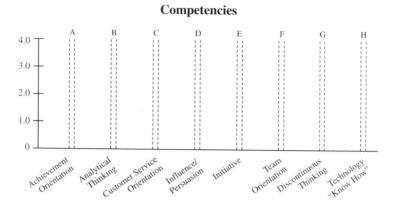

Team Leadership Style

Climate

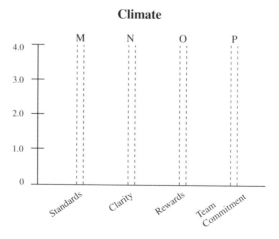

218

COMPETENCIES

Competencies can be thought of as energizers supporting the effective use of team leadership styles. A competency is a personal characteristic that has been shown to cause or predict outstanding job performance. Competencies mark the difference between average job performance and outstanding job performance. They are what outstanding performers do more often, in most situations, with better results.

The following eight competencies have been identified as critical to reengineering initiatives.

Achievement Orientation	A concern for competing against a standard of excellence. The standard may be one's own past performance (striving for improvement) or the performance of others (competitiveness).
Analytical Thinking	Understanding a situation by breaking down its components; determining the implications of a situation in a methodical way.
Customer Service Orientation	A desire to help others meet their needs. It involves focusing effort on discovering the needs of a customer or client and meeting them.
Influence/Persuasion	Understands.
Initiative	Habitually taking action and seizing opportunities.
Team Orientation	Taking on a role as leader of a team; using authority in a fair and equitable manner. Giving positive feedback and support to encourage others to feel they are making an important contribution to the team.
Discontinuous Thinking	Suggesting genuinely new ways to organize work. Proposing radical alternatives to present practices.
Information Systems Technology "Know-How"	Demonstrating in-depth technical knowledge in recommending use of information systems to improve work flow (e.g., networked computers, client server shared databases, etc.). Staying informed by reading information systems literature.

TEAM LEADERSHIP STYLE

Team leaders influence group climate with their styles and practices. Managerial style is defined by a person's typical behavior in a variety of managerial situations. Team Leadership Style is a function of the following:

- a team leader's personal characteristics (motives and values)
- the style a team leader has seen superiors, "mentors," and other team leaders use
- the organization's espoused values about "the right way" to manage
- the specific situations and people with whom the team leader deals

The following four team leadership styles have been identified as integral to reengineering readiness.

Authoritative	A team leader who provides long-term vision; gives employees clear direction.
Affiliative	A team leader who maintains good personal relationships among employees by listening to their concerns and expressing sympathy during times of stress.
Democratic	A team leader who builds commitment and generates new ideas by encouraging employees' participation.
Coaching	A team leader who develops others; who helps employees identify their unique strengths and weaknesses.

CLIMATE

Organizational climate refers to the atmosphere in the workplace. The climate strongly affects individual and organizational performance by arousing (or discouraging) motivation and commitment in a work group. McBer has identified six elements that affect organizational climate. The following four elements were distinguished as the most critical for successful reengineering initiatives:

Standards	The extent to which people perceive the way management sets high standards and challenging goals.
Clarity	The extent to which people are clear about procedures and expectations.
Rewards	The extent to which allocation of rewards is perceived to be based upon superior performance.
Team Commitment	The feeling that management and fellow employees cooperate to get work done.

Reengineering Team Readiness Profile

On the graph below, mark your Team Climate Index score from the scoring worksheet on the vertical axis, and your Management Readiness Index score on the horizontal axis. Then plot the point at which they intersect.

This will indicate whether the person you are rating is prepared to implement change in a work group or other organizational unit through a reengineering approach. As the key below indicates, if the person's point of intersection between the two indexes falls:

- in the dark gray area (Caution), individuals and teams should review climate, competencies, and managerial styles before proceeding with reengineering

- in the light gray area (Team Development), develop the reengineering team by training and including people on the team who bring missing skills to the team

- in the white area (Go), go ahead with reengineering-based change efforts

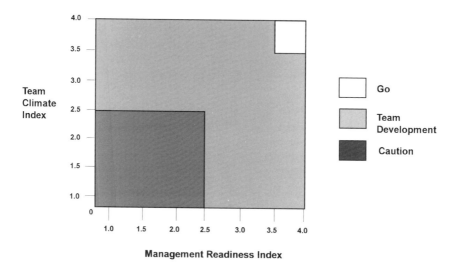

Bibliography

Ackerman, J. (1993, May 22). The Incredible Shrinking Office. *The Boston Globe*.

APTICOM (1993). Philadelphia: Vocational Research Institute.

Automated Case Management System (ACMS). Bucksport, ME: Training Development Corp.

Axel, H. (1994). Outsourcing HR Services. *HR Executive Review* Vol. 1, No. 2. New York: The Conference Board.

Ayre R. & T. Stevenson (1994, April 12). Electronic-Mail Software, *PC,* 13, (7).

Bowen, W. (1986, May 26). The Puny Payoff From Office Computers, *Fortune*.

Career Search (1993, August). A Unique Database for Employee Information, DATABASE 14,4.*I*, 63–65.

Carkhuff, R. (1969). *Helping and Human Relations*, Vols. I & II. New York: Holt, Rinehart & Winston.

Cerciello, V.R. (1991). *Human Resource Management Systems*. New York: Lexington Books/Macmillan.

Currid, C. (1994). *Reengineering Toolkit*. Rocklin, CA: Prima Publishing.

Dalziel, M. and Schoonover, S. (1988). *Changing Ways*. New York: American Management Association (AMACOM).

Davenport, T. (1993). *Process Innovation: Reengineering Work Through Process Technology*. Boston: Harvard Business School Press.

Davenport, T.H. & Short, J.E. (Summer 1994). The New Industrial Engineering: Information Technology and Business Process Redesign, *Sloan Management Review*. Vol 31, No. 4, 11–27.

Davidow, W.H. & Malone, M.S. (1992). *The Virtual Corporation*. New York: HarperCollins.

Davis, S. & Davidson, B. (1991). *2020 Vision*. New York: Simon & Schuster.

Decisis Corp. (1994). *In Compliance: Helping Ensure Consistent, Fair And Legal Human Resources Decisions*. Sebastopol, CA: Decisis Corp.

DeGrace, P. & Stahl, L. (1993). *The Olduvai Imperative*. Englewood Cliffs, NJ: Yourdon Press/Prentice Hall.

Desatnick, R. and Detzel, D. (1993). *Managing to Keep the Customer*. San Francisco: Jossey-Bass.

Drexler, E.K. (1992). *Nanosystems: Molecular Machinery, Manufacturing and Computation*. New York: John Wiley & Sons.

Falcone, A.J., Edwards, J.E. and Day, R.R. (1986). *Meta-analysis of Personnel Training Techniques for Three Populations*. Paper presented at the Annual Meeting of the Academy of Management. Chicago, IL.

Fitz-Enz, J. (1990). *Human Value Management*. San Francisco: Jossey-Bass.

Forres, S.E. & Liebowitz, Z.B. (1991). *Using Computers in Human Resources*. San Francisco: Jossey-Bass.

Frantzreb, R. (1991). Selecting Computer Systems and Software for HR Management. In Forres, S.E. & Liebowitz, Z.B. (1991). *Using Computers in Human Resources*. San Francisco: Jossey-Bass.

Geer, C.T. (1994, August 15). For a new job, press #1, *Fortune*. 118–119.

Greengard, S. (1994, July). New Technology is HR's Route to Reengineering, *Personnel Journal*, 32C–320.

Hammer, M. (1990). Reengineering Work: Don't Automate, Obliterate, *Harvard Business Review*. July–August.

Hammer, M. & Champy, J. (1993). *Reengineering the Corporation*. New York: HarperCollins.

Handy, C. (1990). *The Age of Unreason*. London, UK: Business Books.

Handy, C. (1994). *The Empty Raincoat*. London, UK: Business Books.

Harrington, H.J. (1991). *Business Process Improvement*. New York: McGraw Hill.

Harris, D. (1986, January). Beyond the Barrier: New HRIS Developments. *Personnel*.

Harrison, R. (1985). Role Negotation: A tough minded approach to team development. In Bennis, et.al. (eds). *Interpersonal Dynamics*. Homewood, Il: Dorsey Press.

HayGroup (1994). Haypoll: Touch-Tone Telephone Survey. Philadelphia: Hay Research for Management.

Ho, R. (May 23, 1994). Mellon Bank: A Case Study. Paper presented at the Saratoga Institute Human Resources Effectiveness Conference, Scotsdale, AZ.

Hunter, J.E., Schmidt, F.L. & Judiesch, M.K. (1990). Individual Differences in Output Variability as a Function of Job Complexity, *Journal of Applied Psychology* 75: 2842.

Ishikawa, K. (1988). *Guide to Quality Control*. White Plains, NY: Unipub.

Johansson, H.J., McHugh, P. , Pendlebury, A.J. & Wheeler, W.A. (1993). *Business Process Reengineering*. Chichester, UK: John Wiley & Sons.

Johnson, H. (1992). *Relevance Regained*. New York: Free Press/MacMillan.

Johnson, H. & Kaplan, R. (1987). *Relevance Lost: The Rise and Fall of Management Accounting*. Boston: Harvard Business School Press.

Jones, C. (1986). *Programming Productivity*. New York: McGraw Hill.

Jones, C. (1991). *Applied Software Measurement*. New York: McGraw Hill.

Kennedy, J.L & Morrow, T.J. (1994). *Electronic Job Search Revolution*. New York: John Wiley & Sons.

Kennedy, J.L & Morrow, T.J. (1994). *Electronic Resume Revolution*. New York: John Wiley & Sons.

Kotter, J. (1985). *Power and Influence*. New York: Free Press.

Kugelmass, J. (1995). *Telecommunting*. New York: Lexington/Free Press.

Main, J. (1981, June 29). How to Battle Your Own Bureaucracy: Intel Has a Way to Measure Office-Worker Productivity—and Raise it 30%, *Fortune*.

Mansfield, R.S. & Mumford, S. (n.d.). A Competency-Based Approach to Intercultural Relations. In Mansfield, R.S. (1982). *Advanced Intercultural Relations Workshop Design*. Boston: McBer and Company.

Manzini, A.O., & Gridley, J.D. (1986). *Integrating Human Resources and Strategic Business Planning*. New York: AMACOM.

Martin, A. (1993). Technology and the HR Back Office: Engineering with Interactive Systems Efficiency. *Solutions*. April, 1993.

Martin, J. (1990). *Rapid Application Development*. New York: MacMillan.

McGee, J. & L. Prusak (1993). *Managing Information Strategically*. New York: John Wiley & Sons.

McDonell, E.D. (1993). *Document Imaging Technology*. Salem, MA: Probus Publishing Co.

Mehler, M. (1993). Notes Fanatic. *Corporate Computing*. 161–164.

Merck & Co. (1993). *WEIS: World-Wide Employee Information System*. Whitehouse Station, NJ: Merck, Inc.

Merck & Co. (1993, September). Removing the Barriers between Employees, Managers and Information. Paper presented at the Tesseract Users Group (TUG) Conference, San Francisco, CA.

Meyer, C. (1993). *Fast Cycle Time*. New York: MacMillan.

Meridian Bancorp (1993, September). *TESS: The Employee Self-Service System*. Reading, PA: Meridian Bancorp Inc.

Mundel, M. (1983). *Improving Productivity and Effectiveness*. Englewood Cliffs, NJ: Prentice-Hall.

Norman, D. (1988). *The Design of Everyday Things*. New York: Doubleday.

Nunemanch, N. (1992). *LAN Primer*. San Mateo, CA: M&T Publishing.

Pasmore, W.A. & J.J. Sherwood (eds.) (1978). *Sociotechnical Systems: A Sourcebook*. La Jolla, CA: University Associates.

Porter, M. (1985). *Competitive Advantage*. New York: Free Press/MacMillan, p. 46.

Quinn, B.J. (1992). *Intelligent Enterprise*. New York: Free Press.

Rummler, G. & Brache, A. (1990). *Improving Performance: Managing the White Space on the Organization Chart*. San Francisco: Jossey-Bass.

Rummler, G. (1988). *Organizations as Systems*. Warren, NJ: Rummler-Brache.

Sansome, P.G. (1968, April). *Cost Benefit Analysis of Information Systems: A Survey of Methodologies*. Atlanta, GA: Georgia Institute of Technology.

Schor, J. (1993). *The Overworked American*. New York: Basic Books/Harper Collins.

Sloan S. & Spencer, L.M. (1991). Hay Salesforce Effectiveness Seminar Participant Survey Results. Atlanta, GA: Hay Management Consultants.

Solutions (1993, April). Technology and the HR back office: Engineering with Interactive Systems Efficiency. *Solutions*. 8–9.

Spencer, L. (1994). The Right Stuff for the New Dynamic. In Berger, L. and M. Sikora. (1994) *The Change Management Handbook: A Roadmap to Corporate Transformation*. New York: Irwin.

Spencer, L. and R. Page. Integrated Human Resource Management Information Systems, In Tracey, W. (1994). *Human Resource Planning and Development Handbook*. New York: AMACOM.

Spencer, L. & Spencer, S. (1993). *Competence at Work*. New York: John Wiley & Sons.

Stalk, G. & Hout, T.M. (1990). *Competing Against Time*. New York: Free Press/McMillan.

Truax, C.B. and Carkhuff, R. (1967). *Toward Effective Counselling and Psychotherapy*. Chicago: Aldine Publishing.

Turney, B. (1992). *Common Cents: The ABC (Activity Based Costing) Performance Breakthrough*. Portland, OR: Cost Technology.

Ulanoff & Mace. (1994, March 19). Electronic Forms Software: Filling in the Blanks, *PC*, 13, (6).

U.S. Department of Commerce. (1993, Dec 21). *Integration Definition for Function Modeling (IDEF0) FIPS UB 183*. Washington, DC: Dept. of Commerce.

Walker, A. *Reengineering the HR Function*. (1992, January). Human Resource Planning Society Professional Development Workshop, Amelia Island, FL.

Walker, A.J. (1986). New Technologies in Human Resource Planning. *Human Resource Planning*, 9 (4), 149–159.

Walker, A.J. (1993). *Handbook of Human Resource Management Systems*. New York: McGraw-Hill.

Weinberg, R.B. (1993). *Human Resource Certification Institute Certification Study Guide*. Alexandria, VA: Human Resource Certification Institute.

Weizenbaum, J. (1976). *Computer Power and Human Reason*. San Francisco: W.H. Freeman.

Whiteley, R.C. (1991). *The Customer Driven Company*. Reading, MA: Addison-Wesley.

Yankelovich, D. & Immerwahr, J. (1983). *Putting the Work Ethic to Work*. New York: Public Agenda Foundation.

Index

References to tables and figures are set in **boldface**.

A

Accident safety inspection reports, 114
Accounting firms, and outsourcing, 25
Acculturation, 181–182
Achievement motivation, 147–148
Action Software, 49
Action Technology, 119
Activity-based costing (ABC), 53–65
  activity value analysis (AVA) in, 61–65
  definition of, 53
  expected value analysis with, 60–61
  labor costs worksheet in, **59**
  of personnel information transactions, before and after reengineering, 22, **23**, **24**
  traditional cost accounting compared with, 53–54
  types of, 54–60
  validation of data in, 61
  work flow analysis with, 57–60
Activity value analysis (AVA), 61–65
  ratios and graphs created with, 62–65
  steps in, 62
Administration of human resources
  costs of present human resource systems for, 16, **17**
  impact of reengineering on, 17, **17**
  training and, 113
Administrators, 167
Agents, *see* Smart agent software
Albrecht function points per programmer month (AFPPM), 145, **146**
America On-Line, 117
American Compensation Association (ACA), 124
American National Standards Institute, 73
American Society for Training and Development (ASTD), 124

Analysis
  of competency analysis, 139
  Impact Changeability Analysis Report with, 175–176, **175**
  Integrated Human Resources Management Information System (IHRMIS) for, 123
  of job competency requirements, 128
  of managerial style, 140
Analytical thinking, 148–148
Approvals
  personnel information transactions work flow with, 22
  reengingeering and changes in, 95–96
Architecture
  in client-server systems, 40–41, **42**
  example data fields in, **127**
  file-server, 41
  in Integrated Human Resources Management Information System (IHRMIS), 125–127, **126**
Artificial intelligence, 45–46, 48, 142
Artisoft, 47
Aspen Tree Software, 117
Assessment
  of competency in performance management, 132–134, **135**, **136**
  development objectives for, 134
  implementation of micro reengineering with, 174–175
  Integrated Human Resources Management Information System (IHRMIS) for, 123
  of job applicants, 130
  of organization readiness for reengineering, 165
  of reengineering team readiness, 210–222
AT&T, 50

Automated case management system
    (ACMS), 205–208
Automation
    implications of reengineering for, 25
    resistance to, 30, 31
    savings with, 90
    user-friendliness and, 32
    use of, in reengineering, 86–87
Avantos, 118–119
Awareness seminars, 168–169, 173

B

Bard, Mark, 157
Base salary, 55
Benefits administration, *see* Compensa-
    tion and benefits
Budgeting templates, 110
Bulletin boards, 49, 119
Business Process Systems and Services
    (BPSS), 114
Business Week, 26

C

Capital costs
    in activity-based costing (ABC), 56–57
    return on investment analysis of, 195–
        196
Career Centers (CCs), 205–208
Career Design Software, 119
Career Navigator, 119
Career planning, 119, 134
Cash outlay costs
    direct, 54–55
    fringe, 55
CC Mail, 48
CD-ROM
    employee assistance using, 120–121
    services delivery using, 22
    training using, 22, 29, 92
Certification
    of HR professionals, 99, 119
    for reskilling competency, 173
Champion, 167
Champy, J., 90
Change
    executive leadership for, 159
    macro reengineering and pace of, 165–
        174–167
Changeability, Analysis Report on, 175–
    176, **175**

Charts, organizational, 128
Client-server systems
    key concepts of, 40–41
    typical architecture for, 41, **42**
    use of, in reengineering, 47
Coaching, 118, 158
    expert systems for, 112
    future scenarios for, 8–9
    performance management with, 132
Compensation and benefits
    activity-based costing (ABC) analysis
        of work flow with, 57–60
    administration of, 139–140, **141**
    benefits of reengineering for, 193–194
    expert systems for, 112
    future scenarios for handling, 3–5
    implementation planning and, 170
    institutionalization and, 180–181
    Integrated Human Resources Manage-
        ment Information System
        (IHRMIS) for, **126**, 139–143
    integration of HR functions and, 26
    labor costs and, 55
    on-line systems for, 114
    overhead costs and, 56
    paperless transactions for, 91
    reengineering and changes in, **116**, 120
    Society for Human Resource Manage-
        ment (SHRM) findings on, **104–
        105**
    surveys of, 10
Competency, 144–147
    analysis of, 128
    costs and levels of, 87
    cross–disciplinary teams and, 89–90
    definition of, 144
    economic value of superior perfor-
        mance and, 144–145
    example of, 147–148
    expert systems for modeling, 112
    functioning at highest level and, 88
    future jobs and, 151–156
    of human resources (HR) staff, 29
    multiskilling in, 87
    performance management and, 132–134
    programmer productivity and, 145, **146**
    reengineering and, 87, 148–151
    reengineering team readiness and, 214
Compuserve, 115, 117
Computer-assisted instruction (CAI), 29,
    32–33, 119, 173
Computer literacy, reskilling for, 171–173

Computers
  connectivity of, 40–41
  evolution of, 38–39
  power of, 37–39
  user-friendliness of interface in, 42–44
  See also Personal computers (PCs)
Concurrent engineering, 96–97
Conference Board, 25
Connectivity of computers, 40–41
Consultant teams, 168
Control
  as a byproduct of another task, 96
  reengineering and changes in, 94–96,
    195
Cost accounting
  traditional methods of, 53–54
  See also Activity-based costing (ABC)
Cost-benefit analysis, 16
  templates for, 111
Cost-of-quality rule, 60–61
Costs
  controls and, 95
  cross-disciplinary teams and, **89**
  of HR, as a percentage of total com-
    pany costs, 27, **27**
  "Human Organization," as a percentage
    of total company costs, 28, **28**
  impact of reengineering on, 17, **17**
  of personal computers, 46
  of present human resource systems, 16–
    17, **17**
  of personnel information transactions,
    before and after reengineering, 22,
    23, **24**, **46**
  temporary offices and, 94
  value analysis of, in work flow analy-
    sis, 78
  worker competencies and, 87
Creative destruction in the corporate life
    cycle and, 33–34, **33**
Critical Success Factors, 165
Cross-disciplinary teams, 89–90, 97
Customer Do It Yourself (DIY)
  examples of, 84–86
  macro reengineering using, 12, 84
  Phase I of reengineering with, 18
  services delivery and, 88
  triage rules for choosing, **13**
  workflow output and, 69–70
Customers
  approval decisions and, 95–96
  "downstream," in work flow analysis,
    66

implications of reengineering for, 29–
    33
  as part of information system, 83–84
  service orientation toward, 149

D

Databases
  automation and use of, 86–87
  data organization in, 126–127
  data retrieval from, 109–110
  Do It Yourself (DIY) concept applied
    to, 84–86
  example data fields in, **127**
  including information from customers
    and suppliers in, 83–84
  Integrated Human Resources Manage-
    ment Information System
    (IHRMIS) with, 123
  key-word searches of, 109
  processing information close to end-
    users of, 83
  sharing on a network, 83
  types of data in, 110
  See also Document databases
Data entry, 142
  examples of on-line, 113–114
  reengineering and changes in, 113–121
  work flow and direct entry of, 68
Decentralization
  Integrated Human Resources Manage-
    ment Information System
    (IHRMIS) for decisions on, 124
  implications of reengineering for, 26–
    27
Decision support, 110–113
  expert systems for, 111–113
  Integrated Human Resources Manage-
    ment Information System
    (IHRMIS) for, 123, 143
  spreadsheet templates for, 110–111
Decisis, 112
Delivery of services, *see* Services deliv-
    ery systems
Delrina Form Flow, 49
Department of Defense, 74
Desktop publishing (DTP) software, 68
Destaffing, *see* Staffing/destaffing
Diagnostics, using interactive video
    screens, 85
Digital Voice (IBM), 43
Direct cash outlay costs, in activity-based
    costing (ABC), 54–55

DIY, *see* Customer Do It Yourself (DIY)
Documentation of work flow analysis, 78
Document databases
 employee and labor relations using, 121
 paperless transactions using, 91
 training using, 119
 use of, in reengineering, 49
Do It Yourself (DIY), *see* Customer Do It Yourself (DIY)
Dovetail Software, 117
"Downstream" customers, in work flow analysis, 66
Dragon Dictate, 43
Drake Beam Morin, 119
Drucker, Peter, 160
Dumb terminals, 40

E

EASY, 120
Edify Corporation, 86
Edify Electronic Workforce, **45**, 49
EIS, *see* Expert Information System (EIS)
Electronic filing, 94
Electronic Forms Designer, 49
Electronic mail (e-mail) systems
 future scenarios using, 7, 11
 organization development using, 121
 paperless transactions using, 91
 performance management with, 118
 travel limitation using, 91
 use of, in reengineering, 48
Electronic newsletters, 91
Eliza, 31, 120
Empathy, and customers, 30
Employee Access System, 120
Employee and labor relations
 benefits of reengineering for, 194
 implementation planning and, 170–171
 institutionalization and, 181
 reengineering and changes in, **116**, 121
 Society for Human Resource Management (SHRM) findings on, **106–107**
Employee assistance programs
 Integrated Human Resources Management Information System (IHRMIS) for, 140
 reengineering and changes in, **116**, 120
Employee Reengineering Teams (ERT), 174
Employee Self-Service System, 120

Empowerment
 customer perception of, 30
 people in reengineering and, 16
 supervisors and, 158
Entrepreneur, 167
Equity analysis, 139
Ernst and Young, 94
Error rates
 controls and, 95
 in paperless transactions, 21
E-Span, 117
Ethical issues, and expert systems, 112
Exception control
 future scenarios using, 3
 personnel information transactions work flow with, 21–22
 reengineering with, 95
Executives, future jobs for, 159
Expected value analysis, 60–61
Expert Information System (EIS)
 candidate selection with, 130
 competency assessment with, 134, **135, 136**
 compensation and benefits using, 120
 decentralization and, 26, 27, 125
 decision support with, 111–113
 destaffing decisions and, 124
 employee and labor relations using, 121
 example of, 111–112
 future scenarios for training needs assessment using, 9–10, 143
 help desks using, 88–89
 human resources (HR) staff roles and competencies and, 29
 organization development with, 140
 personnel information transactions work flow with, 21–22
 Phase III of reengineering involving, 25
 resume scanning with, 118
 services delivery using, 22
 staffing and destaffing using, 115
 training and development using, 134, **137**

F

Fair Labor Standards Act (FLSA), 139
Fax communication, 48, 93
Fifth Generation programming language, 44, **45**, 143
Filing, electronic, 94
File-server architecture, 41

Financial services, outsourcing of, 25
Flexibility
  scale for measuring, 155
  supervisors and, 158
Florida Power & Light, 183
Forms flow software
  use of, in reengineering, 48–49
  vendors for, 48
Fortune (magazine), 38
Fourth Generation programming language, 44
Fragmentation, 124–125
Freelance, 71
Fringe cash outlay costs, 55
Functions, *see* Processes
Future scenarios, 3–12
  approaches to reengineering HR, 11–12
  benefits information inquiries, 4–5
  employment, 6–7
  on-line coaching and training, 8–9
  personnel information and benefits administration, 3–4
  team placement, 7
  training needs assessment, 9–11

G

General systems model of work flow, 65, **66**
Goals. in performance management, 131–132
Grammar, in work flow analysis, 73–75
Graphical user interfaces (GUIs), 43, 123
Greentree Computer Assisted Employment Interview, 117
Grievance handling
  expert systems for, 113
  on-line systems for, 121
Groupware software, 121

H

Hammer, Michael, 12, 90
Handy, Charles, 87
Hardware
  Phase II of reengineering of services delivery and development of, 22
  for reengineering, 46–48
Head-count reduction
  impact of reengineering on, 17
  implications of reengineering for, 195
  work flow reengineering and, 22

see also Staffing/destaffing; Work elimination
Help desks
  competency levels and, 88–89
  employee assistance using, 120–121
  expert system database with, 88–89
  organization development using, 121
  training and, 119
  voice-response software for, 32–33, 85
Help systems
  data retrieval and, 109
  training with, 92
Heroes and heroines, 181–182
Hiring decisions
  benefits of reengineering for, 196–197
  Integrated Human Resources Management Information System (IHRMIS) for, 129–130
  on-line systems for, 115, 118
  parallel processing in, 98
Holiday Inn, 166
Hot bunking, 94
Hoteling (temporary offices), 92–93
HRXpert, 120
Human Resource Information Systems (HRIS)
  benefits of reengineering for, 185
  elements of, 123
  evolution of, 122–124
  Integrated Human Resources Management Information System (IHRMIS) differentiated from, 124
Human resources (HR)
  as a percentage of total company costs, 27, **27**
  future scenarios for, 3–12
Human Resources Certification Institution (HRCI), 99
Human resources (HR) professionals
  certification of, 99
  reengineering implications for roles and competencies of, 29
Human Resource System Professionals (HRSP), 124
Hypertext, and data retrieval, 109

I

IBM, 43, 47, 114, 183
IDEF work flow analysis, 74–77
  elements of, 75
  example of, **75**, **76**

IHRMIS, *see* Integrated Human
      Resources Management Informa-
      tion System (IHRMIS)
Impact Changeability Analysis Report,
      175–176, **175**
Implementation, 161–198
   of new work flow after analysis, 79–80
   relationship between macro and micro
      reengineering in, 163, **164**
   reskilling for computer literacy in, 171–
      173
InCompliance, 112
Individual Employment Plan, 206–207
Individual Software, 119
Industrial engineering, 16
Information systems technology (IST),
      37–50
   categories of reengineering savings for,
      184, **186–191**
   evolution of computers in, 38–39
   as key ingredient of reengineering, 15
   power of, 37–39
   for reengineering, 46–50
InForms, 49
Innovation, scale for measuring, 155–156
Innovators, 167
Inputs, in work flow analysis, 67–69
Institute for Human Resources, 120
Institutionalization, 179–181
Integrated Human Resources Manage-
      ment Information System
      (IHRMIS), 122–143
   advantages of, 141
   architecture of, 125–127, **126**
   concept of, 125
   disadvantages of, 142
   elements of, 123
   evolution of, 122–124
   future scenarios for employment using,
      6–7
   HR processes covered in, 125, **126**
   Human Resource Information Systems
      (HRIS) differentiated from, 124
   implementation planning and, 171
   institutionalization and, 181
   integration using, 26
   interfaces between existing systems
      and, 123, 127
   issues driving development of, 124–127
   multiple applications supported by, 123
   personnel information transactions
      work flow in, 21–22

   processing information close to end-
      users of, 83
   technical advances and future of, 142–
      143
   use of, in reengineering, 50
Intel, 50, 95
Interactive video (IV), 29, 85
Interactive Voice Response (IVR) sys-
      tems, 86
   employee and labor relations using, 121
   future scenario for benefits administra-
      tion using, 4–5
   organization development using, 121
   paperless transactions with, 91
   training with, 119
Interfaces with computers, 42–44, 142
   keyboards, 42–43
   pen notepads, 43
   physical interfaces, 42
   programming languages, 44
   screens, 43
   voice recognition software, 43–44
Interviews of job candidates, 115, 117,
      118, 129–130
IVR, *see* Interactive Voice Response
      (IVR) systems

J

Job Ads USA, 117
Job description, in organization, 128
Job design, *see* Organization and job
      design
Job evaluation, 139
Job Search, 117
Job matching services, 117, 131, 205–206
Joint application development/rapid appli-
      cation development (JAD/RAD)
   cross-disciplinary teams and, 90
   networks for, 48

K

Karou, Ishikawa, 65
Keyboards, 42–43
Key-word searches, 109
Kiosks
   employee and labor relations using, 121
   employee assistance and, 120
   human resources (HR) staff and use of,
      29, 85
   organization development using, 121

personnel information transactions
  using, 113
services delivery using, 22
use of, in reengineering 46–47
Knowledge base, in an Integrated Human
  Resources Management Informa-
  tion System (IHRMIS), 123
Knowledge engineers, 157
Knowledge Point Software, 115
Kugelmass, J., 92

L

Labor costs
  in activity-based costing (ABC), 55, **59**
  components of, **55**
Languages, programming, 44
LANtastic, 47
Leadership styles, 149–150, 215
Legal issues, and expert systems, 112
Lighting Word, 119
Local area networks (LANs)
  client-server architecture using, 41, **42**
  use of, in reengineering, 47
Location, and customers, 29
Lotus Development Corporation, 48, 49,
  71, 86, 91, 93, 98, 109, 119

M

Macro reengineering
  definition of, 12
  implementation and, 163–174
  planning with, 165–174
  relationship between micro reengineer-
    ing and, 163, **164**
  rethinking work in, 81–82
  triage rules for, **13**
  vision and, 163–165
Mail systems, *see* Electronic mail (e-
  mail) systems; Voice-mail systems
Mainframe computers, 40
ManagerPro, 118–119
Managers and management
  analysis of style of, 140
  automation and, 87
  command and control styles of, 151,
    152
  decentralization and, 26, 27
  fragmentation of, 124
  future jobs for, 157–158
  integration of HR functions and, 26

personnel information transactions
  work flow and, 22
Society for Human Resource Manage-
  ment (SHRM) findings on, **100–
  101**
Market research, 115
Master-slave systems, 40
Mellon Bank, 88–89, 91, 120
Merck, 120
Meridian Bancorp, 120
Messaging, with e-mail, 48
Mice, as computer interfaces, 43
Micrographics Draw, 71
Micro reengineering
  definition of, 12
  Do It Yourself (DIY) concept applied
    to, 84–86
  Impact Changeability Analysis Report
    on, 175–176, **175**
  implementation and, 174–182
  relationship between macro reengineer-
    ing and, 163, **164**
  resistance to, 178–179
  vision for, 174
Microsoft Corporation, 47, 48, 49, 71, 86
Middle managers
  automation and, 87
  future jobs for, 157–158
Models
  data retrieval and, 109–110
  expert systems for, 112
  trend analysis with, 111
Moore, Gordon, 37
Moore's Law, 37, 43
Motivating employees
  achievement and, 147–148
  benefits of reengineering for, 197–198
  expert systems for, 112
  learning and, 156
  Phase III of reengineering involving, 25
  work and, 156
MS Mail, 48
Multimedia, 48, 142
Multiskilling, 87, 88

N

National Metal Trades Association
  (NMTA), 139
Natural programming language systems,
  44, 49
Needs assessment for training
  data retrieval for, 110

future scenarios for, 10–11
Integrated Human Resources Manage-
    ment Information System
    (IHRMIS) for, 134
Netware Lite, 47
Networks
    connectivity of computers and, 40–41
    evolution of, 40–41
    Personal Digital Assistants (PDAs) on,
        13–14
    sharing central databases on, 83
    telecommuting with, 93
    use of, in reengineering, 47–48
    See also Local area networks (LANs);
        Wide area networks (WANs)
Neural network programs, 45–46
Newsletters, electronic, 91
NOAC principle, 65
No Paper (paperless transactions), 90–91
    electronic filing and, 94
    error rates in, 21
    examples of, 91
    Phase I of reengineering with, 18
    personnel information transactions
        work flow in, **20**, 21–22
Notes, 49, 91, 93, 98, 109, 119
Novell, 47

O

Office (WordPerfect), 49
Offices
    reengineering and changes in, 92–94
    temporary, 92–93, 94
On-line Career Center, 117
Operations analysis, 16
OPTUM, 120
Orders, parallel processing of, 97–98
Organizational climate, assessment of, 216
Organization and job design
    definition of, 125–126
    implementation planning and, 169
    institutionalization and, 179–180
    Integrated Human Resources Manage-
        ment Information System
        (IHRMIS) for, **126**, 128–131, 140
    reengineering and changes in, 115,
        116, 121
Organization development
    implementation planning and, 167, 171
    institutionalization and, 181
    readiness for reengineering and, 165

Outputs, in work flow analysis, 69–70
Outsourcing
    categories of reengineering savings for,
        184, **186–191**
    compensation and benefits using, 120
    implications of reengineering for, 25
    macro reengineering using, 12
    rethinking work and, 82
    of training, 119
    triage rules for choosing, **13**
Overhead costs
    in activity-based costing (ABC), 55–56
    fully loaded, 56
    in traditional cost accounting, 53, 54

P

Pagers, 40
Palmtops, *see* Personal Digital Assistants
    (PDAs)
Paperless transactions, *see* No Paper
    (paperless transactions)
parallel processing, 96–97
Payroll
    outsourcing of, 25
PCs, *see* Personal computers (PCs)
PDAs, *see* Personal Digital Assistants
    (PDAs)
People, 144–160
    competency and, 144–151
    future jobs and, 151–156
    as key ingredient of reengineering, **15**,
        16
    processes and involvement of, 86–90
    reengineering adaptation by, 159
Performance management
    achievement motivation and, 148
    benefits of reengineering for, 197–198
    cycle in, 132, **133**
    expert systems for, 112
    implementation planning and, 170
    institutionalization and, 180
    Integrated Human Resources Manage-
        ment Information System
        (IHRMIS) for, **126**, 131–138
    integration of HR functions and, 26
    on-line systems for, 114
    reengineering and changes in, **116**,
        118–119
    steps in, 118
Performance support systems (PSS), 142
Person, in a database, 126

Personnel information transactions
costs of, before and after reengineering, 22, **23**, **24**
databases and, 110
entering into a database, 83
future scenarios for handling, 3–4
networks for common access to information on, 83
technology and costs of, 46
use of, in reengineering 46–47
work flow after reengineering, **20**, 21–
22
work flow in present human resource
systems, 18–21, **19**
Personal computers (PCs)
connectivity of, 40–41
evolution of, 38–39
as key ingredient of reengineering, 15
power of, 37–38
use of, in reengineering 46–47
Personal Digital Assistants (PDAs)
benefits information inquiries using, 4–
5
evolution of, 39
future scenarios using, 4–5, 6, 7
job hunting using, 6
networking of, 13–14
reengineering using, 12, 13–14
Phones, *see* Telephones
Planning
for careers, 134
communications and, 169
data retrieval and, 110
expert systems for, 113
for individual employment, 206–207
for job succession, 131
macro reengineering implementation
and, 165–174
for training and development, 137, **138**
for workforce, 128
Policy manuals, 91
Portability of competency, 158
Position, in a database, 126
PowerPoint, 71
Price Waterhouse, 166
Problem-solving workshops, 178–17
Process, 51–160
activity-based costing and, 53–65
choosing functions for reengineering
and, 99–109
as key ingredient of reengineering, **15**,
16
rethinking work and, 81–82

Society for Human Resource Management (SHRM) findings on, 99–109
work flow analysis and, 65–80
Process Charter, 49, 71
Processing steps, in work flow, 69
Processing system, in work flow analysis,
65
Prodigy, 117
Productivity
categories of reengineering savings for,
184, **186–191**
power of computers and, 38
of programmers, 145, **146**
reengineering and TQM compared for
gains in, 14–15
worker competencies and, 87
Professional in Human Resources (PHR)
certification, 99
Programming languages, 44
Psychotherapy, software for, 31

Q

Quality, customer perception of, 29–30
Quality control, 95
Quinn, James Bryant, 82

R

RAD, *see* Joint application develop-
ment/rapid application development (JAD/RAD)
Recruitment
Phase III of reengineering involving, 25
Society for Human Resource Management (SHRM) findings on, **102**
travel limitation in, 91–92
Reengineering
business case for, 183–198
categories of savings for, 184–185,
186–191
categories of service for, 115, **116**
choosing functions for, 99–109
concepts in, 81–98
creative destruction in the corporate
life cycle and, 33–34, **33**
customers and, 29–33
definition of, 12
implications of, 25–29
key ingredients of, 15–16
new elements of, 13–15
order of battle in, 17, **18**
phases in, 18–25

productivity gains with, 14–15
rethinking work in, 81–82
return on investment analysis of, **192**,
  195–196
technology needed for, 46–50
total quality management (TQM) compared with, 14–15
triage rules for choosing, **13**
vision for, 2
Reengineering teams
  consultants on, 168
  employees on, 174
  organization of, 167, **168**
  readiness assessment of, 210–222
  roles in, 167
Reliability, and customers, 29–20
Reordering systems, 84
Resistance to micro reengineering, 178–
  179
Reskilling, for computer literacy, 171–173
Response time, and customers, 29
Restrac, 118
Resumes, 6
  screening, 117, 118
  tracking, 130
  writing, 119
Resumix, 118
Return on investment analysis of reengin-
  eering, **192**, 195–196
Role, in a database, 126
Roles, in reengineering, 167

S

Safety
  applications for, 121
  Society for Human Resource Manage-
    ment (SHRM) findings on, **108**
Salary, *see* Compensation
Scitor, 49, 71
Screening of job candidates, 117
Screens, as computer interfaces, 43
Sears, 183
Security
  benefits of reengineering for, 194
  data retrieval and, 110
  Society for Human Resource Manage-
    ment (SHRM) findings on, **108**
Selection of employees
  expert systems for, 112, **130**
  job matching services for, 117
  Phase III of reengineering involving, 25
  travel limitation in, 91–92

Self-managing work groups, **153**, 154
Senior Professional in Human Resources
  (SPHR) certification, 99
Service quality, customer perception of,
  29–30
Services delivery systems
  automation and, 86–87
  competency levels and, 87–88
  costs of present human resource sys-
    tems for, 16, **17**
  customer perception of, 30
  decentralization of, 26–27
  impact of reengineering on costs of, 17,
    17
  Integrated Human Resources Manage-
    ment Information System
    (IHRMIS) for, 141
  Phase II of reengineering involving, 22
Shapeware, 71
Shumpeter, Joseph, 33
Smart agent software
  automation using, 25
  future scenarios using, 6, 10
Smart terminals, 40
Society for Human Resource Management (SHRM)
  certification by, 99
  findings of, 100–109
Software systems
  compensation and benefits using, 120
  employee assistance programs with,
    120
  error trapping and exception control
    with, 95
  job design with, 115
  organization development using, 121
  performance management with, 118–
    119
  Phase II of reengineering of services
    delivery and development of, 22
  for reengineering, 48–50
  staffing and destaffing using, 117, 118
  telecommuting and, 93
  training and development using, 119
  work flow charting with, 71
  See also specific types of software
Software vendors
  outsourcing and, 25
Solow, Robert, 38
Spinaker, 119
Sponsor, 167
Staffing/destaffing
  implications of reengineering for, 27–29

institutionalization and, 180
Integrated Human Resources Management Information System (IHRMIS) for, 125, **126**, 129–131
implementation planning and, 169–170
on-line systems for, 115
See also Head-count reduction; Work elimination
Strategic planning
costs of present human resource systems for, 16, **17**
impact of reengineering on, 17, **17**
integration of HR functions and, 26
Phase III of reengineering involving, 25
Stress management, 170
Suppliers
as part of information system, 83–84
"upstream," in work flow analysis, 66
Systems integration, and outsourcing, 25

T

Tax preparation software, 95
Teams
climate of, 150–151
competencies for reengineering and, 149
cross-disciplinary, 89–90, 97
facilitation of, 158
future scenarios for, 7
as key ingredient of reengineering, 16
leadership styles for, 149–150, 215
self-managing work groups and, **153**, 154
technical professionals and, 157
See also Reengineering teams
Technical experts, 167
Technology, *see* Information systems technology (IST)
Telecommuting, 92–94
benefits of, 93
candidates for, 93
limitations of, 94
Teleconferencing
employee and labor relations using, 121
employee assistance using, 120
hiring interviews using, 118
software for, 50
training with, 119
travel limitation using, 91–92
use of, in reengineering, 49–50
white-boarding software with, 49, 50

Telephones
advantages of, 46
as a computer interface, 43
costs of, 46
as a dumb terminal, 40
employee and labor relations using, 121
hiring interviews using, 118
voice recognition software on, 43–44
voice synthesis software on, 44
Templates
decision support with, 110–111
data retrieval and, 109–110
job descriptions using, 115
Temporary agencies, and outsourcing, 25
TESS, 120
Testing
Individual Employment Plan with, 206
job candidates and, 117
on-line systems for, 114
training programs with, 119
Therapy, software for, 31
Time sharing, and dumb terminals, 40
Total Quality Management (TQM), 65, 95
customer focus of, 29
micro reengineering and, 178
reengineering compared with, 14–15
Touch-screen technology, 43
Touch-tone telephones, *see* Telephones
Training and development
achievement motivation and, 148
awareness seminars for, 168–169, 173
benefits of reengineering for, 194
CD-ROM provision of, 22, 29, 92
communication and distance learning in, 92
computer-assisted instruction (CAI) for, 29, 32–33, 119
data retrieval and, 110
development advisor for, 137–138
future scenarios for, 8–11
help systems for, 92
implementation planning and, 170
institutionalization and, 180
Integrated Human Resources Management Information System (IHRMIS) for, **126**, 134–138
integration of HR functions and, 26
needs assessment for, 10–11, 110, 134
on-line provision of, 8–9, 113
phases of reengineering involving, 22, 25
problem-solving workshops in, 178–17
reengineering and changes in, 113, **116**, 119

reskilling for computer literacy in, 171–173

Society for Human Resource Management (SHRM) findings on, **103**

teleconferencing in, 50

for using personal computers, 46

Training Development Center (TDC), 205–208

Travel, reduction in, 91–92

Trend analysis, 111

U

United HealthCare Corporation, 120

"Upstream" suppliers, in work flow analysis, 66

Usability testing, 46

cross-disciplinary teams and, 90

work flow analysis with, 79

V

Value analysis, in work flow analysis, 78, 80

Variance analysis, 111

Vendors

of e-mail, 48

of networks, 47

outsourcing and, 25

forms flow software, 49

Video conferencing systems

networks with, 47

Visio, 71, 73

Vision, for reengineering, 12, 163–165

Voice annotation, with e-mail, 48

Voice-mail systems

organization development using, 121

travel limitation using, 91

Voice recognition systems, 15, 46

automation using, 25

as computer interfaces, 43–44

help desks using, 32–33, 85

networks with, 47

See also Interactive Voice Response (IVR) systems

Voice-response software

paperless transactions with, 91

travel limitation using, 91

Voice synthesis software, 44

W

Weighted application blank (WAB) systems, 117, 137

Weizenbaum, Joseph, 31

Welch, Jack, 82

White-boarding software

networks with, 47

teleconferencing with, 49, 50

use of, in reengineering, 49

Wide area networks (WANs)

client-server architecture using, 41, **42**

job posting using, 129

personal digital assistant (PDA) connections on, 4–5

use of, in reengineering, 47

Windows for Workgroups, 47

WordPerfect, 48, 49, 86

Work-analysis methods, 16

Work distribution reports, 65

Work elimination

macro reengineering using, 12

triage rules for choosing, **13**

see also Head-count reduction; Staffing/destaffing

Work flow analysis (WFA), 65–80

activity-based costing (ABC) for, 53, 57–60

activity value analysis (AVA) for, 61–62

charting steps in, 71–77

charting symbols in, 72, **73**

general systems model in, 65, **66**

grammar in, 73–75

implementing new work flow from, 79–80

inputs into, 67–69

outputs from, 69–70

processing steps in, 69

steps in performing, 70–80

"upstream" suppliers and "downstream" customers in, 66

worksheets for, 71, **72**, 79

Work flow charting, 16

Work Force Solutions (WFS), 114

Work fragmentation charts, 65

Worksheets

labor costs, in activity-based costing (ABC), **59**

work flow analysis, 71, **72**, 79

.